The
Sylvia
Factor

The
Sylvia
Factor

The Aftermath of World War II

Lee R. McEwen

HILLSBORO PRESS
Franklin, Tennessee

Printed in the United States of America

03   02   01   00   99   1   2   3   4   5

Library of Congress Catalog Card Number: 98-75446

ISBN: 1-57736-130-X

Cover design by Gary Bozeman

Published by
HILLSBORO PRESS
An imprint of
PROVIDENCE HOUSE PUBLISHERS
238 Seaboard Lane • Franklin, Tennessee 37067
800-321-5692

To the Girl in the Moon

and

the Love that Bonds Husband and Wife

CONTENTS

Arkansas Governor Mike Huckabee.

FOREWORD

LEE MCEWEN IS A CHARACTER. HE'S EARTHY AND HONEST.
Few people have lived some of the experiences that Lee has, but
beyond having lived out some of the most fascinating moments on
this planet, Lee has a wonderful and compelling capacity to tell
about them in his writings.

In the twelve years I've known Lee, I have always been entertained by his ability to express himself with a disarming candor
that makes you genuinely want to hear more.

You're going to love this book. You will probably come to feel
that Lee is your friend, too. Set aside some time to read. He will
capture you in his unique web of storytelling that will make you
all but believe *you* have just returned from World War II. Happy
reading!

Mike Huckabee
Governor, State of Arkansas

PREFACE

THE SYLVIA FACTOR: THE AFTERMATH OF WORLD WAR II IS a true story. Some names of places have been changed, and names of some of the characters who are still living and some who are now dead were changed to prevent invasion of their privacy and/or the privacy of living relatives, etc.

On the other hand, some of the characters in the story are identified by their real names. Examples of those are Mr. Dwight Voorhees and Chief Engineer Jim Mallard.

A story could be written about such men, simply titled *The Chiefs*, because, indeed, were it not for men of their caliber and awesome patience, America would have been in dire circumstance during War II. At the beginning of hostilities, our country—just as it is today—was among the nations of the world with a *pitiful* Merchant Marine. As it was, this country had to depend on many foreign seamen to man the thousands of ships to which our merchant fleet grew, almost overnight. And it was men like Dwight Voorhees and Jim Mallard who served far beyond the call of duty, by teaching and training young ignorant lads from the cotton fields and log woods; from the other side of the tracks; from wherever they came. These men even stuck their necks out in order to better serve their country in time of dire need, allowing us "ignorant" lads to sail in positions that would not have been permitted, except men like Voorhees and Mallard put their engineer's, mate's, and skipper's license on the line. In short, risking their own license, they guaranteed our ability to perform.

Indeed, a book could be written about such men, and the fantastic variety of goofs (foul-ups) which they endured while teaching us to be men. Many incidents were humorous (most were), some were sad, and some downright stupid. But all reveal a very important factor about our nation when we get into a big war that is never told other than with casual mention. In World War II, instead of being the great powerful nation that we were, America would have been a floundering wimp, choking on the awesome output of its war material supply, were it not for the U.S. Merchant Marines.

Part One

The *Tout-de-suite* Plumber
in the First War-Bride Ship

CHAPTER 1

LINER AT LANDING STAGE, LIVERPOOL

BOB, MY BAY PONY, SNORTED AS I REINED HIM IN BEFORE we turned north to cross a shoddy wooden bridge over a wide creek, lined on both sides with big cottonwood trees and willow bushes.

I was uneasy this mildly cool morning in late September 1942. But ole Bob was feeling frisky as usual. He was just under eleven-hands high, black mane and tail, and a tan coat smudged with a brush of smoky tint, and only seven years old. He loved to run and didn't like it when I pulled him up. However, a sense of foreboding clutched me and I held his reins taut, hesitating before crossing over into "no-man's-land."

My heart pounded as I sat there astraddle his bare back, peering into the murky twilight. Thoughts raced in my mind about past predicaments when I had ventured across the creek; to me it was the dark badlands as menacing as any through which heroes in cowboy movies ever had to ride their faithful pony.

The creek ran due east. The big cottonwood trees on its south bank grew along a line between the creek and the graveled road.

3

Across the creek, a narrow dirt road ran due north. East of the dirt road, spread for dozens of square miles over the flat Mississippi River delta black land of eastern Arkansas, was the Yanktown Cotton Plantation. West, a three-mile-wide scope of pristine woodland bordered the dirt-road ditch and stretched north alongside the road for another four miles.

The road was on the plantation's private property, but it was not posted. Also, the grown-ups claimed that the county maintained the old rickety bridge to keep it passable (barely) and that the county kept the dirt road graded. Considering that, I believed it was not sinning one iota when I sneaked onto the plantation and recruited help to get my daddy's cotton picked.

However, the riding boss had threatened to shoot the tires off any pickup truck he caught "sneaking" cotton pickers off the plantation. Therefore, to be on the safe side, I always rode my pony when on "dangerous rustling" missions, which was early morning each time, when I sneaked in and out of the shacks, recruiting cotton pickers to gather at a rendezvous off the plantation's property. Then I would race home, jump into Dad's old rattling 1937 Ford pickup truck, and roar back to smuggle them to our modest eighty-acre farm. By then, most of the dew had dried, and they could start picking cotton.

The women, old men, and children didn't have to report each day to a riding boss as did healthy fathers, and they were eager to slip away and earn extra money for picking cotton. We paid them the going rate that all small farmers paid, which was from twenty-five to fifty cents more per one hundred pounds picked than what the plantation paid. Poor white and black families (called day workers instead of sharecroppers) lived and worked on the plantation, which furnished each family a long, three-room shotgun shack, rent free.

Anyway, it was easy for a fifteen-year-old lad to reason that such efforts to rustle cotton pickers to get his daddy's cotton picked were all right in the eyes of the Lord. Indeed it was a single-minded task of the utmost importance to me; the old folks could blow and brag all they wished about how great "Prezeeedent Rooozeeevelt" was, but my daddy was the top dude in my book;

except at times when he "tore my tail up" with an elm switch or his razor strap, I didn't believe there was anybody as tough and as smart as my daddy, Rooozeeevelt included. (Even at age fifteen, I thought President Roosevelt was a big fibber. And I also had a sense of distrust for anyone who smoked ready-rolled cigarettes in one of those long fancy cigarette holders like he did. I thought, as a man, he was sissy for doing so.) And so, Dad was the only top ramrod in my book, and, like he always said, "come hell or high water" I was dead set on getting his cotton picked any way I could. I swelled with pride when he bragged about my efforts to get it all out of the fields before Christmas.

It was by no means an easy task, because a lot of young men had gone into military service, and many other folks had left the country to go to nearby Memphis and other big cities to make war stuff. Therefore, cotton pickers were difficult to find in a normal way.

But regardless of what I thought the Lord might have thought about my efforts, they were never all right in the eyes of Mr. Bean, a big potbellied riding boss. He threw a fit every time my little pony outran his big black gelding at Fourth of July picnics. Therefore, I believed he was obsessed with determination to keep me chased off the plantation—and keep me away from blond-haired Prissy. As time passed, his tactics changed to that of trying to run me down.

He was the father of pretty fourteen-year-old Priscilla Fay, who had golden hair and who giggled and wiggled when folks called her Prissy Fay, which she was called most of the time. I liked Prissy, but she sure did slap my jaws a lot when I tried to find out about girl-things and such stuff.

Anyway, during cotton harvest, my single-minded purpose drove me with determination to get our cotton picked before winter weather downgraded its value. Nineteen forty-two had been a good year. It looked like the forty acres we had planted in cotton were going to yield at least two bales per acre. And I thought that if I could get it all picked in time to sell for the best price, Dad's stern face would light up and he would surely give me a big pat on the back and brag about what a good job I had done.

These thoughts ran through my mind as I sat astride my pony, squinting across the bridge into the gloaming, unable to make out the dirt roadway much farther than a hundred yards beyond the other side the creek.

Birds had started a noisy twitter in the woods, but everything seemed tranquil. Still, I felt ill at ease.

Bob chomped at his bits and pawed at the graveled road. Occasionally he slung his head around to look at me. He did this when he got impatient and aggravated. We had more or less grown up together and had an understanding of one another— most of the time. He was an easy gaited fox-trotter, except we usually didn't do much fox trotting. Instead we raced the wind. But sometimes, just out of the blue, he would buck like the devil when I did something he didn't like.

This early morning, true to form, he laid his ears back. But I was alert, and before he dropped his head to buck, I slapped him sharply on the side of his neck and pulled hard on his reins while digging my bare heels into his sides. He snorted and did a few crow hops, slinging his head, then he settled down.

I always rode him bareback, even though Dad got a saddle for me from Sears and Roebuck—for a whole $24.88! That was in exchange for my promise that I would quit chewing tobacco. However, when I got an unpleasant taste in my mouth, real or imagined, I sneaked a chaw of Days Work. Of course, Dad eventually caught me and he took the saddle away then warned me never to use it again; he said a man always kept his word. This puzzled me, because I was only twelve years of age at that time and I failed to see how that should apply to me.

It was a handsome saddle of polished fine, tan leather engraved with fancy designs. But, actually, Bob and I didn't much care for it. He would always swell his belly, and I had a difficult time getting the saddle girths tight. Anyway, I preferred to ride him bareback. I would grab a handful of his long black mane, dig my heels to his sides, and no other horse around could outrun him. Whether it was at Fourth of July races or riding along a road and other riders making a challenge, ole Bob always left them looking at our backsides.

I eased up on the reins and kneed Bob forward, trying to hold him to a walk as we picked our way around the holes in the bridge. But he really felt his oats, and, as we ventured north up the dirt road, he started slinging his head against the tight reins and began prancing, snorting, and chomping at his bits.

After a couple hundred yards, the birds suddenly hushed their twitter. The cool air felt heavy, and everything was eerily still and deadly silent. My heart thumped so hard I seemed to feel its beat in my eyelids. I again pulled Bob to a stop and gazed all around.

It was still dark and unfriendly in the woods to my left, where big tree branches stretched out over the dirt road. Twilight was slowly soaking the night off the endless white blanket of cotton to my right, which spread east to the horizon, as far as I could see.

I probed the gray daylight ahead, alert that I might see Mr. Bean charging down the road at me on his big black gelding like I had seen him do many times in the past. He always reminded me of Hoot Gibson, who was a popular cowboy in the western movies. In fact, folks often referred to Mr. Bean as "Ole Hoot." And when I ventured onto the plantation, I usually pictured myself as though I was Buck Jones, one of my heroes in the cowboy movies, warily riding my pony through the badlands, wherever they were, "way off somewhere way-a-way outch yonder in the big ole wild cowboy West. . . . "

But this particular morning, I felt too uneasy to feel much cowboyish even though the road appeared to be empty. The birds remained strangely quiet, but all I could see in the distance were specks of light from kerosene lamps faintly dotting the windows of a long row of shotgun shanties that faced the road.

Warily, I once again nudged my pony on.

A loud flurry of wings fluttered in the trees.

My innards jerked into a knot.

Bob's ears pitched forward. A big rock jumped up out of my belly and stuck in my throat; my heart pounded in my ears.

A huge black shadow had leaped out of the woods and blocked the narrow road.

My pony snorted with a sling of his head as I hauled back on the reins. About twenty feet away, there sat Ole Hoot stuffed in black cowboy clothes astride his tall black horse, wearing a smirk under his wide-brimmed black cowboy hat. His balloon butt squirted out over the silver-trimmed edge of his black saddle.

He was an intimidating figure; always gave me goose bumps. And on this morning he looked especially scary amidst the gloaming, like a big sinister blob. He looked lots meaner than that Hitler rascal I had seen in the movie newsreels, who Dad and all the grown-ups cussed.

Sitting there with his roly-poly belly wrapped around the saddle horn, Mr. Bean smirked like a fox with a rabbit in its paws. He growled, "I got yew now, yew little trespassing runt."

Things didn't taste good, and I snatched a plug of Days Work from my overall's bib pocket and gnawed off a jaw full. Bob kept chomping at the bits and pawing the dusty road.

Mr. Bean kneed his horse forward, saying, "That double-talking sheriff ain't gonna have any excuse this time, yew little ragged-assed fart. I'm a taking yew to him, personally!"

I felt trapped. I couldn't dart off to the right. It was unthinkable, because no decent person would run a horse through a lush field of open cotton boles, knocking cotton all over the ground to rot, even if it did belong to some Yankee plantation owner. Such a terrible act just simply was not done in cotton country if it could be avoided at all.

And there wasn't time to wheel my pony about for a full-speed run without risking him breaking a leg running across the shabby bridge full of cracks and holes.

There was only one choice, although the woods were dark and foreboding, and a run through them was risky. Nonetheless, I squared Bob around while squirting a stream of amber that plopped dust at the big black's hoofs.

Mr. Bean grabbed for my pony's bridle reins.

I jammed my heels to Bob's sides.

In one leap, he cleared the road ditch and, with a couple more powerful lunges, was at full speed, dodging through big oak, hickory, ash, and maple trees.

I bent low, with my right hand full of his flowing mane and my left hand gripping the reins, leaving plenty of slack to give him his head. My bare heels dug hard against my faithful steed's sides.

He didn't need guiding; he seemed to know which low branches I would clear. The trees were a blur in the twilight as he dodged through them without breaking a stride.

Hoot howled, "YeeeOwwwEeee, yew won't get away this time, yew 'baccer-spittin' fart blossom. I'm a gonna hogtie yew!"

My buddy was really strung out, his pounding hoofs planting acorns. My rear flashed a big red patch in the seat of my overalls at the bellering riding boss.

There was a sharp yelp followed with loud cursing.

I pulled Bob up, and we swung around to see Hoot spread-eagled on the forest floor.

I thought: Yep, no matter how the movies show it, a dude just can't ride tall in the saddle while chasing an outlaw through a bunch of big trees with low-hanging branches.

We stopped a few feet away to make sure he was not hurt, much.

His foot twisted in a stirrup when he got raked out of the saddle. He sat up, jerked off a boot, still groaning and moaning and cussing. I took a big breath and sighed in relief.

His blazing eyes shot me with hot buckshot. Gasping to regain the breath knocked out when his belly smacked the ground, he shook a fist and puffed, "I'm a, I'm a—Yew just wait, yew grinnin' little shit-ass—If it's the last thing I ever do, I'm a gonna catch yewr stinkin,' shaggy, sneaky hide."

Bob and I retrieved the big man's horse, and Mr. Bean flung an arm up and tried to grab my ankle when I handed his horse's reins to him. Bob snorted and jumped away.

Bean sat there roasting me with the furnace in his eyes.

I pushed a mop of sun-bleached brown hair off my forehead, squeezed my chaw with my jaw, and aimed an eye in his direction. I hesitated with lips pursed. Watching him nurse his foot, I suddenly felt sorry for him, realizing he would have plenty of misery for awhile, getting his heavy frame around on that bum ankle. I turned and squirted amber in the other direction.

Silently tipping my hand in a mock salute, I wheeled Bob about like we were headed for home.

Mr. Bean raved after us, "Smirk while yew can, yew little pesky hard-tailed highbinder, but I'm a gonna catch yew and yew can just bet on it. I'm a gettin' me some baling wire and I'm a gonna run yew down then wrap yewr shifty hide up so tight yew can't spit. Yew gonna choke on that 'baccer when I do!"

We left him sputtering and fuming, howling louder and louder, as I rode in a wide circle through the woods, still anxious to recruit cotton pickers now that the coast was clear, for the day, at least.

Even so, I was troubled about Mr. Bean's twisted ankle; I worried about what affect it might have on Prissy's feelings for me. I didn't have to wait long to find out.

PRISSY FAY THREW A QUART JAR OF PEANUT BUTTER AT me. It bumped my shoulder then rolled about six feet along the graveled road.

I was surprised—the glass jar didn't break—it didn't even crack!

She had asked me to get the twists out of the leather strap for her book satchel. When I did, she sucked a sharp breath and squealed, "Stop that—L. R. McEwen, yew're hateful. Yew are a, a, a pure D old devil, is what yew are!"

Then she remained poised, her blue eyes shooting darts while she stomped a foot at me, all the time making her little twisty butt wiggle with captivating rhythm. It was a sunny afternoon in early October 1942, just a few days after her father was raked out of his saddle when he chased me. She kept fussing up such a storm, I couldn't understand another word she jabbered.

Of course, she could have fixed the shoulder strap herself, but I figured that she wanted to do a little flirting with me.

Curly blond-haired Priscilla Fay was always flirting with us boys. Whether walking to and from the consolidated school at

Cottonbelt Junction, at school, or at church, she was always flirting. And it seemed she wanted to brush her little springy cup cakes against us boys' chests and do all the flirting, but didn't want to be flirted at.

She sure did keep me confused.

Because, heck, all I did when I got the kinks out of the strap was sort of nudge one of her little ole blooming touch-me-nots. What I mean is, it was not like I planned to do it on purpose. It was, well . . . darn it, I couldn't help myself. After all, there they were, all stuck out, like plump ripe peaches. I mean, they didn't flop at all. . . ! I often wondered if she wore props.

Once, when we were walking together, we passed old man Morton's barn. It leaned like it would flop down at any moment, except he had it propped with wooden poles. I don't know why I did it, but suddenly the thought popped into my mind. It was not like I was trying to be a smart aleck, but I asked Prissy politely and sincerely if she had started wearing props. She slapped the fire out of me.

She was always popping my jaws, for no good reason that I could ever determine. Except, it was always when I was trying to learn things about girls. For example, like at a ball game, she would get all excited and give my leg petty patty slaps and squeezes, but when I patted her knee and maybe slipped in a little squeeze of one of her soft cozy legs, she just slapped the devil out of me.

She kept me confused, all the time. Heck, I never once ever thought about popping her jaws when she squeezed my leg!

At age fifteen, I could never get Dad to tell me anything about girls without him snickering at me like I was funny. For that matter, in 1942 with the world at war and grown-ups all pre-occupied with excited gossip about the best way to win the war and about cotton prices maybe going to a dollar a pound—if the war lasted long enough—I decided that the trial and error method was the only way I could learn about anything. If it wasn't excited jabber about higher-priced cotton, Dad and the grown-ups were all-time talking all about how great President Roosevelt was and all such.

As the oldest son of a hardworking father who was deter-mined to own his eighty acres outright, which were surrounded with big cotton plantations, I missed much school helping him. And so, I came to the definite conclusion after long hours of soli-tude in self-communion that it was up to me to find out about things—especially about girls—in life that confused me.

And girls my age certainly were no help.

I would ask most politely about some little something I sincerely wished to know concerning girls; like did any ole boy ever make a girl feel like a log chain was dragging through their hind end with them expecting every link to be a hook, and they would smirk and say snooty things like, "Boy, what a dummy. You're crazy if you think a girl is silly enough to talk to you about such personal stuff."

And, even when I tried to get close enough to listen to a bunch of girls jabbering, they would clam up the instant they noticed me. (Little did I know, of course, that in the near future I would be a bumbling plumber in the first war-bride ship, where I learned lots of girl stuff—among other things—by listening to over nine hundred women jabber each voyage.)

Somehow, the girls of my youth didn't seem fair, when all a young lad wanted was to find out about girls; just what all did girls think when they sized up some boy. It didn't seem at all unreasonable to me that a healthy boy wanted to know about such important matters.

Even at that early age, I adopted a policy of getting right to the point without beating around the bush. Because, as his oldest son, I was depended on by Dad in such matters as paying cotton pickers, getting cotton ginned, and sometimes taking livestock to market, and I learned that the buyers didn't give a "young squirt" any breaks; they would go through a spiel of crap, trying to snooker me on prices. I loathed it when grown-ups, like the buyers, gave me a lot of malarkey. And so, I vowed to myself that I was not going to be a part of the BS method of selling my goods, or myself, in life.

Anyway, with Prissy, it was not that I was ever trying to be naughty. Heck, I was not even being personal, much. It was just, well, I simply had that healthy urge to find out.

In short, finding out about stuff that puzzled me was more important than all that phooey about the birds and the bees. Dang it, I was not a bird and I was not a bee. Besides, I already knew lots about birds and bees and bulls and cows and boars and sows. I wanted to know about girls!

But trying to find out about a girl like Prissy and cozy up to her was frustrating. However, one of the times when she let me be the boy who got to walk her home from church, I supposed she decided it was time for me to graduate from the hand-holding stage. She crooked an arm and let me bounce along with my arm linked with hers.

But, wow! When a healthy girl and boy get all out of step with one another . . . bouncing along a graveled road with a big moon smiling down and a warm summer night's breeze is making all the crops smell like vanilla tea cakes fresh out of the oven, mixing in with the sweet smell of that Camay soap most girls seemed to use, a young'n's heart gets all fluttery, sort of like he was astraddle a real long see saw with his hind end hanging way out over the edge of a high cliff.

When just a little boy, I sometimes watched my older sisters wash their faces and I was fascinated when they left a bunch of soap suds to dry without rinsing them off. Mom told me that girls did that because it was like perfume; that it made them smell good. And, for sure, it smelled cozy to a lad, bouncing along under a smiley moon winking at him.

With all that feel-good smelling, I got out of step and all, bouncing along with my arm in Prissy's. And when she got to bouncing down and I was bouncing up, why, naturally, my arm got to bouncing up a little too much and one of the bounces bounced one of her little spongy touch-me-nots.

She slapped the fire out of me.

We kept bouncing along in awkward silence until finally she sighed, and said, "Well, alright. Since yew don't know how to hold a decent girl's arm proper, yew can just put yewr arm around my waist. But mind yew now, I said my waist!"

Well, I sure did. But before long my arm was getting a mite tired with me straining to keep it snugged proper around her. And, too, what with us getting all out of step again, why, naturally, when she got to bouncing up and me bouncing down, my reckless hand just accidently sort of cozied down on her little ole butter ball butt. She slapped the fire out of me again!

It's not the easiest thing to do, walking with a pretty girl along a bumpy gravel road without your ignorant hand sort of moving around with the bounces, trying to find out about things.

But, by golly, I got to hug Prissy Fay all the way around that night.

I felt the four-mile walk to her house and two miles back home was worthwhile because she let me put my arms all way around her for cozy squeezes. She gave me little giggly smacks, twisting and wiggling, hugging me like an on and off switch, bouncing her softies on my chest. But, dang it, before I could really get to mojoing, her daddy bellered for her to get on in the house.

Walking home from school that day, I picked up her jar of peanut butter, and she poked it back into her book satchel, still fussing and blabbering.

"Lee Roy McEwen," she rasped through clamped teeth, "it's a good thing that jar didn't break or yew would have to pay my mothhhuh a whole quarter for it." She jutted her chin at me and prissied on down the road, still jabbering away. "And yew can just keep yewrself to yewrself. I don't want the likes of yew walking with a decent girl like me, Leeeee Roy."

Darn it. She would really get my goat the way she made a face when she called me Leeeee Roy. My folks and everyone called me L. R. Prissy Fay did also, except when she really wanted to corncob me. Anyway, I poked along behind, just watching her little ole derriere wiggle in time with her blabber jabber. She could jabber as much as a flock of wild mallard ducks feeding in a rice field. At times, just wiggling and prissing, she seldom let up, just 'ack, 'ack, 'ack.

When she did finally catch her breath, I tried to get her to being nice again. I cleared my throat, and said, "Uhm, uh, Prissy Fay, does peanut butter really cost a whole quarter, now days?"

She flung a sneer over her shoulder, scoffing, "Why, of course. Yew don't think the store at Cottonbelt Junction gives it away, do yew, Leeeee Roy?"

Looking back, it seems that my whole relation with Priscilla was like an ongoing contest; a matter of which side would win in each encounter. I sincerely wished to get *my side* back to being nice and all. But *her side* was playing hardball and riling me to no end, by keeping on with that Leeeee Roy bit.

I snorted, "Humph, appears to me like that's too much to pay for just a piddling dab of peanut butter."

"Really," she scoffed, "and just how would yew know, Leeeee Roy?"

"Well, Miss Smarty, anybody with any gumption has heard tell that before the war started, you could buy a little ole quart for just nineteen cents at that Kroger store in Marked Tree. And, anyway, it sure looks to me like your folks would save lots of money if your mama made your own peanut butter, like my mom makes for us."

"Ha." She stopped to stare at me like I was a dummy. I got in stride with her, with her face still calling me a dummy, and she goes on, "Well, I'll have yew know, my mothhhuh has more impor-tant things to do than mess around making piddling stuff like peanut butter. An—an—and if yewr daddy didn't give his money to that little old Baptist missionary and mess around working on little ole churches all over Poinsett County, why, why, why, he might have the money—Yew might get to know how good store-bought things are. Homemade peanut butter! Yuggg-E!" She squeezed her eyes with a curl of her nose.

OoooWee. I really did want to get my side to being nice but, dad-gum-it! Her uppity side kept putting a burr in the seat of my overalls. I suddenly didn't like the taste in my mouth, and I snatched a plug of Day's Work from my overall's bib pocket. I gnashed off a big chaw and chomped on it, desperately trying to think of something to get my side even. I spurted a stream of amber a couple of steps ahead of her side. She almost plopped a strutting foot in it but managed to hop the sanitized spot.

"Ha." She smirked and poked her tongue at me.

By now both of us were really stepping it off, and I puffed, "Prissy Fay Bean, you don't know what the heck you're talking about. If my dad wants to help that little preacher dude, that's nobody's business but Dad's—and the Lord's." By including the Almighty, I was sure I had gotten even.

"Ha," she taunted with her curled nose flung in the air, adding, "gets drunk on that old Floating Palace honky-tonk at Marked Tree then he goes off with a preacher on Sundays to build churches. Yewr daddy is some child of God's, alright. He's a big ole hypocrite, if yew ask me, Leeeee Roy."

OoooWeeee. Then, I really did want to kick her little ole twisty rear. I grasped for something to say. Anything!

"Well, uh, uh, yeah, I can tell you something, Miss Aster, at least he ain't no big-butted riding boss like your daddy, riding herd on poor folks to grow cotton just to make some Yankee plantation owner rich. My dad might belt down a few slugs of sko-cat and rub elbows with the devil now and then, but he works real hard so's we can get our own farm paid for. And, Miss Smarty Bloomers, that ain't easy to do with just eighty acres that's surrounded with big plantations choking the heck out of you."

"Ha," she cut in, "like daddy says, nobody twisted yewr daddy's arm to make him sneak in and get that swampy little dinky eighty acres. Daddy says yew folks are trying to get too big for yewr britches—especially yew, Leeeee Roy. If yew don't stop stealing our cotton pickers, Daddy's going to put yew in jail."

I shrugged. "I don't know what you're talking about. Even if I was, he'd have to catch me—but anyway, Smarty, we're getting our farm paid for. And you can tell 'em all, by doggies, us McEwen's ain't doing it by shorting folks on the going rate for picking cotton and all such."

I watched her face flow red; I knew I had hit a raw nerve and figured I had scored big.

But then, for some reason, I suddenly felt pangs of pity for her; though I didn't know why I should be feeling sorry for Prissy because, after all, she got to eat store-bought peanut butter and go to school regularly. I was always envious of my friends who were so lucky, especially those who got to attend school every day.

The fire in her eyes and sassy jut of her chin were gone, and she looked away. I no longer desired to keep butting heads with her and decided to cut out. At least, I was even again, or so I thought. Intending to cut across fields and woods, I started up the Cotton Belt Railroad embankment, which paralleled the graveled road on its left, going south.

But as I reached the top, she called, "L. R.," in a pettish tone she often used.

I paused with a foot on a rail and looked back. She stood there, tilting her head from side to side, making her long springy curls dance like she was Shirley Temple.

I wondered what she was up to. One thing I had learned about girls, most of them had plenty of tricks when dealing with an ole boy, and one had to really stay on the ball to keep ahead of Prissy's side.

Most farm girls like my sisters often curled their hair with a home perm, like those that were advertised on billboards along the roads to Marked Tree and Memphis. And over the radio, there was a lot of advertising for home perms, mixed with that for Carter's Little Liver Pills, Sloan's Horse Liniment, and Antiphlogistine Salve. But Priscilla was always going on and on and on about her mothhhuh taking her to Marked Tree or Memphis to get her hair all pampered at one of those fancy beauty parlors.

She kept dangling those pretty curls at me, like she did to all boys.

A rolling store rattled by, hiding her in a swirl of dust.

While she fanned the gritty cloud, I silently waited for her side to make the first move. Finally she purred, "Ohhh, now for goodness sakes, L. R., say something. Heavens, yew shouldn't get so angra. After all, I was only telling yew what my daddy and everybody says. Yew never see me getting angra like that—bu, bu, but never mind about a little thing like that. We're not mad at each other, are we? Hmmmm?"

I dropped my face and kicked at cinders on the rail bed, convinced my side was coming out the winner on this go around. Not wanting to appear too eager, I waited—about two seconds. Then I mumbled, "Nahhh, don't reckon. Nah, I ain't mad. What about you?"

Stealing a peek, I ducked my face again.

She sweetly purred, "Oh, yew old silly thing, yew, I told yew I didn't get angra. Of course, I'm not mad. Why, why, why, uh . . . I'll even let yew carry my book satchel the rest of the way, if yew wish. Hmmmm?"

I felt my side slipping, and started to shake my head. But, somehow, I just couldn't get it to move. I just stood there with my mouth open and stared at her. After all, she was all smiley, tilting her head and sort of looking sideways at me out of one eye real cute-like, while jigging her shapely leg, making her little ole butt twitch and wiggle.

Yeah, I did. I didn't want to hurt her feelings again. Yeah, I went on and carried the whole works, heavily loaded with books, peanut butter, and girl stuff.

A mile and one-half south of Cottonbelt Junction, the road crossed the wide creek. Actually, it was a deep drainage canal like many that were dug a mile apart, way back sometime after Reconstruction Days, and they ran west to east throughout the flat fertile Mississippi River Delta in eastern Arkansas. The old folks claimed that Yankee carpetbaggers and East Tennessee scalawags gobbled up the swampland at private government auctions for as little as five to twenty-five cents per acre, then the "Damn Yankee Giverment" dug canals for them, which provided a permanent network to the Mississippi River that drained the entire delta.

But the canals had long been hosts to clusters of willows and big cottonwood trees, and were often referred to as creeks. Across the bridge, we took a branch road that crossed the railroad. It was the same road which ran east along the creek that bordered the Yanktown Plantation on the south, much farther on. Our farm was also bordered by the creek on the south, but it was only half a mile east of the Cottonbelt Junction Road. At our place, another graveled road branched off to the south. There, a plantation field hand always waited in a mule drawn wagon to carry Priscilla and other children on to their homes.

I paused with her and kicked at loose gravel.

Prissy gave my cheek one of her little flirty pats, taking on a superior air to coo, "Now, remember, L. R., it was yew who agreed that we shouldn't be angra at each other. An, an, and, even, if Daddy does think yew're a stinker, I don't care what he says. I think you're sort of . . . Ohhh, I wish yew'd quit chewing that ole 'baccer. Yew would be real pretty if yew didn't have that nasty stuff stuck in yewr jaw."

"Awww, it ain't nasty, Priscilla Fay." I chuckled. "Matter of fact, it's the best stuff there is to take a bad taste out of your mouth—and besides, an ole boy can't be pretty. Us ole boys are handsome."

Priscilla had a habit of telling boys we were pretty, but little did I realize that this would be the last time she would tell me or fuss about me chewing tobacco. I stayed out of school for days on end without seeing her while I hustled to find cotton pickers.

The cotton bolls were all fully opened, needing to be picked the second and final time before the full impact of winter weather. Mom and Dad were concerned but allowed that the Lord would find a way to get it all out of the field before too much rainy weather set in.

This would be my last cotton harvest. Even with a war on, I had no idea that I was soon to embark on a long zigzagged journey that would eventually take me to foreign countries and cover hundreds of thousand miles of ocean, often on course only when I crossed it.

Chapter 3

LINER AT LANDING STAGE, LIVERPOOL.   69418

I CONTINUED TO WORK MANY HOURS EACH DAY TO GET the cotton picked.

Dad "horse traded"—something he delighted in doing—as a sideline in a modest way; buying, selling, and trading livestock to provide our family with bare necessities like clothes and food staples that we could not raise on the farm. Also, he did indeed spend much time with the county missionary, helping him organize rural churches. Then he sometimes physically helped construct the simple wood frame and concrete block buildings in which to have Sunday School and Sunday preaching.

As timber was rapidly cleared and new, fertile land put into cotton production for soaring wartime prices, little communities grew up all around our area of the Delta.

For example, thirty miles from Marked Tree—about fifty miles northwest of Memphis—a wilderness area of several thousand acres of cypress trees, thickets, and huge rattlesnakes was opened to homesteaders. This area of the black fertile delta was called Dyess Colony.

In his youth, Johnny Cash, the popular country singer and actor, kept one eye out for rattlesnakes while he picked cotton there as a farm boy. The community became more sophisticated, and today it is simply called Dyess, Arkansas. Also, about thirty miles southeast of our place, near a fork in a road known as the "Y," several thousand additional acres of government swampland in the mighty Mississippi River floodplain opened to home- steaders. (A little known fact, Arkansas has a greater number of rivers, bayous, creeks, and moving bodies of fresh water through it than any of the other contiguous forty-eight states.)

I remember well the summer night in 1942, sitting on a rough board for a bench under a brush arbor at one of the little settle- ments southeast of our farm near the "Y." Dad was holding forth, helping raise funds to build a church before cold weather.

He was still a *believer* even though he was apt to raise a little hell at Marked Tree a few Saturday nights during a year. And when he told a preacher or anyone else that he would do or help do something, he would go all out to get it done. He and Mom called that "keeping your word and having sticka u-nus." That night, Dad was up there stomping around on the makeshift podium made of rough two-by-twelve boards, waving his arms and shouting appeals to a ragtag group of sharecroppers, field hands, and a few families who hoped to someday own outright their little farm plots.

I sat at the back nodding as I dozed, and he startled me when he stomped, and shouted, "Now, listen to me. The Lord is looking down on us here tonight." Sounding just like a hellfire and brim- stone preacher, he bellered on, "And I'm here to tell you that we can't afford to turn our backs on Him. No, sir! Whyyyy, my dear brothers and sisters, at this very moment, many of us have friends and loved ones waaaaaay off across them big salty ponds, waaaaaay away on outch yonder, and bullets are just a whining all around them."

He could make his voice tremble and quiver just like those preachers who always scared the devil out of me.

Dad wailed on, "Bombs are dropping allllll around them. Wounded comrades are allllll around them. The dying and dead are allllll around them. They're shivering in muddy foxholes. They are wet and hungry. They—All—Wish—They—Were—Here—Tonight. And what are we doing? Huh? Just—What—Are—We—Doing?

"We are gathered here tonight all safe and cozy, with allllll the comforts of home. And we are counting on the Almighty to keep our soldier boys safe and to bring them allllll home in one piece. Are we going to let the Lord down? Are we going to let our soldier boys down?"

He paused and slowly swept a solemn gaze over the congregation. Then in a somber tone, he went on, "Nooooo, I'm here to tell you, just like Prezeeedent Rooozeeevelt always says, we ain't got nothin' to be afraid of but fear itself. Yessir, it's the old devil, is who our great prezeeedent is talking about. And yawl know that we can't afford to refuse the preacher a big donation to build a church right here on this very spot to the everlasting glory of the Lord. Now, yawl all know that, don't you?"

Wiping sweat from his brow, he went on, "Of course you do. Glory, we all have to make sacrifices. Why, even our prezeeedent drys his coffee grounds and uses them over and over." With a rising voice, he added, "Do we think we are any better than our great leader? Of course we don't. And we have to give. We have to give until it hurts!"

Suddenly thrusting his fist down with a bang, he shrilled, "Then give some more! And to show just how much we need to open our hearts and pockets, I'm going to give the first thousand dollars." He again banged the lectern with his fist, and I knew he danged well meant it.

That was big money in those days; indeed, when America got into the War, one could still buy a new Chevy pickup truck for $790.

My mouth popped open and, gazing up through dried leaves at the stars, I failed to stifle my groan, "Good Lord, where in the holy hell is he gonna get it?"

A seven-year-old neighbor's child seated by me gasped. When she gave me that look, I knew I was in a heap of trouble. She hastened to declare, "I ummm, the old devil is sure gonna get you. I'm sure gonna tell your daddy."

Heckfire, the Lord knew I was not being sacrilegious or anything. It was, just . . . well, there I sat wearing the only overalls I owned that didn't have those blamed red patches, and Dad was giving away a thousand dollars which I knew he would have to borrow, what with having to use cotton money to pay on the loan for the farm and have funds to operate.

The child kept her word; she tattled, while Dad glared at me. As we bumped along home that night, I hunkered in the back of our rattling pickup truck in silent torment.

As soon as we were all in the house Dad never said a word. Just shot me with both eyes and got his razor strap. I was strong at age fifteen and was almost as big as he, but I got to my feet at the command of his eyes. He smoked my rear with that blazing strap.

As usual after such punishment, Dad would wait until after a cooling-off then he would say things like, "Son, it hurts your poor old dad a lot worse than it does you for me to have to whip you, but your poor old dad has to make sure his kids grow up proper. Now, give your poor old pappi a big hug and we'll forget the whole matter." At the time, I could not understand why Dad always insisted that we hug him after he had "torn our tails up" with his razor strap. And he also demanded that we tell poor old dad that we loved him. He then never failed to end such matters with the reminder, "And don't you ever forget, as long as you sleep under your pappi's roof and poke your feet under my dinner table, you won't ever be too big for me to tear your tail up when you need it."

Missing school so much, as I had the past three years, Mr. Britton, the school principal and also my first-year algebra teacher, sent assignments for me to study at home. But there was little time for anything but farm homework. In the cotton belt, the custom was to work from sunup until sundown. But regardless of how much cotton needed to be picked, most folks took Saturdays off and went to town. In the cotton belt, it was simply the way of life for poor farmers; cotton harvest was the only time during the year when children had a dime to see a picture show or a nickel for a cone at the ice cream parlor.

However, the grown-up men went to town each Saturday throughout the year whether there was any money for pleasure or not—although, many often found a way to pay twenty-five or thirty cents for a quart of beer to chase down a few healthy snorts of sko-cat. But even if they did nothing but sit on a bench and whittle on a stick while watching the world go by in the little cotton towns, all during a week of hard work, folks looked forward to Saturday.

However, my parents were from the poor red clay hills of Tennessee, an area that many conjurors of labels now refer to as Appalachia (where my older siblings and I were born), and Dad and Mom's work ethic was "make hay while the sun shines." They didn't merely say it, they meant it. We all worked from daylight until it grew too dark to see. Then by the light of a kerosene lantern we had to milk the cows and tend the needs of the other farm animals. Therefore, we didn't go to town many Saturdays. In foul or fair weather, there was always plenty of work on the McEwen's little eighty acres. When not working in the fields, there were fences to repair, wood and logs to cut, pigs to castrate, lye soap to be made from animal fat. . . . The back log of work for all of us to do was always waiting.

In the fall, there was the chore to get the cotton picked during the day. We got our first radio in 1938, and Dad liked to listen to Mr. District Attorney, the Grand Ole Opry, and other similar radio programs, and so, at night, I hitched a team to the wagon and hauled the cotton two miles to the gin at Cottonbelt Junction. I usually waited in line with other cotton wagons until the wee hours in the mornings; I could catnap at intervals while waiting to keep moving my wagon up in line.

In short, I never turned in one homework assignment for algebra. Yet, Mr. Britton gave me a B average for the year, thus I was not required to take final exams; he simply passed me on to the tenth grade.

He understood my situation. He came out a couple of times and talked to Dad about me missing so much school. I once overheard him say that I had a promising future if I finished high school.

Dad responded, "Oh, yeah, Teacher, my boy's got all his marbles, alright enough. He's my right hand . . . and you don't have to worry, that boy won't have any trouble catching up on learning all about what that confounded X-stuff equals and such. Yes sir, I'm going to see to it that my kids get enough education and have it better than their poor old mama and I had it. Yes siree, that's what life is all about. Making sure your young'n's have things lots better'n their poor old pappi and mama—just look at this rich, black land! The Lord's will, we're gonna get it all paid for, come hell or high water. It's lots better'n that red soggy clay I was raised on back up home in Tennessee when I was a growing up. Don't you worry about my boy, Teacher, he catches on fast."

With America producing and sending Lend-Lease war supplies to England and Russia, within a year or so, cotton had jumped from eight and nine cents per pound to twenty cents. After the United States got into the war, it soared to over forty cents. Farmers sitting around shooting the breeze in the general store at Cottonbelt Junction mused that the Lord sure worked in mysterious ways, that cotton would go to a dollar per pound if the war lasted long enough.

Primarily, it merely became a form of idle gossip. Many would go home at night and worry about sons away *over there* in the battlefields of some far off land.

Dad never tried to pin me down about how I recruited cotton pickers, but I overheard him telling Mom that when he was in Marked Tree one day the sheriff told him that Mr. Bean was complaining about my *alleged* trespassing. He chuckled while saying that the sheriff said he kept telling Mr. Bean he would see what could be done when the riding boss caught me.

Mr. Bean made a few other half-hearted attempts but he never caught us. As long legged as was his big sleek horse it was no match for a little bay pony with powerful forelegs, a strong heart, and a special kinship with the barefooted lad who grew up with him.

However, Mr. Bean did indeed slam the damper tight on his daughter's and my boy-girl relation. Except Priscilla assured me that we would still be good friends and that I could still carry her books. But I never knew whether her side won or mine.

Perhaps it was a draw.

Anyway, we never again bounced along arm in arm from church under a big yellow moon. The road I was to travel was full of holes from which the unexpected often jumped out at me, and my life would be vastly different from hers. I kept trying to grab the world by its tail, and it thrashed about and slammed me on the deck time after time.

CHAPTER 4

LINER AT LANDING STAGE, LIVERPOOL.

69418

WE GOT ALL THE COTTON PICKED, AND DAD WAS PAID TOP price for it. But the winter dragged on. I was able to attend school more often but was so far behind my tenth-grade classmates that it was utter confusion and torment for me. Showing up for class each day, I felt like I was naked, stumbling blind through a frigid cave where sinister creatures fluttered all around, pricking every pore of my body. My skin crawled and my stomach balled into a wad that ached so much it made me sick.

Most classmates smiled with kindness as I stuttered and stammered when called upon by the teacher during verbal question-and-answer periods. But the snickers from others and their leering faces gave me the urge to flee the room and hide. The long school days seemed to never end.

Finally, in the tenth grade I accepted the chilling fact that I was not learning. It was a bitter pill to swallow because I fervently longed to finish high school; I wanted to be somebody.

In our area if children got a good eighth-grade education it was considered fair to middling; thus, they could measure cotton-planting acreage which the government allowed for each forty acres farmed, measure log-feet to prevent shortage at the sawmill, and figure the fair share of their sharecrops each year. They would be smart enough to get by.

If any were lucky enough to go through high school and get a diploma, they were really in tall cotton. They had a chance to get a job with the government or be a mail carrier, a game warden, or rural school teacher, etc., and become well-off folks and get to really be somebody.

The opportunity to go to college, especially for renters' and sharecroppers' children, was so remote that few ever thought about it. A common topic when old folks gossiped was, if kids expected to ever get to be somebody, they had darn sure better get that high school diploma.

I really wanted that diploma. With it, I was certain I could capture the golden crown in life. But I wanted to earn the right to have a high school diploma. When missing several days at school before I reached junior high school, I managed to study my books on my own, or with Dad's help, and catch up. I had no trouble learning; school had been easy and satisfying. I yearned for it to be that way, still.

Mom knew my frustration. Often she would comment, "Son, you just might have to settle for learning a skill of some kind." Also, I would overhear her feeding such thoughts to Dad, "Roy, that boy needs to go off and learn him a good trade."

On a cool misty day in early spring of 1943, it all became crystal clear. A chill swept through me. I shivered as the anxiety and frustration froze out of me. At that moment, I came to terms with my lot in life. I admonished myself that there were young Americans far away from home fighting and dying and that I had no cause to feel sorry for myself.

Yet, I still could not keep the lump out of my throat, knowing that I was not going to finish school. I was all alone on the back forty, driving an old steel-rimmed A-model John Deere put-put tractor, cutting open the land with a bush-and-bog disk plow.

My heart ached in my self-communion.

It hurt.

I stopped the tractor.

I cried.

I gazed long into the drab overcast. A lone hawk gracefully glided low, circling over a cornfield. The past year the stalks had grown tall and sturdy, holding big ears of golden corn. Now they were all bent, broken, and weather-beaten.

The big predator soared higher and circled back. I killed the tractor's motor and watched.

I then wished I hadn't. A little rabbit darted out of the cornfield and scampered over open ground I had already plowed. It tried to reach the cover of a fence row, too far away.

With a mighty flap of its powerful wings, the hawk swooped down and snared the frightened rabbit with its talons.

I know of nothing more pitiful in the wild animal world than the chilling cry of a little rabbit that, surely, knows death is at hand. Its death knell seemed to linger in the stillness long after the dismal mist swallowed the hawk and its prey. Then all was quiet and I remained motionless for a spell. I wondered what humans thought those few seconds of time when they knew raw danger or death was near. I would know in days to come. After turning the fly wheel and cranking the tractor, I crawled back up on the seat. I gazed into the solid overcast and pondered about what my future would be like. In the gray mist I could see nothing but blank empty vastness.

A shiver again swept over me and I shrugged it off. I sighed and thought that whatever my lot in life, somehow the Lord just had to help me get to be somebody. I then vowed I would bust a gut trying.

A brisk breeze dried the tears and matted my eyelashes. I wiped them with the tattered sleeves of my faded denim jacket, then with a final sigh, I shoved the hand clutch forward on the old John Deere and kept on put-putting.

Since that day I have never shed a single tear. Oh, yes, indeed, I have traveled the oceans to far places, witnessed war tragedy, and experienced much in life that caused me to have tears many times through the years, but they have all been inside.

After crops were laid by that summer, I went to Memphis to stay with my sister Lillian and her family.

A very tenacious young mother was Lillian. She worked for $38.90 per week making raincoats for the military, and she made sure that her four little daughters had clothes to attend school. Dad made it plain that I was to find a job and start learning a trade before crops were ready to harvest, or that I would have to come back to the farm. I got a job as a welder's helper earning 52 cents an hour with Pidgeon & Thomas Iron Company, where LCTs (landing craft for tanks) for the United States Navy were built.

I thought being a helper was for kids. I had to keep working but wanted to learn to weld and wished to attend welding school at night. But there was only one public vocational school in Memphis at that time; to attend, one applied through the State Employment Office.

The elderly lady who interviewed me threw a fit when she learned I was working ten hours per day. Where I worked, there were only two ten-hour shifts per day, six days per week. Of course, employees were paid overtime for the extra time over eight hours per day and over forty hours per week, and so one either worked ten hours per day or they didn't have a job. Luckily, I had not yet told her where I was employed. She quickly informed me that at only sixteen years of age, I was already working two hours each day more than the Tennessee Child-Labor Law allowed.

She asked me to repeat my name. I instantly realized I had blundered into the wrong chicken house and I muttered that my name was McNut, jumped up and headed for the door.

She scampered after me, yelling, "Young man, you get yourself back here this minute, and I mean it!"

I outran her.

At work, when I caught an electrode not being used by a welder, I grabbed it and practiced welding on scrap metal. After I got the knack to keep the welding rod from sticking, I learned, and eventually passed all navy welding tests. Then I felt like I was right up there with the grown-ups, doing something important to help in the war effort.

The hope to really get to be somebody and find that pretty woman when I got grown was constantly in the back of my mind. I never went back home, except to visit. . . . A product of a time and circumstance, on my own in the turmoil of a world at war . . . as such, I felt uneasy at times, all alone without Dad and Mom to turn to for a guiding hand.

Author at age sixteen on his own in 1943 in the turmoil of a world at war.

But I got advice of sorts when I left home. Dad's was short and to the point. However, when Mom added her advice to his, I was faced with a dilemma: Dad surely sensed a loss when his oldest boy left home, but in his gruff manner he hid it to growl, "Son, anybody gives you any stuff just knock the stuffing out ov 'em." Mom hastened to counter, "Now, son, don't you go to paying any attention to that. You just always turn the other cheek and the Lord will take care of the rest—and always hang on to your sticka u-nus. You'll need lots of sticka u-nus to get by in this old world."

Mindful that I was not finishing high school, I felt pangs of guilt about my sticka u-nus (tenacity).

Dad was a tenderhearted man in many ways, but he still had that toughness developed from a hard life in the hills of Tennessee as a boy and as a young farmer-blacksmith at Hollow Rock. He was a hard worker and did the best he knew to support a large family. Though poor, he always remained ambitious in his own way; he, too, wanted to get to be somebody by owning his own farm, free and clear—a noteworthy and grand accomplishment back then for those who had been poor tenant farmers all their lives.

Therefore, I have never blamed him for my lack of formal education. He personally had a good 3-R eighth-grade education, especially in 'rithmatic. Perhaps unconsciously, he could not understand how X equaling an unknown quantity or number would be of any great value in life to his son. I don't know. . . . But I know he did the best he knew how to do, and I never could blame him or Mom for my lot in life.

They loved us, they fed us, we were healthy, they whipped our hard tails when we disobeyed or did wrong, and we grew up loving one another, respecting God, country, and our parents.

After I learned to weld all positions, I was paid $1.20 per hour, the wartime-freeze maximum allowed for a qualified welder. I felt I was in high cotton!

I bought a 1940 Chevrolet club coupe that had a narrow back seat. And soon I had several new friends. Including myself, on occasion, there were three couples, with lap seating, crammed inside the little car.

My first date in Memphis was with Cora Ann, the sixteen-year-old sister of Howard, a friend with whom I worked. She went on and on and on about her ever loving high school prom.

Finally, I said, "Yep, Cora Ann, your hairdo looks just dandy. Did your mama give it to you?"

She came unglued! Looked at me, well . . . sort of strange. But, heck, I didn't know. They never had any high school proms back over there fifty miles across the Mississippi River in those old cotton fields. With all the stuff I had heard on the radio and had seen advertised on highway billboards about home perms, I just naturally thought that the high-school-prom business was some kind of fancy hairdo for girls.

I soon realized that I had many rough edges but didn't think I was a dummy; I knew I was ignorant but believed I was smart enough to know it. And I was well aware of the sudden changes in my life and that things were moving swiftly. I had lived in Memphis as a child and was confident it was only a matter of a little time until I could adapt to city ways. Even so, the process was full of blunders.

Cora and I dated frequently with Howard and his various dates. He was a couple of years older than I and he always had several girls on the string. His sister was a nice girl, pretty, and not a bit flaunty about her looks, and I could hug her all the way around on occasion, with proper conduct.

Howard usually selected the fun places, some that would normally be off-limits to young'n's barely dry behind the ears. But, in wartime, heads looked the other way. And, although we had lots of clean fun going to places like Maywood, a sandy-bottom spring-fed swimming hole in Mississippi only about thirty miles south of Memphis, we also tried to act like grown-ups and so we sometimes went to a few nightclubs.

Once we tried a fancy new place which Howard had discovered, but we were not allowed admittance without a necktie. I never knew how to tie a tie but, having been accustomed to improvising with baling wire and such on the farm, an idea popped into my mind. While removing my shoes, I asked Howard if he knew how to tie a bow tie. He got the idea and already had his pocket knife open when I snatched off my bright yellow socks. Cutting the socks into strips, he fashioned a crude bow tie for him and me.

Cora and some of Howard's dates had been teaching me to dance, but this night I never got to hug Cora on the dance floor. As soon as I put my cheek next to hers, she sniffed and drew back with an anguished frown, keeping me at arm's length.

I felt rejected because I knew darn well that my sock bow tie could not possibly be stinking like she let on. I had taken a good soaking bath after work then put on new socks, after giving my feet a generous sprinkling with Mexsana powder.

Howard's date didn't seem to mind his tie, because they danced and belly-rubbed each time the band played. Of course she was getting a little bourbon flirty and, too, maybe she liked the smell of that Mexsana powder. But I don't guess Cora did. We sat out the rest of the evening, with her looking me over like she was appraising a box of Cracker Jacks, wondering about the prize inside.

She was a delightful girl but I don't think she was really mature enough to appreciate a country boy who was pretty good at improvising with baling wire, yellow socks, and stuff. She never asked me anything about my station in life, just got into my car ready to go, and gleefully chatter on and on about her cottonpickin' high school prom.

Early one morning, after we had seen Howard off on the train when he was drafted into the army, I took Cora home before I went to work. I proudly wore my big orange badge across which was emblazoned Qualified Welder. Maybe more attention had, indeed, been given my car, because she had never asked about my work and she was surprised to learn I was a welder.

After all those dates, and me thinking I'm getting to be hot stuff, she exclaimed, "You . . . A kid like you, a welder . . . ! A first-class welder?"

"Nope," I fumed, "I ain't no first class—I'm lots more'n a first class. I'm a qualified welder. I can weld any damn—uh, danged thing they throw at me."

She didn't mean to make light of my skill but, nonetheless, I felt sick inside, thinking that a pretty girl like her failed to recognize my worth as much as my own self-appraisal. I thought, "Man O man, girls are sure hard to figure. . . . I'm as old as she is and she thinks I'm a little ole kid. Dang it, she can't even milk a cow or ride a bucking mule. . . . All she knows is high school proms."

If encounters with a variety of situations and trial-and-error are a good teacher, I had a master. Whether the incidents were embarrassing, humbling, frustrating, or sad, they were fed into my subconscious and reviewed from time to time. I spent hours with my face secluded in my welding hood, burning rod after rod, often not even raising my shield each time I inserted a new welding rod into the electrode, just thinking about things. It did not occur to me that I was seeking logic; rather I thought of it as trying to make sense out of things, to figure how to keep from making so many blunders. Each event, simple, complicated, big, or little, was food for thought.

If the joke was on me, so be it. I had sticka u-nus and, by dang, I was going to bust a gut to be somebody and find that real pretty woman who matched the image of my dream girl; one who wanted to live with me the rest of our lives. I excused my stumbles and fumbles by rationalizing that it was merely a matter of learning about city ways and girls and such.

But I had no idea that I would soon make a sudden jump to advanced schooling, competing with adults where, literally, no one pulled their punches on a teenaged lad; not even a big amazon whose physical wrath I was to feel.

LINER AT LANDING STAGE, LIVERPOOL 69418

CHAPTER 5

LATE SUMMER OF 1944, THE NAVY STOPPED CONTRACTING for LCTs in Memphis, and workers were released from their wartime job-freeze to find employment elsewhere. Some went to Oak Ridge, Tennessee, to work on a super secret project—later revealed to be related to the development of the atomic bomb.

Albert Sloan, a friend on the job, and I went to Panama City, Florida, to help build Liberty ships in the Wainwright Shipyard. The tires were worn out on my Chevy, and the Ration Board gave me a big hassle about granting permits to buy gas and new tires for the trip. I sold the car. Therefore, we made the 570-mile trip by bus, laying over for hours at bus stations and changing coaches several times during the day-and-one-half journey. Daylight one morning found us humming along U.S. highway 231 southward. I began to detect a rotten odor unlike any I had ever smelled. I sniffed and frowned at Salty—he had recently spent three weeks in Navy Boot Camp, then he was discharged for some reason, and he was prone to swagger and use salty lingo like a real sea dog. We called him Salty. He addressed any male as Mate or Mac.

SCENE OF THE WAYS AT THE WAINWRIGHT SHIP YARDS PANAMA CITY, FLORIDA   116-P

Wainwright shipyard under construction at Panama City, Florida, after outbreak of World War II — there were six ways. Six Liberty ships per month were built in this shipyard.

I was sure that Salty needed to go to the toilet. We were still some forty miles from Panama City, and as we drew nearer, I kept wondering if the whole bus load of passengers needed to visit the outhouse; I was certain the whole lot had eaten a fill of beans back at the rest stop in Dothan, Alabama. I had done my share of plowing behind gassy mules but it would have taken a barn full of mules to gas the air that strongly.

I learned that the foul odor was coming from a paper mill at Port Saint Joe, near Panama City. Of course there are now paper mills scattered all over our Southland, but I had never been exposed to paper mill odor until that day. I never got used to the stink. A gray-haired native who lived at Saint Joe, also a welder at the shipyard, commented that the odor smelled like money to him.

Unaccustomed to hearing such comments equating the paper mill with employment for an area, I failed to understand. Therefore, I responded by saying that any money I ever had sure didn't stink like that because back on the farm we used old mail-order catalogs to wipe with.

He called me a smart-assed punk.

Salty and I shared a room on the second floor of the white frame Elizabeth Hotel on Harrison Street in Panama City—the population then was said to be a little over eleven thousand.

Cora and I wrote to each other, but she was prone to tone her letters as though she thought of me as a kid. Little did she know in her safe haven of beautiful easy-going Memphis that it was a fast moving world which the kid was trying to grab by its tail.

Soon, pretty Stella Buford with fluffy, creamy blonde hair caught my eye. She was one of a twenty-one-member welding crew to which I was also assigned. We called her Repete. A friend of Stella's was also part of our crew, and we called her Pete. Both Pete and Repete were nice young ladies and were treated as such.

Although Stella was three years my senior, we hit it off from the start, to the disgust of my buddy, Salty. He could not understand why a pretty young woman like her would give any attention to a kid like me.

I must admit, I too wondered about that, because she was, indeed, a very beautiful and bright young lady. But once when she

First Baptist Church at Panama City, Florida, 1944.

and I were discussing our age differences, she said she thought I was an original and that she found that appealing. That original part, I didn't understand, but a pretty girl like her thinking it was appealing boosted my self-esteem.

Salty was also a year my senior but one would think he was old enough to have sailed around the Horn in Clipper Ships, the way he would sling old sea-dog terms about. He often referred to others as lubbers—spent only three weeks in Navy Boot Camp, and calling others lubbers . . . !

Stella and I went to movies and church, etc., and I had no desire to cast an eye about for other girls. And there were, indeed, several women working at the yard; it was reported that over half the welders at Wainwright were women. Many were wives with husbands in military service.

A few of the women welders were tough, as I learned about one woman in particular when I worked overtime one evening. She was a thirty-four-year-old stout amazon—I mean she was tall as a pine, chesty and strong.

I normally worked on way number-4 but, to work overtime that evening, I was assigned to a different leaderman on number-6 way. The utility man assigned a welding cable to me, and I traced it all the way from topside, in and out of compartments, through tangles of other cables, to where it dropped down into a deep-tank compartment aft of the engine room bulkhead. I tugged on the cable from the deck above and felt a slight response.

Planting my feet, I pulled harder, hoping I could free it.

Cursing and squealing blared from below.

I peeked over the edge and saw the tall big-boned woman hanging on, jumping around like King Kong swinging on a vine, raising all kinds of racket. I shouted that she had my cable.

She howled like a panther with her tail in a trap, then snarled, "You little son of a bitch, bring your shitty ass down that ladder, I'll show you whose cable this is!"

Other workers were snickering at me, and, besides, no decent country boy could live it down if he let a girl rustle his welding cable. But just as I stepped from the ladder, she picked a haymaker up from the deck and jarred me. I stumbled back over a tangle of cables and electrical cords and plopped on my rump. She came at me again, twirling the brass rod holder at the end of the cable. Before she let it fly at my head, a gray-haired gentleman slapped her with his open palm.

She looked surprised.

So was I when recognizing the man to be the one who had called me a smart-assed punk, regarding the paper mill stink and smell of money.

Things really got hot and loud. She called the older welder a sneaking son of a bitch and threw a roundhouse haymaker at him. He ducked and pinned her arms. She kneed him in the groin and spit in his face, and he popped her again with his open hand.

I just leaned back on my elbows and watched the show.

The commotion got the attention of her leaderman and also that of the quarterman. A leaderman was over a single crew and a quarterman supervised four or five leadermen and crews. *Ma Barker* was still cussing and raising cain, even at the quarterman. But the grizzle-haired welder was as calm as a flushed toilet. The quarterman asked if he had hit the woman, and he told him, no, that he only slapped her because she had put herself in a man's place.

The quarterman said, "Oh, well then, she shouldn't have done that." Then he tried to learn why the lady was so upset, and she pointed a finger at me and one at the older man, and let go with another sputtering stream of nasty talk.

The older welder finally ended the controversy by informing the quarterman he had witnessed the particular welding cable being assigned to me and that the kid was merely trying to get it from Big Mama—his words.

The boss checked and learned that the woman had not bothered to check out a cable from the utility man but, instead, had just grabbed the first one handy. The quarterman took the cable from the enraged woman and handed it to me. I pulled it over into the engine room and went to work.

Stella didn't work overtime that day, but my good buddy, Albert, hastened to fill her in, and then some. He told her that Mac got the hell beat out of him by a girl I had messed with.

And, of course, I had a well-defined swollen jaw that would seem to verify it.

Poor Salty. He sure tried . . . he was my friend and I liked him, but didn't think I needed any more friends like him, all at once, with me trying to cope with predicaments that kept jumping out of holes along the path I trod.

However, I had never gotten as much petting from Mom when I was a little tot as what Stella gave me when she learned the straight of the incident. Each morning for two or three days as we got our welding gear from our big locker at the head of way number-4, both Pete and Repete would coo and purr over me, petting my swollen jaw and giving it little brushes with their lips. I wished I had been popped on both jaws by the slugger.

Heroes brought back from overseas for recruiting duty often made pep talks at the shipyard. Usually it was during a break for a ship launching. I would listen in awe and get all fired up; I was going to join some branch of service each time I heard one of those brave soldiers or sailors tell their war story; in fact, I had already tried to join the Seabees before I was eighteen.

Dad would have signed the papers but Mom sent them back unsigned, writing that when I became eighteen and the matter was out of her hands, that was one thing; but if she sent me off beforehand and if I got killed, she couldn't forgive herself—a concern not unusual for mothers of the time when it came to giving their consent for an underaged son to volunteer to go to war.

I was disappointed, because as a welder, I had been offered some type of little stripe by the Construction Battalion of the navy—known as Seabees—after basic training. However, at the time, it would only be a few months until I could join up without parental consent. Salty offered me the benefit of his wisdom on the matter. He told me outfits like the Seabees or Merchant Marine would be too rough for a kid like me. He urged me to join the Paratroopers or real Marines. He pretended to be sincere, just like he was really concerned about me getting soft duty . . . !

The Wainwright shipyard was one of over twenty in the USA from 1941 through 1945 that built more than 2,700 Liberty-Class ships. (The *Patrick Henry*, the first Liberty ship, was launched

September 1941 in Baltimore; a total of fourteen were launched in America that day. Building Liberty ships was the largest ship-building effort by any nation ever.) Add to that over 500 Victory ships built for the Merchant Marine, and all the other ships built such as the fighting ships of the navy, and that created an urgent need for welders. And so, the welding superintendent kept pressuring me to stay on the job. He tried to butter me up, insisting that I was a vital part of national defense, that my country needed me right where I was, that he had influence with the draft board, and that he could get me deferred from military service for the war's duration.

But I saw those ships leaving every five days through St. Andrews Bay, slipping on out into the Gulf, and a longing tugged inside my chest as I watched them fade over the horizon into the wide expanse of the unknown. I had helped build those ships, and they were sailing to faraway places I could only dream about. As ship after ship left Panama City, the urgency within me grew.

Often, when the day shift ended, recruiters for the United States Maritime Service training base at St. Petersburg were waiting outside the shipyard's gate. They really latched on to young lads and hung on, painting glowing word-pictures of all the exotic places that would be ours to see, if we would just sign on with them. Their persistence reached such a point it seemed they would make me something like an admiral. One aggressive recruiter outright promised that I could also finish high school, if I would just sign up; he hooked me by making the additional promise I could become a marine engineer, in short order—a ship's officer, fancy uniform, gold braid, and all.

Hot dog . . . ! Finding my dream girl ought to be easy, if I could get all decked out in a fancy officer's uniform, I thought.

My first cousin, Glen, Mom's twin sister's son, was like a big brother to me. He was regular army, artillery sergeant, in before the United States got into the War II shooting, and he wrote me a V-letter from somewhere in Italy, in reply to my request for advice. He stated he had learned how to destroy in order to serve, but if I had a chance to learn something constructive, like becoming an engineer, and still serve my country, then I should go for it. Thus, I joined the Merchant Marines, where fate held in store a big surprise—a human first—for which it selected me to eventually blunder through.

After a short visit home, I returned to Panama City and worked a few days longer as a farewell gesture.

There were six construction ways at the Wainwright shipyard, and we launched six ships per month. And just before I left, we launched a ship named in honor of Wendell L. Willkie, who was defeated as the Republican candidate in 1940 when he ran against Franklin D. Roosevelt for President of the United States. Old-timers quipped that winners sometimes got big sleek ships named in their honor but losers had to settle for fat squatty Liberty ships.

Now, I really don't know who first started the bottle-bouncing-off-the-bow act in launching ships, but Mrs. Wendell Willkie was at the Wainwright yard and she did the best bottle-bouncing performance I have ever seen. She well outdid Miss Margaret Truman (daughter of Senator Harry S. Truman) when she did her thing with the champagne bottle on the prow of the Battleship *Missouri* when it was launched 29 January, 1944, at the Navy Yard in Brooklyn, New York. It seemed to me that Miss Truman just sort of petted the *Mighty Mo* with her champagne bottle—her delicate whacks were shown many times in movie newsreels and, later, on television.

Author at age eighteen, April 1945. This picture was taken on a visit back to Memphis a few days before entering Maritime Service Training at St. Petersburg, Florida.

But Mrs. Willkie's bottle-banging effort never was shown by any newsreel that I ever saw. And she really slammed the bottle hard on the prow of that Liberty ship named in honor of her late husband, and, still, it didn't break!

June 1945. Author while on special thirty-two-hour pass from training at St. Petersburg, Florida.

Peanut butter jars and champagne bottles surely must have been tough stuff back then. . . . Anyway, at each launching, a man grabbed the bottle at the last second and gave it a hard whack to give each ship a good send-off with a splash of bubbly.

Stella and I were together the night before I left to report to the Maritime Training Station. She made me promise that I would not get a potbelly.

I even had a special picture made of myself to give her just before we parted. Then, out of the blue, she stunned me by commenting that she would make up her mind between me and a boyhood sweetheart who was in the army, to whom she said she was engaged, when he got back from overseas.

Stella was really a sweet and pretty girl but I didn't think I was yet ripe enough to be plucked. Anyway, I had not thought about such serious matters happening so soon.

I could understand her thoughts on the matter since she was three years my senior. But the implied suggestion that I should agree to be one of two bulls in the holding pen, waiting to know which one would eventually be selected, was not at all appealing to me.

I let the subject ride until later.

Flags everywhere were at half-mast when we reached Birmingham, Alabama, from where my group of Merchant Marine Volunteers would be sent by train to the Maritime Training Station. And I learned that President Roosevelt died at Warm Springs, Georgia, on that day, April 12, 1945.

CHAPTER 6

LINER AT LANDING STAGE, LIVERPOOL.   69418

THE MARITIME TRAINING STATION AT ST. PETERSBURG WAS on a landfill that spread out into the bay. The main gate was at the north with direct access to a city street.

There were about 120 in my group. Upon arrival we were greeted at the entrance by a chief petty officer who cautioned that any of us who had second thoughts and wished to change our minds could do so before relinquishing our enrollment papers. But, he added, that once we surrendered the papers, our bodies, our thoughts, and our very souls would belong to Uncle Sam for the coming weeks of training.

He waited, then asked us to pass through the gate. When we were all inside, he ordered a second-class petty officer to take possession of each packet of our enrollment documents. When they were all secured, he then told us, "Now, I don't know, and don't want to know, and don't care, what the recruiting people told you men, but whatever it was, just forget it and we'll get along just fine. Their job was to get you here." He paused, scanning our faces as we let the sobering news sink in; I felt a ship sinking in the pit of my stomach and I swallowed hard. I really wished for a big chaw of Days Work, but had stopped chewing because a welding shield over my face and spitting tobacco juice had not been compatible.

The chief went on, "I know that many of you were probably promised the *golden skyhook* by the recruiters. They perhaps told you men that you could receive special training." He paused to flash a devilish grin, then added, "Ahhh, yes . . . you thought you would become glorified deck or engineering officers and the like, that you would strut in dashing uniforms all splashed with gold braid." He jutted his chin, to snap, "Forget it. It ain't going to happen, except for a very limited number of you."

He again paused, and I felt the urge to tell him to cut out the crap and get on with it. Finally he said, "After brief training in seamanship, most of you men will be shipped out as wipers, ordinary seamen, or messmen." He again paused and looked us over, one by one. Then clearing his throat, he took on a gung-ho tone, and added, "Very good.

"Now then. Men, we'll do the best we can, but our country needs merchant seamen to man ships for the big push in the Pacific. Yes, I said the big push. That's what you're here for, and we're going to get you aboard those ships as soon as possible. . . ." He let it dangle.

"Are there any questions," he asked in a sharp tone that indicated he did not wish to hear any. Feet shuffled and there was mumbling among us but no one spoke up.

Finally I blurted, "No sir, I ain't got any questions, but I want my dadgummed papers back."

He did a double take, then barked, "What's your name, sailor?"

"It's McEwen, but I ain't no sailor."

He rubbed his chin, looked at me long, then drawled, "Welllll, son, you are now.

"McEwen, huh?" He turned to the second-class petty officer and ordered, "Make a note on McEwen, I think we have us a boll weevil who's going to be a troublemaker."

The petty officer took on a smirky grin and scribbled on his pad like he relished the opportunity.

Heckfire, I was not any trouble maker . . . ! It was just a case with me, that what was right was right. I got extremely upset when someone lied to me, and there I believed that Uncle Sam, my own government, had lied to me. I was a bitter, frustrated young man.

However, the chief deserved a medal for telling us straight. Few would get special training, and within a couple of months I would find my *tender* butt bounced around out on the North Atlantic. But not before the United States Maritime Service Training Station at St. Petersburg knew that a boy from the log woods and cotton fields had been there.

Little Red, who became a good pal, forewarned me. He had an older brother who was in the navy, and had received advice from him on what not to do while in training. Red solemnly scolded, "Mac, you should have kept quiet at the front gate. Now you have drawn attention to yourself. They're sure gonna be after your country ass."

Everyone was passing out advice like old pros and I took Red's comments with a grain of salt. However, it was only a matter of hours when, everywhere I turned, I got the feeling that all the Maritime personnel knew who I was.

We were marched to our barracks and, within a day or so, processed and issued uniforms. I was assigned a lower bunk at the far end of the long building, well away from the large head and shower room. The next day, late in the afternoon while I was taking a shower, they pulled a fire drill.

We had been instructed to drop everything when we heard the signal for abandoning ship or heard the fire alarm and report immediately to our mustering stations. Therefore, I snugged a big towel around me and "laid to," as they called it. They were not going to have reason to call me a troublemaker, because, by golly, I was going to obey orders to the letter.

The long administration building was centered on the base. And stretching along the east side, between the building and the seawall, a street accessed the main gate. My assigned mustering station was on the east side near the front gate. Women who worked in the offices were leaving for the day, rushing towards the gate, until they spotted me, standing at attention, front row center, bare as a peeled banana except for the towel.

My group was mustered within five feet of the street, and the ladies giggled and snickered to one another as they paused along.

Some jerk behind me jerked at my towel, and I tried to hang on. The petty officer barked for me to come to attention. It was the front-gate second-class petty officer, whom we tagged Bean Pole.

I obeyed.

The rascal behind me jerked my towel off leaving not a single thread for cover.

The passing ladies giggled and a few stopped briefly to howl with unrestrained laughter.

I dashed to the rear of the muster.

Petty officer bawled that he had not ordered me to fall out, and he barked for me to fall back in and come to attention, on the double.

I did.

There I stood, naked as a 'coon's eye in a spotlight.

Petty put me on report.

I appeared before captain's mast early next morning, and was declared guilty of being out of uniform, conduct unbecoming a seaman, and breaking ranks without an order. Also, I got a stern lecture about the Maritime not tolerating goldbricks. I was restricted to the base for two weeks. That meant I had to work or pull extra watch duty on weekends and also after training exercises each day during the week; I also had to work or stand watch until 11 or 12 P.M.

Before I finished that off, while in a hurry after chow one evening to get a shower and have a few leisure moments before turning-to for my penalty duty, I snapped the lock closed on my locker with the key inside.

The barracks office put me on report for that.

I was charged with carelessness not in keeping with good seamanship. I got another week's restriction and a stern lecture about the Maritime not tolerating goldbricks.

I became terribly frustrated. I earnestly tried to do my best and had no problems with my regular training routines. I climbed the ropes and cargo nets and kept pace with the best going through the obstacle course; my physical condition still retained much of the toughness from my hard work on the farm.

Although I believed I already knew how to row a boat, I put my back into the lifeboat training and paid attention to my instructors and was careful to obey every order, and thought I observed all the rules. I didn't know what, but I felt like something sinister was stalking me. I even got put on report while working off punishment details.

For example, we goldbricks were cleaning the big spacious office of the main administration building one night. Another hard-driving petty officer asked if I could run the big industrial-type buffing machine. I had never used one before but figured it would be easier than tussling with a double-shovel plow in new ground, and so I assured him that I could.

I flipped the switch on the big centrifugal floor polisher and hung on while that scooting, whirling sucker dragged me all over the big office. It knocked chairs and wastebaskets across the room, and it bumped desks, knocking typewriters, staplers, ash trays, and other stuff to the floor.

Petty officer jumped up and down, screaming, "Turn it off, turn it off, turn it off!"

I shouted back for him not to worry, that I would get the hang of the buzzing bull before I was through. After all, I had tussled with a big hard-rimmed tractor in new ground. I had sticka u-nus and was not going to let a little squirrely machine get the best of me.

Petty officer danced a jig as he darted about until he found the receptacle and jerked out the electrical cord's plug-in.

I was put on report for that little bulldogging escapade, was told I disobeyed an order to turn off the machine, and that I had destroyed property vital to the war effort.

That added another two weeks restriction and extra duty to my growing backlog. And the presiding officer at captain's mast assured me that the Maritime knew how to handle goldbricks— had I been required to remain on that base until I worked off all my extra duty, I don't believe I would have ever left unless I was granted a parole. Two special passes were the only times I left the base during my entire tenure there.

One was a forty-two-hour pass for being with the crew who won a lifeboat race. The race was held one Saturday afternoon to entertain the yacht people of the area. It was supposed to be a volunteer affair. However, a boat was a man short for the oars. I was nearby, policing the area for trash, and Bean Pole *volunteered* me by pushing me into the boat.

Several lifeboats were towed a mile out into Tampa Bay, lined up with bows even, then we were ordered to race back to the base. But when each of us feathered our oar while waiting for the starting signal, I discovered that my oar was actually one used for a rudder. It was bigger and longer and weighed two or three times as much as a rowing oar. Someone had sneaked an oar-switch into that boat. I then suspected why Bean Pole was so determined to get me into the boat as part of the twelve-man rowing crew. But all the others happened to be fairly husky lads, and they told me to boat the tiller oar to keep it out of their way. Those strong pistons really bent their backs and won the race. And so, that got me my first pass from the base.

I tried to make it way up to Panama City and back, but waiting for bus connections, and buses running behind schedule, caused me to be six hours late getting back to the base.

It was a fruitless trip, anyway. Stella was peed-off at me. I had written her a letter in which I said that after thinking it over, I decided I didn't want to be one of two bulls waiting in a holding pen. She thought my analogy was absurd and could not understand why I felt that way if I really cared for her.

She played me the recording of her favorite song, "Beautiful Dreamer," but I didn't get to hug her all the way around when I left. Woe was me. Finding out about girls continued to be a bumfuzzling endeavor.

Back at the base, I was put on report for being AWOL, and I received an additional two weeks restriction with extra duty.

Boxing matches were held one Saturday afternoon to entertain citizens of St. Pete. My pal, Little Red, and I volunteered to participate; we went the prescribed three rounds with each other, faking our wildly swung haymakers. It was called a draw and we each were given a special thirty-two-hour pass.

We rented a room at a moderately priced hotel then took a look at the pretty city. At the end of the Million Dollar Pier we met two nice young ladies from Nashville, Tennessee. They were first cousins visiting an uncle to both.

He was a grand old man; a snow-white-haired gentleman and apparently a man with a comfortable retirement, as a former executive for a railroad. His niece Alice Jordan and I enjoyed each other's company from the start. She was a pleasant and attractive young lady who planned to start college soon in Nashville. She, too, had long golden hair, but she acted more refined than Prissy Fay—she didn't call me Leeeee Roy.

The old-timer beamed when he learned I was born not far from McEwen, Tennessee, and we got along great. We warmed up to each other, talking about hunting and country life. I recalled how, growing up on the farm, I mimicked wild mallards by pressing the end of a fist to my mouth and blowing hard through the hollow. And, except when my hands and lips were extremely cold and stiff, I seldom used a duck caller when hunting.

I remembered the days when mallard ducks darkened the sky in the rice growing area of the Arkansas Delta, and I sometimes stood hail calling and chattering the feed-call merely to watch in awe as ducks funneled down to cover a rice field. They can see far when flying and, when conditions were right, after one flock started dropping, others joined to paint a crisp blue sky full of blotches like big tree leaves fluttering to settle on the water. At such times, the flooded fields looked as though they were a shimmering carpet of greenhead mallards. Truly a spectacular sight.

Alice's uncle got a kick out of my reminiscences and duck calling exhibition, and I felt at ease with my newfound friends, until I pulled a real boo-boo.

That Sunday evening he took us to Pass-a-Grille Beach for southern fried chicken. There I was, in the company of high-class folks, with a personal dilemma facing me. I simply never thought it practical to use a knife and fork to eat fried chicken, no matter what etiquette experts advised on the matter. But I tried. Tightly gripping the fork, I jammed the tines to the plate to anchor the drumstick. I applied so such pressure that, when I used my knife, fork, chicken, and all scooted off the plate and across the table. I felt naked. However my new friends politely ducked their faces and wiped at their mouths with napkins. No one made the slightest snicker, but anger at myself raged within me. I shook my head in my mind and grabbed the drumstick with my hand, thinking it was a silly, dumb thing for Mac to try and whittle crispy fried chicken off little bones with a knife and fork when a leg already offered a ready-made handle.

Whether the uncle thought he was helping a country lad save face or whether he welcomed the excuse to join in, the jolly-faced man grabbed a drumstick, heartily chuckling, "I'll shovel coal with you. Son, let's show 'em how to enjoy fried chicken."

Doris Day singing "Going to Take a Sentimental Journey" to the fine music of Les Brown and his Band of Renown was the top tune during this time and was heard everywhere. Now, when I hear that pretty wistful song, it brings back fond memories of some warmhearted folks who once upon a time made a lonely boy's day one of great joy.

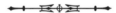

But, alas, good times must sometimes end, and it was soon back to the base, where my boo-boos continued.

After I had eaten noon chow one day, a soft drink machine took my nickel but failed to dispense my "Co'Cola"—no, not Coca-Cola. Back then few of my peers called it Coca-Cola, and we didn't call it Coke. Even though Coke became a registered trademark, to us coke was something used to make steel. It was Co'Cola to us; we said it all as one word: "Ko-Kola."

I humped the machine with my shoulder then let it drop with a jar. Co'Colas started shooting out as coins clattered from the coin-return slot.

The silver-haired delivery man appeared out of nowhere and threw a jigging fit. Then he stomped to the officer-of-the-day's office down the hall.

Acting like he was eager to show what a great guy he was, the O. D. fawned all over the soda pop man. Then he put me on report, and I was charged with some malarkey about lacking an attitude compatible with building goodwill among the local citizenry. Another week's restriction was added on, along with a declaration that the Maritime knew how to deal with goldbricks, and that I had better shape up because I definitely was not going to ship out until I did.

I worried in torment about it—hell's bells, all I had done was try to get my Co'Cola jarred out of the stingy machine . . . !

But the more that was piled on the more I bowed my back. I gritted my teeth and resolved to show them that I was not a dumb goldbrick. I was attentive to my training instructors and made high scores on the little tests we were given for tying all those knots with ropes, boxing the compass, swimming, and jumping off the high tower into the swimming pool. They told us that jumping off the high tower was a required test to determine if one would jump off a sinking ship.

I guaran-dang-teed them that if a ship was sinking I would jump. Didn't do any good. They made me jump off to prove it.

No big thing, I had jumped out of trees at the old swimming hole higher than that twenty-foot tower.

All girl stuff, I thought.

But they made the biggest to-do about lifeboat handling, so it seemed to me. We were told over and over about ship disasters at sea; and especially about the chaotic way lifeboats were handled in the 1934 disaster of the ocean liner *Morro Castle*, in which 134 lives were lost within sight of Ashbury Park, off New Jersey's coast. (Later on down the trail, there would be cause for the *Morro Castle* to have a special meaning to me.)

Our spirits soared May 8 (V-E Day), when President Truman announced the allied victory in Europe; Germany's unconditional surrender became effective at midnight May 8–9. The last German U-Boat sunk was by a British plane on May 9. Unfortunately, the ceasefire was too late reaching the mountains of northern Italy when the last American killed in Europe, my cousin, Sergeant Connie McEwen, from Camden, Tennessee, was killed a day later. I would greatly miss Connie's grinning face—he was like a good-natured big brother—he put me astraddle my first horse when I was only two years of age.

Anyway, I was determined to finish basic training and get on to the good stuff.

Three or four trainees from my group were going to be selected to take special training, and I refused to let myself believe that I would not be one of them. Therefore, as first choice, I listed engineer-officer's training at Kings Point, New York, and asked for training to become a radio operator as my second choice.

But Little Red and I soon learned we were going to a shipping pool in Charleston. We were classified as messmen.

No special training, no nothing—I was going to be a kitchen-jockey messman! One heck of a way to get to be somebody, I thought. I failed to see how there could be any great need for mere messmen to finish off the rest of the war with Japan. I appealed my classification without success. In effect, according to my interpretation, I was told I was too dumb to take the special training I wanted.

I was totally drained and bitter. All hope was gone. I thought, Uncle Sam had not been square with me in the way they got me to join the Maritime. I told Little Red that I was going to "crawl the fence" and return to the shipyard where I could do real work. Whether he snitched, or whoever, the chaplain had me hauled before him. A tall rawboned man with bushy eyebrows, he patiently listened as I poured out my grief and disgust.

"Dang it, Preacher, I don't like it when people lie to me," I blurted. He nodded as though he understood and tried to console me with kind words of encouragement.

It didn't take. I continued to sound off. "Unless he gets to be somebody, how can a dumb ole boy ever find a pretty, decent girl who'd ever want to be his mate for life? Now you just answer me that—besides, what the hel—uh, heck, does a Catholic preacher care about an ole boy from the sticks; an ole hard-tailed Baptist, at that!"

Man, he came alive. Snatched me by the arms and pulled my face to his, scolding, "Now, you listen to me, my young hotheaded friend. I care very much about what happens to you. I care about all of God's creatures!" He was scaring the holy hell out of me and I drew back from his glare.

A faint grin touched the corners of his mouth, and he went on, "Now, if you really desire to become an engineer as ardently as you claim and if you want to, as you say, get to be somebody, then you will take a berth aboard a ship." He released my arms and paced about, then in a softer tone, continued, "Lee, that's certainly one of the best places to learn."

Shaking a long bony finger in my face, he added, "And, young man, you listen, I sense enough about you already to know that you really don't want to crawl the fence and be a quitter. Why, if you did that, it would put a black mark on your record for the rest of your life. Now we don't want that, do we? Of course not. Just take my advice and stick it out. You appear to be sincere, and I'm sure things are going to turn out well for you."

I mumbled that I sure did hope so and started to the door with my tail dragging.

He followed and gave me a fatherly pat on the back, with a final comment, "Do me a favor, Sailor. Never worry about getting to be somebody. You are somebody. We are all somebody; we're God's children. And don't ever forget it."

I never crawled the fence, but I didn't get out of St. Pete without leaving additional footprints of my having once passed that way.

While waiting to be shipped, I still had to work at diminishing the penalty duty I had piled up. I was assigned to the main galley as a flunky. The burly chief cook with tatoos all over hairy arms ordered me to watch a large floor-mounted electric mixer into which he had dumped a bushel of boiled potatoes. He had already seasoned them, but he pointed to a stack of butter and ordered me to cream the potatoes by adding butter.

As the mixer hummed, I occasionally tossed in a pound of butter. But the spuds seemed slow in taking on that rich creamy look like Mom always made. And so I tossed in two chunks at a time. After the twelve pounds were gone, the potatoes still didn't appear to be as creamy as Mom's. I approached the chief for more butter. I shuffled my feet as I waited while he finished giving instructions to a cook trainee.

Finally he growled, "Well, Boll Weevil, what do you want?"

"Sir, I need some more butter, if you don't mind." I flashed him an eager grin.

His eyes leaped over to the empty spot on the stainless steel table top where his butter had been. He whipped the deck with a towel, and bellered, "You mean that you used all my butter? That's all the damned butter allocated for the whole damned meal. You damned cotton-patch sailors are going to scuttle me yet before this damned war is over!"

His safety valve stuck and he blew up. For sure, he put me on report. It didn't do him a darn bit of good, though.

There was no butter for bread rolls at noon chow that day, but I never heard one single complaint. Everyone said those were the best mashed potatoes they had tasted since leaving their mother's cooking.

I thought to myself, hotdog, at last, I finally did something that made people think I was a pretty good ole boy.

After midnight that same day, for my last night to have extra duty, I was assigned to patrol a firewatch from the main gate westward along the front fence. I was really beat. For several days, I had little sleep or rest.

The first-class petty officer on duty at the gatehouse surely read the fatigue in my face. After about an hour, he hinted that he couldn't see me if I went to the head in the back room then lay my face on a desk top to grab a few winks.

It was some of the soundest sleep I ever enjoyed, until jarred awake when the whole base seemed to come alive.

During the course of training, clumsy attempts to get released from the Maritime with honor were sometimes tried by those who decided they didn't want a tour of the world by sea. And one of the most common attempts was the walking-in-your-sleep malady. This happened quite frequently. Perhaps a few were legitimate strolls but most such snoring-walks were suspect.

Anyway, while I was away from my patrol, lost in dreamland in the back room, a sleeping beauty dozed by in the silent night. If he was dreaming about falling, he would always be able to tell his grandchildren it is not true that if one ever landed when having such a dream it would be fatal.

Could have been, though. He walked off the blooming seawall near the front gate.

When the tide was in, as we were all aware, it would have been a short drop. But the tide was out. He dropped about twelve feet and sprawled across a small boat that was tied up in a manner which allowed it to rise and fall with tides.

He woke up.

He woke the whole slumbering base.

Seldom does one ever hear such bellering and carrying on.

And adding confusion to the melee, some clown sneaked an abandon-ship signal over the high-volume public address: repeating over and over, seven short blasts followed by a long

First week in July 1945. Author while on overnight pass from "shipping pool" in Charleston, South Carolina, from where the author would be assigned July 11 to the U.S. Army Hospital ship Larkspur.

blast—indeed, just like a fire drill, everyone was required to fall out and muster when they heard an abandon-ship signal.

There sure was a lot of commotion going on around the old United States Maritime Training Station at St. Pete that night.

But to my surprise and relief, nothing happened to me because of the leaving-my-post boo-boo. The petty officer simply reported he had granted me leave from my patrol to relieve myself in the head.

Fortunately, the snoozing cruiser's wake-up only sprained an ankle and cracked a couple of his ribs, I was told.

And so, I was allowed to board the train with my group and travel on to Charleston. There I would be assigned to a ship, which, after three voyages, would be selected as the very first ship assigned to a particular delicate duty.

The unusual experience was so unique that less than two or three dozen people out of the whole human race ever had such an adventure. To narrow the focus even more, I was one of two who were the first two people to ever do so. Also, my ship led the way; it was the very first to carry out this once-in-a-lifetime type duty. After which, many new rules and regulations immediately went into effect to govern the crews who manned all the other U.S. Army transport ships that were selected for this very delicate and special assignment.

CHAPTER 7

LINER AT LANDING STAGE, LIVERPOOL.

69418

LIFE AROUND THE BARRACKS AT THE SHIPPING POOL IN Charleston was boring and restless. There was plenty of time to reflect, ponder, and to hope for the future despite my despair.

The fields did not appear fertile, and the prospects for a good yield in my life seemed slim. But I would picture Dad and Mom saying, "Son, where there's a will the Almighty will find a way for you. You've just gotta have sticka u-nus." And so I resolved to keep plowing, come what may.

A popular new song of the time by Bing Crosby was heard each day over the radio: "You Belong To My Heart, Dear, Now And Forever." It added to my melancholy longing; somewhere out there, I knew not where, someone belonged to my heart.

July 10, 1945, aircraft from carriers began bombing targets in Japan, preparing for an invasion by American forces. That day, Red and I signed on with the U.S. Army Transport Service, Water Division, called the ATS. (It would be changed to Army Transportation Corps.) We were assigned berths aboard the United States Army Hospital Ship *Larkspur*. Crewmen referred to her as the *Larkspur Motion*.

U.S. Army Hospital ship Larkspur *coming into port at Charleston, South Carolina, during* World War II. *In 1900 at Bremen, Germany, the keel was laid for the ship, and she was outfitted at Bremenhaven, a few miles downstream on River Wesser. Named the* Breslen, *she was a German raider during World War I. After that war, the U.S. Navy confiscated the ship. Having left Germany as a "man of war," she would return on a mission of mercy forty-six years after her birth at Bremen/Bremerhaven. The* Larkspur *served in the Atlantic during War II, bringing sick and wounded American warriors home from Oran, North Africa; France; Germany; and England. She was later recommissioned as the U.S. Army Transport* Bridgeport *and would have the honor to bring the first shipload of war brides to America.*

She was an ancient old lady, named the *Breslin* when built in Bremen, Germany, in 1900, and outfitted at Bremerhaven in 1901. As a raider in World War I, she preyed on allied ships, then was confiscated by the U.S. Navy after War I. However, her old twin quadruple-expansion reciprocating steam engines had seen their best days. She was too slow, even, for ten-knot convoy speed. But she was a good riding ship with a thick hull of riveted plates, and the U.S. Army made her into a hospital ship for World War II service in the Atlantic, where she traveled alone. She was a tough old girl I would soon learn.

I was assigned to the ship's mess as its only waiter, in which I was to serve seventeen so-called chief petty officers: chief quartermaster, boatswain, chief electrician, and chief plumber, etc.

The ship's mess was on D-deck, forward of the long saloon mess room on the port side. The pantry was aft of the saloon mess. Ship's officers, army-officer doctors, and the forty army-officer nurses dined in the saloon mess.

I had to skip and hustle to get chow to serve my bunch because I often had to wait in line behind the nine waiters who served the officers. Thus, sometimes it was quite awhile before I got chow to feed disgruntled diners in my mess room, and I often got chewed out for taking so long.

July 11, 1945, we got underway for Cherbourg, France. At sea, with all the crew aboard, I discovered that I was serving chow to thirty-one men instead of seventeen. But what the heck, the best chow came from the officers' pantry, and I could not blame the assistants to the chiefs for getting in on a good thing. But they also bitched and demanded pampered service just as though they belonged. I could have had the parasites barred but didn't want to be a snitch. I figured that I would tolerate them if they could tolerate me—I bitched right back at them.

Heads were turned and poker games were allowed in the ship's mess at night, and I was told that, as caterer, I would receive generous tips. However, I was not concerned about how many tips I could get. I was still in a state of bitterness and disgust. And my attitude soured even more after Lee Hi, the ship's carpenter, jogged into the mess room a few minutes before supper chow that first evening at sea.

The grinning clown sat down and jabbered in his broken English, "Ahhh, you Lee me Lee. Me you be good buddies. We be good shipmates. Lee Hi show how play good ploka. Lee Hi allee time play ploka Lee Hi good ploka player. Allee time nobody beat Lee Hi play ploka. . . . "

Jabber, jabber, and all that time the cheerful "ploka" player was squeezing juice from lemon slices, making a glass of lemonade. There was none left!

Of course others wanted a slice of lemon for tea when they came in to dine that evening. But the pantrymen refused to give me anymore. They had supplied me with seventeen slices of lemon for the meal; seventeen men were all I was supposed to serve and seventeen slices of lemon were all I could get.

My chow hounds took it out on me. They told me time and again how good their waiter was the previous trips and how much they had rewarded him in tips.

I fired back, suggesting they could stick their tips where the sun didn't shine. And I was quick to tell one and all that I was not going to sea to be an eighty-dollar-per-month waiter.

I was not a good waiter and, by golly, I got few tips. Actually, I was given only one tip for the whole voyage. A permanent-crew army sergeant, who operated our radar, gave me five dollars when we returned to Charleston.

The sarge never once bitched at me. He was a friendly, easy-going man, and we used to have long talks; he often had coffee in my mess while chatting with me. He told me about his father who had been a mariner in World War I.

Once he offered, "Mac, you should get off these ships. You're still young, and you can find something better. . . . My dad was a piece of crap under people's feet after the shooting stopped in Number One, and it'll be the same way for American Merchant Marines when this one is all over."

My treatment as host of the poker games was even worse than it was when I served regular chow. Often when losing a big pot, the loser would vent his anger at me: "Why did you bring me rye with baby shit all over it? I wanted white bread and mayonnaise," or, "This coffee is like warmed over piss!"

It didn't matter that I had just returned from the pantry with a pot of hot coffee, and that the loser had distinctly told me he wanted a sandwich made with ham and mustard on rye. It was very hard to please one who had just lost a big money pot.

The volatile Larkspur Poker Club had a thing about tearing up cards and flinging them out the porthole when a diehard player lost a big pot. And, although I had to plead with the two Red Cross ladies stationed on board to give me a new deck, some of the disgruntled poker players raved at me each time, grumbling that I took too long, and they always told me what a stinking waiter I was.

Finally, I again suggested what they could do with their tips and their poker games in my mess room, and I pulled a sit-down on them.

Little Red was a waiter for the saloon mess, and after supper chow the second night at sea, I turned the poker club catering over to him. He took their flack and just grinned at them. (He made more in tips than he did in salary; overall, he made more each trip than many of the ship's officers made!) And after I finished serving chow each day, I went below and worked until midnight, learning to be a fireman.

I enjoyed it down in the fire room. Everyone taught me little important functions, and for the first time since welding in the shipyard, I was doing something more to my liking.

Still, a feeling of foreboding bothered me from time to time, especially when I was able to hit the sack for a short night's sleep. I would tell myself such apprehensions were known by millions of other young men who had crossed that wide ocean, headed for a war zone. Mindful that they had a far greater reason to feel anxiety than I, guilt feelings nagged me, and I chided myself for being a softy about my sense of gloom.

We had to anchor inside the long breakwater and wait for docking space when we reached Cherbourg.

Sunken ships which the retreating Germans had scuttled still cluttered the harbor. But they had been tugged aside to open a zigzagged passage through their maze, yet only about two ships could tie up at any one time at the badly damaged docking area.

The bombed-out, shelled-out, burned-out hulls of buildings and piles of rubble that had once been buildings, presented scenes much more dismal than any war destruction I had seen in news-reels at the movies. There was no brightness to the drab scene before my eyes near the waterfront in Cherbourg. The grand terminal building which once welcomed great ocean liners was blasted into jumbled piles of big concrete chunks.

One tried to imagine what it had once been like, but this day it was impossible for me to envision carefree passengers of another time embarking or debarking because I was too stunned by the stark reality of what the war had left in its wake.

Small craft provided ship-to-shore taxi service for those who wished to go ashore. Most who were not on duty did. However, some of us lingered aboard.

Young shipmates, some of whom were first-trippers also, returned to chatter with excitement about their first visit in a foreign country. They tried to swagger with the salty demeanor of a real "sea dog" while describing in detail their escapades ashore: a brief shackup for a five-cent pack of cigarettes—a ten-pack carton only cost us fifty cents aboard ship.

Some compared other bargains: a German P38 service pistol purchased for a few nickel packs of American cigarettes. The enemy must have also done a lot of swapping, because there were quite a number of P38 pistols to be had in Cherbourg; Chanel No. 5 perfume (developed in time for bartering during the German occupation of France) could still be found for a carton of cigarettes. Dealers back in the States would pay twenty-two dollars an ounce to any hustler who could find and bring some back. Cognac brandy was available for a few packs of cigarettes per bottle. I was amazed that such bounty was still available in the war-torn city.

By far, the most popular boast for some young seamen, often no older than I, was about all the zig-ziging they did. One novice chortled that he had used up a whole carton of Lucky Strike cigarettes during an all-night visit with a woman. His companion scoffed at him about his illustrious version, and claimed that the novice merely gave the woman the cigarettes to stop her from laughing at him and for her promise that she would not tell others about his obvious inexperience.

Zig-zig was a term I had never heard before, but it was soon defined by young first-trippers who suddenly felt they had become full-grown studs.

I didn't set one foot on a foreign land my first trip. My heart simply was not in it. Nor did I feel like I was a softy because of my feelings. This torn-up spot in the world, destruction and misery everywhere, and all the talk about young girls selling their bodies for a mere nickel, a pack of cigarettes, made me think of my sisters back home and how lucky they were.

Of course we swaggered and attempted to display the demeanor of a salty seaman, but I found that there were many young shipmates who shared my innermost feelings. Maybe we had not yet clearly shaped our thoughts on the matter, but deep within our subconscious was knowledge which made us realize that when it came to the woman-man deal making for a lifetime, the most valuable asset we had was ourselves. We were zealous, perhaps unconsciously, in our efforts to keep our trade goods undamaged.

Anyway, the drab, forlorn sad scene of war-ravaged Cherbourg seemed to match my mood. And simply gazing from aboard ship without going ashore to rub elbows with it was enough for me on this trip.

In contrast, it warmed my heart to see the overflowing joy of the soldiers, young and some not so young, coming aboard for us to take them home.

Some suffered various serious illnesses, but many were without an arm or a leg. Some with both an arm and leg missing. Still, there were others in far worse condition—there were those who had suffered in such conflicts as the Battle of the Bulge—those whose flesh had literally been frozen off in that most fierce battle, by so many, of War II in its final months.

On the battlefield they had been tigers—tough, mean fighting machines who had marched through a blazing hell with smoking gunpowder for a shield. All their tomorrows had been left back home in the hearts of their loved ones, and now they were going home.

A lump stuck in my throat while I watched brave men come aboard and kiss the deck with tears slipping down their cheeks, and while others reached out a feeble hand from their stretchers to pat a bulkhead or any part of the old ship they could touch.

In spite of my emotion, I did not feel very pleased with myself and this was merely my first trip. For awhile there as I looked on, a feeling of pride touched my heart in realizing I was a small part in the overall effort to carry those men home. All the way back across the Atlantic, I was in awe of all of them. I observed them day after day and was somewhat amazed that several combat soldiers seemed to appreciate those like myself wanting to know firsthand what they had been through.

Talk about it? They had been *over there* and, indeed, they *did* want to talk about it, if we expressed sincere interest and really paid attention to what they could tell us.

I felt a sense of guilt. There I was strong and healthy amidst young men scarred and disfigured for life, and I wondered if I was selfish because I harbored the dream I clung to.

We were on our way back when a radio operator posted one of our daily news flashes on the bulletin board in the C-deck foyer, midships. A surge of excitement swept through the ship upon learning that the "Little Boy" had been dropped on Hiroshima August 6, 1945.

Three days later, when learning that an A-bomb, the "Fat Man," had also destroyed Nagasaki, the old-timers agreed it was all over.

We docked in Charleston, August 14, 1945, the date Japan agreed to surrender. Many shipmates lamented because they would not be in New York City's Times Square to be part of the V-J Day celebration. General Jonathan Wainwright—in whose honor the shipyard in Panama City had been named—was released August 16, 1945, after over three years in captivity, from a Japanese POW camp in Manchuria. And we were all giddy with relief and joy because the burden of War II had suddenly been swept away.

To add to my elation, Chief Engineer Mallard informed me he would request the chief steward to release me for transfer to the engine department. Mr. Mallard really knew how to make a young man feel important; he had started to sea at age thirteen as a cabin boy and he knew the score. I remember him shaking my hand and patting me on the back, telling me that the watch-engineer had reported good things about my efforts to learn a fireman's routine. Then he told me he would be happy to have me as a member of the blackgang.

I was thrilled and full of anticipation. I thought, by golly, maybe the chaplain at the Maritime Training Base knew what he was talking about after all.

But while gathering my gear to move to the engine department's fo'c's'le, I was ordered over the PA to report to the chief steward's office.

There the steward raved, "McEwen, just who the hell do you young people think I am? I'm not running a seagoing boarding house for every lubber who comes aboard and makes one trip then gets the notion to switch to the blackgang. I've just informed Chief Mallard that I will not agree to your transfer." I started to protest, and he waved a hand, adding, "No! My decision is final. I'm not going to listen to any whining dribble about the matter. That is all, now go tend to your mess duties."

Like a snap of the finger, I decided I didn't like that man.

Once again, I felt like a ship was sinking in the pit of my stomach. My disgust fed anger that started slow, rising as I mused aloud, "Welllll sir, I don't know if that's all or not."

His mouth popped open and he stared at me.

I studied the deck for a second, and then it suddenly hit me: Dammit, I was tired of being treated like a kid. Looking him in the eye, I managed to keep my voice even, and said, "Mister, you can take that mess room and stick it." Tossing a mock salute, I left him frowning with wrinkled brow. I went aft and packed my sea bag to head for home and only God knew where else.

But the ship was being dry-docked in the navy shipyard for routine hull inspection, and I failed to get ashore beforehand. As the water inside the huge enclosure dropped, the ship started listing critically. I was already dressed in my best but I went below to see what was going on, why they were not transferring water or fuel oil to trim the vessel.

There was a good reason. Most of the blackgang signed off after each trip to seek a berth in a ship with a more modern power plant, because the old *Larkspur* was indeed a workhorse for members of the blackgang. Most of the power plant had been in the ship since 1900, and the complex ancient machinery needed frequent repairs to keep her clucking main engines turning the props. All controls were manual. The only parts that could be called modern were the three low-pressure watertube boilers that generated saturated steam to two hundred pounds per square inch; they had replaced six firetube boilers. Engine room and fire room crew members referred to their watches down in the hole as spending four hours in hell. Consequently, there was a big turnover in the blackgang trip after trip (it was a break for a novice like me, though, because this turnover made quick promotions possible for those who stayed aboard and would work).

It was after 4 P.M., and down in the hole I only recognized one face, that of an oiler who had been aboard the last trip. New replacements on watch were bumping into each other, running around in the fire room trying to find proper valves by which fuel oil could be transferred to bring the ship to an even keel.

I leaned on a workbench and watched. The scene was very funny—and, anyway, in my frame of mind, I also didn't care what happened. The oiler got the attention of a gray-haired man in faded dungarees and a chambray shirt. Pointing to me, the oiler informed him that I had worked in the fire room the previous trip and that I might know something about the valve setup. Running around like a headless rooster, the old-timer scooted to a stop before me. Tugging at a floppy oiler's cap, he puffed, "Do you? Can you? Lad, will you give us a hand?"

I believed the oldster to be merely a watertender and I cocked an eye at him, to say, "Mister, I know the transfer setup all right enough, but I don't give a hoot if this ship flops over and takes the side out of that damned dry dock."

He frowned as though he had not heard me correctly. Briefly toying with a little shaggy mustache playing under his nose, he studied my face. A twinkle mingled with anxiety in his eyes, and abruptly grabbing the seat of my britches with a hand at the nap of my neck, he wheeled me between the boilers.

Half chuckling, he growled, "Lad, I don't know what your problem is, but you get your fantail around there and start opening valves—and they'd better be the right ones!"

We transferred fuel oil and fresh water from port to starboard tanks, and brought the ship back on even keel.

I discovered that the old-timer was War I navy vintage; he was Mr. Dwight Voorhees, second engineer, who was standing his first watch in the *Larkspur Motion*, having just signed aboard.

A deck officer can sign aboard *any* ship and be ready to get underway immediately. But, when going in a ship of the various types, with different type power plants, an engineering officer would prefer time to familiarize himself with the ship's engine room and the locations of all the many controls, etc.

Anyway, one would have thought I had just helped save a life the way Mr. Voorhees carried on. He grabbed my hand with a hearty shake and slapped me on the back, chortling, "Young man, you can sail in the hole with me, anytime."

I caught a bus and started the weary trip to Memphis. It took nearly two days with late buses and changing buses that didn't make timely connections with other departures.

There was plenty of time to reflect and wallow in misery. My thoughts raced, and I mused that no matter how hard a country boy tried, perhaps fate decreed that such an uneducated person was not supposed to get to be somebody so's he could find a real special, nice girl to share his life. I also thought that even though there were good people in the world, I didn't believe the chief steward aboard the *Larkspur* was one of them.

I had spent my whole life, all that I could remember, putting in long-hour days. Everything I had done, whether before I left home or since, often involved long days.

When Dad moved the family from Memphis during the Great Depression, it was usually long hours of toil on the farm. Even before, in Memphis as a child, Dad refused soup kitchen, bread line, or any form of handouts as he called them, for the family. We removed the sod from vacant lots in our neighborhood, then raised vegetables and peddled them for pennies. I recalled the patches of hot tar on the streets in the summer months that stuck to my bare feet. Yet, my siblings and I, big and little, went up one street and down another, calling out our bargains.

One I remember to this day: "Ros'n' ears, good fresh green ros'n' ears, two for a nickel, four for a dime, dozen for a quarter, make your belly shine."

History reveals that those were tough times for millions, but, as children, we more or less thought of it as life. We peddled our vegetables for whatever we could get. Often we settled for ten or even five cents for a dozen plump ears of fresh corn. We accepted mere pennies at times rather than let it spoil. And sometimes we simply gave unsold vegetables to some needy family at the end of a day.

Dad was laid off for a long time at the Ford assembly plant in Memphis. He then earned what he could delivering the *Commercial*, now known as the *Commercial Appeal* newspaper. He eventually combined what was once nine paper routes. He converted a buggy like those used in trotting or harness racing by adding Model-T Ford wheels and constructing a wooden box underneath the seat to the footboard, in which to carry the newspapers he delivered early each morning.

Before I was old enough to attend school, I helped hitch up our mare, then went with Dad and rolled papers for him to throw onto subscribers' yards, up one street and down the other.

Life was sometimes dull and dreary during the Great Depression, but we managed to have enough food most of the time, and Dad took pride in taking care of his own.

Then we moved to the farm in 1934, and hard work became an everyday way of life for me, even at eight years of age.

And so I felt no sense of dread in regards to working hard at whatever the future had in store. Working long hours or whatever it took, I was eager to do. I yearned to find that pretty woman when I was fully mature, somewhere, somehow, and find a life of love and joy.

But heading for Memphis, it seemed I was losing headway in my efforts to gain a satisfying station in life. My feelings were pretty low when the bus pulled into the station.

However, when I arrived at my sister's home I was surprised because she had been expecting me—I had told no one that I was coming home. Lillian told me that Western Union had telephoned (I had used her address as my home address since the days I worked in Memphis building LCTs and had not yet changed it). Mr. Voorhees had wired me to hurry back to the ship, that I could sign back aboard as fireman on his 4–to–8 watches. No time was wasted. My parents had no telephone and I could not call them; I did try to call Cora Ann, but she was not home. I hugged everyone, said hello and good-bye, and got the next bus back.

All the way back to Charleston, I kept thinking, maybe Mom and Dad were right all along, that the Lord really did work in mysterious ways sometimes.

And once more I was on a cloud. My hopes soared.

But my brief sojourn through the Maritime Base and all my experiences in the shipyards were like Sunday School compared to the encounters that lay ahead for a young road scholar still innocent about many things in life. Fate kept piling up an assortment of unique trials to put me through. The unexpected kept popping out of holes along the trail I traveled—although *hurricane* is the term usually applied to fierce storms fueled by tropical waters, a hurricane is a hurricane under any name.

LINER AT LANDING STAGE, LIVERPOOL.   69418

CHAPTER
8

MR. VOORHEES WAS A STRAIGHT SHOOTER WHO USUALLY
got right to the point. I liked him a lot. Every Christmas season
when Frank Capra's great classic movie *It's A Wonderful Life* is
shown on television, featuring the late Thomas Mitchell in a
supporting role, I am reminded of Mr. Voorhees. The War I navy
man would have made a good double for the popular supporting
actor. The old engineer was a family man with a wife and teenaged
daughter at home in Florida. Also, he had a son he was trying to
get through medical school and another son in the navy somewhere in the Pacific.

He was an easygoing, God-fearing man, but hell on wheels
when he felt the occasion demanded. However, he was patient and
helpful to any young lad, as he called us, if one was willing to
work and get his head on straight, also his term.

It would be a few years later when I learned from Chief
Engineer Mallard that Mr. Voorhees had confronted the chief
steward and demanded he give a young man a break. Whatever

From left to right: First Engineer Dwight Voorhees and Chief Machinist Lynn Miller. Miller's appearance and demeanor was much like that of the songwriter, actor, and entertainer, Hoagy Carmichael. Aboard ship, Miller was nicknamed "Hoagy." This picture was taken on boat deck of U.S. Army Hospital ship Charles A. Stafford, *in early 1947. (The* Stafford *was formerly the Ward Line's Passenger Liner* Siboney.) *Mr. Voorhees was the second engineer aboard the* Larkspur *when the author started to sea. Note the big lightbulbs and their covers sticking up in the foreground. They are the red lights and red glass covers that formed an enormous red-cross on the boat deck, easily seen in daytime and shining bright at night.*

the old Navy man's method, Mr. Mallard said the chief steward hastened to approve my transfer to the blackgang.

When I got back to Charleston, the *Larkspur* had been moved from dry dock and was being loaded with supplies. The next day, we sailed again for Cherbourg, France.

Lighthearted once more, I developed a keen interest about life aboard ship and about the various traits of human nature and behavior. With so many people confined for days and weeks on a relatively small floating tub of steel, it was fascinating to a country boy. In one sense, she was really a floating army post. However, time-honored laws and rules of the sea governed overall; thus, the merchant marine captain was the ultimate master at sea, when and if he chose to exercise such authority.

In his flashy gold-adorned uniform, our white-haired skipper was the image of a tall regal-clad emperor. He was never seen going about the ship; he was the master on the throne, staying always topside near the bridge. He was said to be a British subject, yet he had a strange accent to me. But the old salts scoffed that he was a pussycat, that, instead of exercising his authority as master, he kissed the Army Brass's butt. I suspected he most likely didn't want to rock the boat and jeopardize his relations with his employer.

Mr. Sheaty was the *Larkspur's* first officer. Occasionally one heard the skipper personally paging the chief mate in his high-pitched wail over the ship's public address, "Mr. Shitty, come here, my boy, your captain wishes to speak to you." At other times when one was sunbathing on the boat deck near the bridge, the skipper's voice was carried by the wind, "Mr. Shitty, those are my orders," or, "Mr. Shitty," this or, "Mr. Shitty," that . . . the skipper was often calling for Mr. Sheaty.

He was not being pretentious by the way he pronounced the jovial first officer's name. His accent simply made it come out that way. And it *was* a distinct Mr. "Shitty." The first mate would merely grin and wag his head when paged by the old man.

All in all, life aboard the ship was pleasant. There was genuine respect and friendship between the permanent army crew and the civilian merchant crew members.

The so-called post commander was a doctor, with the army reserve rank of colonel. He was an intelligent man aside from his medical knowledge; he allowed those who knew what they were doing operate the ship. He never tried to throw his weight around and stick his nose in matters he knew nothing about. He, as well as the other army-officer doctors and nurses, gave full attention to providing aid and comfort to our passengers.

And so, life was congenial and peaceful while the old ship still operated as a hospital ship; this would change later when she was recommissioned as a transport, which would haul the first load of war brides to America.

There were some real characters in our crew and one was Lee Hi, the poker-playing carpenter, who had, according to scuttlebutt, been with the skipper for ten years. Also, it was said that he had been the mayor of a large city in China, where the captain had somehow saved him from being hung by rebels.

When Lee Hi perceived himself to be confronted with a threat, his quick response was, "You wanna go see cap'an? Com'on, we go see cap'an!" To my knowledge, no one ever did. We all liked Lee Hi. He was a natural clown, amusing without displaying any pretentious effort to be. But he was a goof-off. A real sure enough goldbrick. Seldom did I ever see him doing anything other than play poker and operate the windlass when we dropped or weighed anchor. That man sure loved to play poker, and he always came out ahead in winnings every trip.

I often marveled about the cheerful man; he never discussed his past. I sensed he had little or no family left back in China and I thought how sad it must be to roam the world cut off from one's homeland.

My second trip, we wiggled right on through the maze of sunken ships and docked as soon as we reached Cherbourg, although cargo ships waited at anchor behind the Contentin Peninsula's breakwater, which extended well out into the English Channel.

A couple of hundred yards inland from the deepwater dock a bridge crossed a small-boat canal that paralleled a long street. And at night, one lone street lamp at the bridge was all the light by which one could be guided in the boarded-up ghostly city. However, once inside, one saw that the local cathouse had plenty of fancy lights. A very colorful place, it was. I had never seen anything like it before.

Cherbourg was still occupied and governed by the U.S. Army, and the whorehouse was supposed to be off limits to all Americans, military and civilians.

But Red and I stumbled upon several merchant seamen and enlisted men who were in line, backed up into the darkness alongside the big building. MPs, a corporal and a sergeant, were on guard at the entrance. However, there were patrons entering and leaving in a steady flow. And at brief intervals, the corporal pointed two fingers, and two more eager studs would rush out of the darkness, each with two dollars ready. The guards split the "finder's fee" and crammed the money into their bulging pockets.

Red asked if I wanted to see what a French whorehouse looked like.

I asked him if he wanted to see what it looked like.

He asked me if we should go in.

I asked him if he thought we should go in.

He said he didn't know, and wanted to know what I thought.

I said I didn't know either, and asked what he thought.

We stood, scuffing our shoes at the cobblestones in a moment of silence. Then I allowed that I would bet it was a lot different than an American whorehouse.

Red agreed and added that he would bet that the difference was like daylight from dark.

I thought so too and allowed that we would never know unless we gave it a look.

He said I might be right about that, and then he asked what I thought.

I said I didn't know and asked what he thought.

We both shrugged at one another.

I supposed he didn't want me to think he was chicken just as I didn't want him to think I was chicken. And so, after a brief wait in a continuous forming line, each of us gave the corporal two dollars and entered the only whorehouse either had ever been in.

Shades of the big woman welder in Panama City flashed before me as a painted buxom woman in a short short skirt, that failed to hide all of her big caboose, welcomed us with open arms.

I careened out of the reach of her offered embrace.

A long row of chairs lined both sides of the gilded cavern, and back of these, facing doors to little rooms on each side, were couches on which embraced couples were raising steam while waiting to pop their relief valves in one of the little rooms. A bar served cognac, which did not at all taste like bourbon. There was black market American beer—for a price. One bottle cost a whole dollar! No decent country boy was about to pay a dollar when he could still buy a bottle of Memphis-brewed Goldcrest at home for just eleven cents. Falstaff and Stag were only sixteen cents a bottle and Schlitz and Budweiser were just twenty-one cents. Business was booming though. The place was full of girls prancing about, flipping their little dainty short flared skirts, showing much of their service equipment. The jukebox blared above all the glee, wailing out American songs and tunes. GIs and merchant marines milled about feeling of the fruit; squeezing plump butts and breasts like wives and mothers back home squeezed tomatoes when selecting them in a grocery store.

Red and I sat gawking, turning red when two cosmetic queens promenaded up and plopped their uninvited tune-up equipment on our laps.

They ran their fingers through our hair and over our bodies, mimicking exclamations of awe as they invaded parts never before known to anyone, except our mothers when they pinned baby diapers on us. With pretentious glee, they acted like they had just found the best watermelon in the whole blooming patch.

The operator on my lap wiggled her tongue in my ear, and cooed, "OoooWeee, nice boy. We make plenty good zig-zig, *oui?*"

Now I was not a bit bashful about hugging a pretty girl all way around, but despite all her makeup and perfume, that gal felt all balmy and sticky, and sort of smelled just like she had been hoeing cotton all day in the hot sun, although I doubted she would know anything about being a cotton hoer. So I thought: No, hell no. You ain't gonna zig-zig this old boy. But I didn't say anything, just sort of squirmed, and I squirmed my situation away from her warm caressing hands.

I looked at Red and his face matched his hair.

His friendly mechanic had his belt unbuckled and his hood open.

The poor lad had both hands cupped over his engine. He flipped his mouth from side to side, but still the merchandiser smeared his face with her painted lips, giggling as she sought to give him a sample of her goods.

I wondered if I looked as rattled as he.

The din in the huge room suddenly hushed when shrieking profanity shrilled from an upper cubicle.

A balcony with guardrails ran along both sides upstairs, giving access to the little side rooms in which clients received service. Red and I sat on the left from the entrance, and we had full view when Lee Hi darted out of an upper room on the right, facing us. He was trying to cover his head with both arms as a young woman raged behind him, striking him with the heel of a shoe—it was his shoe.

Both MPs charged inside, shushing with both hands, pleading for quiet, lest the officer-of-the-day cruised by and heard. The sergeant looked up at the enraged woman and exclaimed, "What the hell is wrong, what did he do to you?"

She screamed in English, and I learned that she was indeed British, "The bloody bahhhstard didn't do anything to me. The freaking freak just rubbed me tootsee while 'e mahhhstabated." The confused sergeant shrugged, and exclaimed, "So? What do you care? Why the hell all the fuss?"

She leaned over the rail and waved a single dollar bill, and squealed so hard she almost choked. "This! The bloody bahhh-stard won't give me me otha bloody Yank dolla! 'E says 'e only pay 'alf, 'e did. Said I didn't do anything . . . !"

The MP motioned for the grumbling carpenter to come on down. Then he urged him to pay up. Lee Hi, still raving in Chinese, refused.

The MP sergeant pleaded with him.

Still, Lee Hi refused, howling his protest, "Me no cotchee putsey. No putsey, no udder dolla. Lee Hi no clazy. Lee Hi no cotchee claps."

The MP wagged his head in disbelief then faked the threat he would take Lee Hi to the MP station if he didn't pay up, and claimed the O.D. would then hit him with a ten-dollar fine.

Lee Hi stood growling a funny grunty chuckle, then chortled, "Hokay, we go. We go see cap'an."

A grinning AB from our ship answered the puzzled look on the sergeant's face, telling him the carpenter meant that he wanted them to go see the ship's captain. The sergeant cursed then thought of a simple solution. He gave the business lady a dollar out of his own pocket.

No one was supposed to use greenbacks. We were told to exchange dollars for occupational script issued by the U.S. Army, and use only that as a medium of exchange. But American cigarettes and dollars were demanded, which I later found to largely be the case in every country, except England.

The sergeant ushered the grumbling carpenter outside. Red caught his racing engine in the zipper and let out a yelp, but finally managed to get it secured back under the hood, then we followed.

Lee Hi stood outside the door wearing only one shoe, which he seemed not to notice, and continued to rant at the MPs in a sing-song rage. The sergeant tried to get Lee Hi to reimburse him for the dollar he gave the whore. Lee Hi slung his head like a mule shaking off a horse fly. He countered by demanding that the MPs refund him a dollar of the entrance fee. He kept getting louder and louder.

I heard an upper window open across the narrow street and saw a face stuck out of the dark frame. Angry French cursing clattered down on the negotiators.

Lee Hi started stomping off, then he wheeled back and got in the sergeant's face once again, shouting, "We go see cap'an. Com'on, we see. Lee Hi no clazy. Lee Hi no cotchee putsey, you owe Lee Hi dolla." He jabbed a finger at his open palm, demanding, "One dolla, right here, you owe. You no pay Lee Hi . . . we go see cap'an."

The corporal cut in and pleaded, "Sarge, let's give that crazy Eggroll a damned dollar and shut him up. He's going to keep on 'til he has the lieutenant down on our ass. Here, I'll give him a dollar." He jerked a bill out of his pocket, and several greenbacks fluttered to the street.

The former China mayor took the dollar and snorted in victory. Eyeing the soldier gathering his scattered money, Lee Hi's face suddenly beamed. "Ah, ha," he exclaimed, "soldiers gotchee plenty dolla. You play ploka? Com'on, we go ship and play plenty ploka."

The two soldiers flung plenty choice words at the happy carpenter and ordered him to get lost, on the double.

We picked our way along the black street.

Red broke the silence with the comment, "Ain't the first time I pissed away a couple of bucks. I didn't see anything in that joint so special, did you?"

"Naw, I saw better looking beetles than those one time when Dad took me to the ole Floating Palace honky-tonk down on the ole Saint Frances River at Marked Tree," I replied, keeping an anxious eye peeled at each doorway we passed.

Our steps echoed loudly in the erie silence of the narrow dark streets, and the buildings seemed to close in to squeeze us. We had already been warned that American seamen were getting their throats slashed for a mere pack of cigarettes.

Red went on, "Besides, I never did want a used car. I'm going to get me one that's nice and classy that nobody else has ever messed with. What about you?"

"Yeah, guess you're right about that. I had me a used car and had all kinds of trouble with the blooming transmission."

"Transmission . . . ? Oh, yeah, a car! Uh, what sort of trouble?"

"Well, when I'd try to shift from low to second it'd try to go into reverse. And when I'd try to go from second to high, it'd go back to low instead. After they took me for a pile of money to fix the transmission, come to find out the little ole selector pin to shift gears was bent. Cost me eighty-nine cents which was all I needed in the first place. But I'll tell you right now, Red, if the little ole selector pin on a '40 Chevy is bent all out of whack, you'll always have a heck of a time gettin' the transmission in high gear, did you know it?"

"Naw, but I'll take your word for it. I never fooled with no used cars. Anyway, I want a new one. When I get one, I want one like a Buick, with a fluid drive transmission."

After a short distance, we turned right, along the canal side-street. Like a dim distant star through the pitch black night, we could see the speck of light far up ahead where the bridge crossed the canal.

Lee Hi stepped on a pebble with his bare foot and hobbled while letting go a stream of singsong cussing. Suddenly he became aware that he had left a shoe. He stopped and looked over his shoulder, mumbling. For a moment I thought he was going back. But with a disdainful wave at the darkness behind us, he chuckled, then said, "Ahhh, we go ship."

He gleefully mumbled to himself then, making the turn under the light at the bridge, stopped and flashed the dollar refund at us, chortling, "See, Lee Hi gotchee dolla back and no cotchee claps!"

Red and I stopped, and he wiggled the dollar under our noses, displayed a serious expression, and said, "You nice young buddies. Alleee time no zing-zing in putsey cathouse no cotchee claps. Alleee time you be like Lee Hi, alleee time you no cotchee claps. Lee Hi alleee time no cotchee claps." It was amusing because he was so happy about the dollar he wrangled back from the MPs. The black plain-toed dress shoes that most seamen wore generally cost six dollars a pair. But I don't think he considered, or maybe didn't care, that by losing a shoe he had come out in the hole.

After a thirteen-day crossing we made Charleston again. We tied up in the navy yard astern the *Reno*, a navy cruiser in from the Pacific with much damage caused when hit by a Japanese kamikaze plane that exploded in her bridge area.

Our ship needed a few repairs, as we often did when making port, and we killed the power plant. But within a few days, the blackgang and shipyard workers made fast work of the repairs.

I liked the repair work, I was learning.

I only went ashore one time to make a short overnight trip to visit my Memphis friend, Howard, who was in the Oliver General Hospital with a broken neck at nearby Augusta, Georgia.

After a few days we sailed again for Cherbourg. There had been another big turnover in the blackgang, and Mr. Mallard promoted me to watertender in charge of the 4–to–8 watch in the fire room. Man, I was really mojoing, I thought. In two trips to France, I had made it from an $80-per-month chow slinger to a $110-per-month watertender. Although I had to pay for my own clothes, and also pay income tax, which was deducted from my monthly salary, I thought I was on my way.

We had as passengers a troupe of 150 USO entertainers when we sailed. Some were very beautiful actresses, all headed up by a strutting show-business person of some sort.

We were ordered not to fraternize with the female passengers; however, some of the officers ignored the directive.

But all of us wore our best when off duty. The pretty girls seemed to appreciate that, because they were nice and thoughtful. They packed close as possible to the boat deck's aft edge to sunbathe in their skimpy bathing suits.

We crowded on the open aft part of C-deck, the main deck, looking up like puppy dogs waiting for a cookie to be tossed; and the lovely beauties flopped about, squirmed and twisted their shapely butterball derrieres. I thought they sure did a lot of wiggling and twisting about just to get the effect of the sun.

The ship's nurses stopped using the boat deck on which to soak in the sun, and I guessed they just didn't care about entertainers. Instead, the nurses climbed a ladder to the top of a little deckhouse at the stern on C-deck. A canvas curtain, stretched all around the guardrail at the top, cut off the view from below on C-deck and from all other decks. But it was baffling to me why the naked ladies sunning on top of the deckhouse had not caught on to the fact there was always a seaman on lookout, up forward, high up in the crow's nest; and he always had binoculars.

And, for sure, no watch in the crow's nest ever gave their vantage point away. They stayed hunkered down when they faced aft to lookout, never exposing themselves above the enclosure.

Had there been any, no danger had a chance of sneaking up on us from the stern during daylight on a sunny day. But on another trip, a lookout looking out aft too long a time let our ship almost bump a floating mine in the English Channel. Minesweepers were busy, but they would not find all the mines laid in the war; ships like the U.S. Army Transport *Alexander* would be getting a bang from one of those blasted things for years to come. However, our quartermaster happened to see the sun's glitter on the mine and gave the wheel a hard turn, and we barely eased past the rascal.

That near miss got the skipper's attention and thereafter he kept a lookout stationed on the bow when we were in the Channel.

So far my third trip had been smooth and I thought tending water was merely child's play. However, we started getting reports by ship's radio about a storm kicking up in the North Sea, which at first caused little concern because we were still more than 600 miles from the English Channel. But we learned that the storm kept growing and that it was marching through the Channel towards the Atlantic, tossing mines upon the shores of France and England, doing considerable damage.

With little less than a day's time before reaching the Channel, I was tossed out of my bunk after midnight.

The ship rolled, heaved, and pitched, then yawed and crashed down a mountain and laid on her port side. A bunkmate stumbled into our starboard-side room and switched on the light. A glance at the porthole revealed a wall of water from the high rolling sea outside the thick glass. My fo'c'sle-mate slammed the deadlight over the porthole and dogged it tight. I didn't feel the throbbing vibrations of the engines and realized that the ship was dead in the water.

The briny mountains rolled taller, and the old girl fell in a trough, and it seemed as though she was going to just stay keeled over while the mad ocean kept jumping up and down on her starboard side. She was down too long and her ribs bent and her ancient hull caved; I would soon learn that her hull cracked along the starboard side just above her normal waterline.

My shipmate and I exchanged anxious looks.

I fumed, "Dang it, reckon she's just gonna stay down?"

He shrugged, informing me that the watch lost water in the boilers and the engines had to be stopped. He said the sea was acting up some but that he had just come from the crew's mess and had been told by the deck yeoman that the skipper thought the storm would peter out in the open water of the Atlantic.

The engines' throb was felt once again, and the ship climbed over the tall tumbling mountains, struggling to make headway. Still she took frequent hard jolts, and I didn't feel as relaxed as my shipmate tried to act. However, I stuffed my life jacket and pillow as props to keep me wedged in my bunk, and finally dozed. It didn't seem long until I was tossed again, sprawled on the deck, pillow and all.

The ship was doing it all, pitching, rolling, and yawing. She fell down a mountain and as she tried to take the next surging cliff on a climb, it knocked her bow around to slide her broached into another deep canyon. There she quivered and shuddered with her old engines churning, doing their best, while mountains of brine rolled upon her starboard side and stomped.

It was not yet time for my morning 4–to–8 watch but I dressed and went below to the crew's mess.

Broken dishes were scattered over the deck, and open cabinet doors flapped and banged. The night messman slipped and stumbled about cursing amid the debris, trying to save the remaining crockery. I straddled a bench and locked my legs, reaching an arm across to clasp the table's edge on the other side. Silently I nursed a mug half-full of coffee with the other hand.

The rolling and pitching increased, and the lunging mountains crashing into her bow were hitting with increased frenzy. I had never been jarred like that riding a tractor over tree roots and stumps or by ole Bob when he took a notion to buck. When a towering wave threw her bow up to hang suspended, a shipmate howled with nervous bravado, "Ride it, you old bitch." The ship shook and quivered and just hung there suspended. Her headway stalled, and she rode the rolling mountain of water back. It seemed an eternity as the fierce onslaught kept her in its mighty clutches and continued to sweep her back, back, back, causing her to quiver with its lashing fury.

I held my breath.

Finally she came crashing down. We learned later that she had been stalled often, making minus headway while being swept back riding the crests of the tumbling mountainous waves.

My shipmate kept up a nervous stream of cursing.

I grimaced and thought, he'd better shut up before he gets the Lord pissed off at us. Keeping a firm grip on the far edge of the table, I sat quietly holding the coffee mug with my other hand. Needing to go relieve myself, I felt frozen to the bench and reckoned I would hold it awhile unless it was jarred out.

The public address speaker crackled early in the morning. Doubtless was anyone asleep, anyway. The skipper announced that he thought the storm would die when it hit the open water, but instead it had grown wide and big (there was not any hurricane center then; storm warnings were limited to that passed on by radio from ships at sea). He told us it had gathered strength from the warmer waters influenced by the Gulf Stream crossing over off the Grand Banks, feeding eastward, on into the Atlantic Currents. He ordered all portholes closed, then advised that the storm had spread too wide to skirt, and that we were too slow to turn and outrun it. He added that we were going to take it head-on and that we would likely feel a little shake now and then while we pushed our way through.

I desperately wished I was back among the cotton fields and log woods. I silently prayed that whatever I had ever done wrong, I wish I had not done it. And I promised I would never do anymore devilish things as long as I lived, if the Good Lord would just hear me and get us out of the storm and on to France.

I went on watch, and catching the ship paused briefly on even keel, I frowned to see less than an inch of water showing in each of the boilers' glass gauges. The hotwell in the engine room, between the starboard engine and hull, where condensed exhaust steam returned and from where the boiler feedwater pumps took suction, was at 212 degrees. Both feed pumps were in use, but the hot condensate caused them to vapor lock and they jerked like strain-haltered rear legs of a horse. Also, making the situation more critical, the steam-operated injector would not function to force feedwater into the three starving boilers.

My chest froze with my eyes fixed on the starboard hull. It was warped and caved in, and its horizontal riveted seam was cracked near boiler-drum level. A solid sheet of ocean was sliding down the hull. Suddenly I realized the sloshing sound beneath my feet was sea water rolling across the double-bottom tank tops just under the floor plates. I shuddered as the sloshing seemed to gurgle in glee. My throat ached like a big heavy rock was stuck in it.

The suction of the fire pump and the ballast pump were tied in with the bilge pumps, and all the pumps were pumping at their maximum, but the water continued to rise, occasionally splashing over the floor plates as the ship rolled.

The jerking feedwater pumps failed to hold enough suction to keep the boilers safely watered, and slowly the level continued to drop in the gauges. I was gripped with a paralyzing sense of panic and had to force myself to give attention to duty.

After what seemed an eternity into the watch, the bridge told us that the sustained wind had peeked at 140 knots—about 155 miles an hour. The telegraph from the bridge stayed on *full ahead*, and the engines hissed and clattered, delivering all the power they had, trying to keep the ship's bow into the storm-crazy sea.

Each time a mountain rolled under the hull from bow to stern, the floor plates wiggled and buckled, and I felt three powerful rolling ripples underfoot—not two, not four or five, but three distinct ripples each time.

A one-hundred-pound anvil tore loose and roared across the floor plates with each violent roll. Over and back, from starboard to port, it jarred the ancient hull like a projectile fired from a cannon; we didn't have time to spare, and also, we couldn't keep our feet anchored to the slick floor plates in order to manhandle the rampaging anvil and secure it. We let it scoot.

A lifeline was stretched thwartships across the fire room, arm-reach high, along a path to tend the boilers' feedwater control reach rods. And, as I tugged myself along the lifeline, squeezing minute turns on valve wheels to rob one boiler to feed another, I hauled myself up with the line to clear my feet and ankles each time that roaring bulldozer came whizzing by.

The water level in the boilers slowly fell until it reached the bottom of all gauges, and finally it dropped out of sight. Spurts shot up into the glasses when the ship rolled, but fear of a meltdown and exploding boilers pounded with a raw ache inside my chest.

A big freckled-face fireman started pulling the fires, closing the oil valves for each burner. I yelled for him to stop. We had to try to keep a full head of steam so the ship could fight the lashing fury and to keep pumping bilges.

He cursed and shook a fist at me.

I rushed over and whacked his wrists with a valve-wheel wrench. He threw a haymaker at me, slipped, and fell on his butt.

I hastened back to tend the spurts of water.

The other fireman re-ignited the dead burners.

The scared fireman—we were all scared—got up and shagged it up the zigzagged ladders.

He stopped far up in the fire room fid'le near a door to the boat deck and leaned on a catwalk rail to look down at us—an oiler had already fled the engine room, leaving Mr. Voorhees with only one oiler, who had to struggle to squirt oil on both engines' hot guides, slides, and bearings.

Control levers had been attached to the butterfly throttle valves in the steam lines, and the old timer stayed glued to those long handles, between the two clucking engines.

Constantly the stern was violently pitched into the air, and each time he flung the levers, shutting off steam, howling, "Noooo, you don't, you wild hellion." Having kept the engines from running away and tearing from their mounts with propellers whirling in air, he waited until the props dropped and again grabbed the sea; then he eased the throttle valves open to start the engines cranking again. He would give a long growling chuckle, then say, "Yeahhhh, that's the way, Babies, bite it. Screw that mean bitch."

The junior third engineer shut down the freshwater evaporating plant in the upper-flat aft and came down to help.

Mr. Voorhees put him on the throttle handles, then dashed in for a quick check of the fire room. He spotted the fireman looking down at us. The engineer charged up the ladders.

The fireman threw a roundhouse haymaker at him.

Mr. Voorhees ducked and whirled him around then grabbed his looped belt and came dragging him back down in the hole.

The fireman was cursing and bellering above the noise of the fire room racket as their feet touched the floor plates. "But Second, that there crazy Arkansas sonabitch gonna blow us all up. He done damned nigh broke both my arms when I tried to pull the fires. He ain't got one damned lick of sense!"

I was so scared that a bitter acrid taste kept seeping up into my mouth. Even so, I could not help but marvel for a few seconds at the majesty of that moment when Mr. Voorhees spoke to the fireman in a tone as calm as a cat purring, "Yeah, but, Son, if these boilers blow, they'll go right out the top. Yeahhh. Why, Son, they'd take you with them, you standing up there like that. Yeah, you'd better stay down here where it's safe."

Then his face froze as he shot a glance at the empty gauges. He barked, "How much water in those boilers?!"

"I, I, I got plenty, I think."

He snatched my shoulders and stuck his eyes into mine. "Think, hell. How much water do you have in those boilers?!"

Scared, nervous, and frustrated, it all boiled over and I got mad. I yelped, "Dammit, Second, I know how fast that water ain't dropping and I've still got enough. I know I have. It's still in that two-inch safety margin below the gauges!"

He probed my eyes briefly, and a faint smile spread in his face. "It's okay, Son, I trust you," he said calmly, "just stick in the hole with me and keep a full head of steam."

He was gone in a flash, back out to talk at his engines.

Soon after, I was puzzled but greatly relieved when for no reason we could then determine, the hotwell cooled down. The pumps took suction and steadily fed water back to a safe level in the boilers. We would later discover that the turbulence had caused a weak thermo valve in a condensate return line to malfunction, which allowed live steam to feed into and overheat the hotwell, until someone topside closed a radiator's steam valve inside a shower room.

That watch was the worst.

The ship was steered in a manner to relieve the damaged starboard side from some of the storm's onslaught. Intermittently the port side started getting a share of pounding from the mighty waves. Thus, the bilge pumps gained on the incoming sea water before I went off watch that morning.

But we were held in the clutches of the storm for nearly two days before we finally broke out. One twenty-four-hour period we backed up sixty-nine nautical miles as the relentless storm kept sweeping the ship back, even though the engines churned with all they had to fight it head-on, trying to make headway.

The English Channel was like a funnel for the heavy ship traffic coming and going, and we had constantly received distress calls for help from other vessels; small fishing boats and schooners were taking on water. Some broke apart and sank. Lives were lost but I never knew how many.

I learned that fierce storms with strong winds were not uncommon across northern France and southern England. But I was told that this was the first storm with such hurricane-force winds for several decades in that part of the world; it had developed in the North Sea. Interestingly, this most powerful storm followed a winter that was also the most vicious of the century, occurring just a few months past in which the Battle of the Bulge, that most fierce battle of War II, had been fought.

On the previous homeward journeys, I had already listened with awe to wounded soldiers who had fought in the frigid winds, snow, and ice, in a frontal counterattack to push the enemy back foot by foot in the Battle of the Bulge. I would hear more from soldiers who had toes, fingers, and flesh frozen off in this terrible ordeal. But, in response, what could a young novice seaman only a couple of years removed from the farm say after listening to those men describe some of the horror they had seen and the terror of some of their battles; men who only a short time before had been young themselves?

A sigh, then the solemn comment, "Yep, war sure is hell, ain't it?" would get a stern look, and the standard reply, "Yeah, and don't let anyone tell you that hell's a warm place. It'll freeze your balls off. I've been there, and I know."

I felt great respect for all soldiers we brought home but, still, I could not help having a special feeling of compassion for those who had not only fought their way ashore on D-Day and slugged it out across France, but who then found themselves in the most brutal and miserable battle ever faced by so many Americans, at a time when it was thought all was over except the celebrating. The gaunt faces of those gallant men are stamped in my memory forever, and deep appreciation is imbedded in my heart for the tremendous sacrifices they made.

Coming off my morning watch after breaking free of the storm, I strolled aft for a breather before eating breakfast. The sea was calm with low swells that lazily rolled under the ship's bow and lifted her in a gentle rock fore to aft.

Several pretty USO ladies milled about near the stern, nervously chattering with great relief.

I nodded to a master sergeant who was going over for occupational duty, then I leaned on the stern rail and looked back over the wake churned by the propellers as we again approached the English Channel. Whether on or off watch, body and mind had been in a constant state of tense strain; I felt spent and shaky.

One pretty sweet thing chirped to her troupe leader, "But, I was just simply scarrrRud to deaaaUth. Landsakes, weren't you?"

With arms folded across his chest, their leader reared back, and scoffed, "Nahhhh, I wasn't concerned. After all, ships cross the oceans all the time."

I did a double take when he glanced over her head with a smirk at me. I mumbled to myself, "Why, you blowhard jackass, I wish I'd had you down in the hole with no water in the boilers and dodging that ankle-popping anvil."

The master sergeant overheard and grinned at me. He then frowned at the man and took a couple of steps to stand by me. Looking squarely at whistle-britches, he softly drawled, "Well, Mister, this dogface was certainly scared. Just an old foot soldier, myself. Been in two world wars. Been shot at, but I always had a small measure of comfort, knowing I could shoot back. Citizen, I can tell you, there's nothing that scares me like the fury of God or Nature, or whatever you choose to call it."

He gave me a knowing wink and another grin. With a slap on my back, he raised his voice, "Well done, sailor, you men can be in my army any day." He strolled off toward a passageway.

I had chatted with him a couple of times before while having coffee and knew that he was going back over for a few months of soft occupational duty before retiring after thirty years in the army. But I never saw the soldier again. We anchored out and he left the ship before we docked.

I have always regretted that I didn't find a way to let that real professional soldier know how grateful I was to him for having made a young man not too far removed from the sticks feel a little more pleased with himself.

However, the old topkick probably already knew that.

The Germans had cleaned tools and material out of Cherbourg. There was talk of crossing over to Southampton, England, to replace the cracked and warped plates, and put the ship's starboard side in good repair. But the sick and wounded were brought aboard when we docked, and they raved to head for home. After caulking the crack in the riveted seam of the hull, we took the Southern Route back across. We had smooth sailing, and thirteen days later we pulled into New York. A few days after unloading, the ship went to a repair shipyard where she was made seaworthy.

With my ship in port for several days, Arkansas was about to meet New York.

CHAPTER

9

LINER AT LANDING STAGE, LIVERPOOL.   69418

THIS RETURN TRIP INTO NEW YORK PROVIDED PLENTY OF time ashore, and, indeed, I got a good look at the great city.

It was also a chance to catch up on all the movies and see many of the big bands of the era. I ate my first pizza, called pizza pies then. I had never heard of them in the South.

Also, I was not prepared for Frank Sinatra.

A shipmate from Brooklyn and I were strolling past the Capitol Theater late one night after having seen our last movie for the evening at another theater. We were held up by a big crowd shrieking and shoving to get to a long black limousine. The mob blocked the vehicle as it tried to exit a narrow street alongside the big theater into Times Square.

Squealing, wailing, moaning, groaning girls, young and some older, were literally crawling over the hood of the limo.

They wrung their hands and cried, "Frankie, Frankie, Frankie, I loooove you." They kept pushing and shoving with tears running down their cheeks. I saw a stream running down one hysterical young girl's leg and I watched slacked-jawed as it ran over the edge of her shoe and made a puddle on the sidewalk.

I asked my shipmate who the heck was that Frankie fellow, anyway.

He looked at me like I had just come in from the cotton patch with an empty sack. "Hehhh, youz kiddin'? Why, dat's Frankie Boy. Frank Sinatra. Jeez, ain't youz ever hoird of him . . . ? He's 'da hottest singer around. Youz didn't know 'bout him down in dem pig trails?"

Perhaps I had seen the popular singer in movie bit parts, but his name had never registered in my mind. I told my friend, "Nope, never came across that dude before. Is he somebody sort of famous like real big singers such as ole Roy Acuff or Ernest Tubbs?"

"Jeez," he exclaimed, "youz for real? Who da hell are 'dey? Never hoird of dem guys. Nobody is like Frankie Boy. I ain't jiving, he's copacetic. He's real gone, youz don't know dat?"

Restaurants had oyster and clam bars up front, and Little Neck clams suited my taste. Shipmates and I would catch up on all the movies and eat clams or oysters on the half shell; we'd see a movie, eat a dozen, and see another movie.

Brooklyn and I took on another dozen, then caught the Seabeach Express subway. The ship had not yet moved to the shipyard and was still at the Brooklyn Army Base. We were sitting across the way, facing a young lady, whom I assumed was dressed in a particular New York-style for some women.

Her toenails were painted red, and she wore a tiny gold chain around an ankle from which a little trinket dangled. The current national fashion for most women was long, flared skirts almost to the ankles, but that young woman wore a short skirt. Even with her legs crossed, I could see the cheeks of her buttocks. Her extremely long fingernails really fascinated me. I had never seen inch-long nails before. I did not think she could pick much cotton with them.

Perhaps I had been staring. I tried not to. When my eyes met hers she gave me the mean eye, and I quickly looked away. But soon I would again steal little peeks at this New York woman-creature. I supposed she might be attractive to others but I didn't think she looked at all like my dream girl.

I mused that I didn't want a woman all painted up like her; I didn't want a woman who seemed not to care what ole boy she showed her butt to. And I darned sure did not want a woman with a pitchfork prong sticking from each finger.

The train slowed for a stop. I was sitting near the door. The young lady crossed over and stood waiting. Then as the door opened, she tapped me on the shoulder.

I looked up.

"Well, Hominy Grits, did you have time to get me undressed?" she snapped, then darted from the car.

I stared with mouth popped open, and Brooklyn stiffed a finger after her and howled with laughter at me.

It sort of got my goat and, to save face, I tried to sound serious and mused aloud that I wondered how the heck that girl could possibly know that I was partial to grits.

Those were the first words of a direct personal nature spoken to me by a New York woman.

We left on another voyage and, while gone, we received a news bulletin that five Navy Avenger torpedo planes out of Fort Lauderdale, Florida, mysteriously disappeared while flying over the "Bermuda Triangle" in the Atlantic Ocean, December 5, 1945.

As usual, my ship had bellyaches and on our return it went into the shipyard. I knew we needed minor repairs but didn't know why she would be in the shipyard for a month. With Christmas near, all but a skeleton crew were given leave, and December 22, 1945, I went home.

I made the rounds visiting friends and relatives.

A married sister with children lectured me about my soul and getting right with the Lord.

I had recently received a nineteen-page handwritten letter from her on the same subject. It contained a long list of scriptures which she urged me to study in the Bible, but I had been busy digging into Mr. Voorhees's marine engineers manuals and had not yet gotten around to her particular brand of soul engineering.

Sis was a devoted mother and wife and a very devout Christian. But after she married, she changed frocks to one gilded with much more straight lace, and she appeared to believe if anyone was not baptized by her brand of preacher they would go to hell, for sure.

As I slithered to the door, she kept on hounding me about being baptized with her brand. She followed me out and stood on the porch, still preaching as I urgently tried to make it into Dad's pickup and start the engine.

I pleaded, "Look, Sis, I really appreciate hearing from you. I always love to get letters from home, but please write me about how everyone is doing and all. Okay?"

"Well, my goodness, L. R.," she insisted. "You never know what might happen to you way out there on that ocean. Mercy sake, I'm just concerned about your soul."

"Yeah, I know, Sis. I appreciate your concern but the war is over and ain't much can happen to an ole hardtail like me."

She kept on, "Makes no difference, your soul is still important to your sister. For heaven's sake, just think . . . what if your soul had gone to the bottom of that old ocean in that storm? You said yourself that bad storms could pop up at anytime. See there? The Lord was sure trying to tell you something. He gave you another chance but He might not be so charitable the next time."

I should have let it go at that but reckon the devil must have been nudging me . . . I just had to get the last word. I popped off, "Ah, sure He will. Why, Sis, you're looking at one crackerjack watertender who can keep steam up with pee and a prayer. So, don't worry, I won't ever have to be scared in any more storms, and. . . . "

Suddenly something grabbed a handful inside my chest and squeezed hard. I momentarily froze. Instantly I was back in the crew's mess, with legs locked around the bench, cringing at my equally scared shipmate who cursed the storm and everything else. And so, I pleaded for understanding, "Look, Sis, why are you so danged worried about me being baptized when you know, darned well, I was baptized more'n anybody when we were young'n's! Don't you remember fussing at me for going up to alter call every time it looked like the preacher was shaking his blooming finger right at me, bellering, 'You're going to hell just as sure as you're sittin' there,' blah, blah, blah."

"Sssst," she hissed, "stop being sacrilegious!"

"Hell's bells . . . ! Whose being sacri anything? Dang it, I'm here to tell you, those fiery-eyed old farts used to scare the devil plumb out of me when I was a little boy. And you oughta blamed well remember. I'd mosey up to alter call so I wouldn't miss out on getting a good soaking before the creeks froze over, to carry me through the winter. And when the creeks thawed, I'd always get another'n' to carry me through a hardworking summer. Why, I got baptized so many times in muddy creeks and rivers, betcha I can still spit up mud cakes. Heck, Sis, how the devil could you forget all that?"

She stood with eyes wide and mouth agape. She was naturally fair complexioned but, nonetheless, her face turned a ghostly

Country baptizing in Muddy Creek. Author at age ten about to get one of several baptizings as a youngster. In his youth, he played it safe and went to alter call every time it seemed a preacher shook a finger at him and bellered, "You're going to hell just as sure as you're sittin' there!"

white and her eyes grew bigger. She moaned, "My goooodness, you're awful. L. R., you are simply awful, awful, awful."

Again, that struck a wrong chord, and I hastened, "No, I'm not. Dad-gum-it, Sis, I'm the sweetest rascal around . . . ain't nothing but goodness in my heart for everybody—as long as some jerk don't try to bend my flesh."

I made it inside the truck with one foot, but before I got seated and the engine started, she came at me again.

Shaking a finger, she proclaimed, "Heaven knows, you do beat all. But, just the same, you and I have always been close, and I'm going to keep on 'til you get right with the Lord. And, young man, you can just put that in your pipe and smoke it!"

I realized two and two were not making four with her, where I was concerned, so I tried to take two and make it one or the other to set her mind at ease about her brother. I urged, "Now, look, Sis, if my ship ever does happen to sink, you can bet the cotton crop that your brother's gonna get a darned good baptizing, so stop worrying about it, will you?"

Her mouth fell open, her face again drained, and she looked all around like she hoped "No One" heard, and cried out, "My God, if I said something like that the Lord would strike me dead."

I couldn't keep from chuckling, then I spoke seriously, "Yeah, I know, Sis, You . . . He probably would, uh . . . with your strong belief—uh, I mean, I know how sincere and all you are about what you believe, and I admire you for it, but, but—but, dammit, me and the Big Skipper's getting along just fine!"

"See there . . . you oughtn't to cuss like that! You're just stubborn as a mule and won't listen to somebody who's trying to show you the path to the doorway for heaven!"

As always, I couldn't win. I merely grinned and blew her a kiss. But after I got into the truck and had the engine running, I rolled down the window, hoping to get the last word. "Keep writing, Sis. And don't worry about me taking the right path. Hell's bells, I might believe in all of 'em. And I ain't bird-terdin' you, the Big Skipper knows them hellfire and brimstone preachers done scared all the hell plumb out of me, and I betcha He'll let me in even if I have to go around to the back door."

I tried to make a fast getaway but let up on the clutch too quickly and killed the dad-gummed engine.

She cackled it tickled her so, then danged if she didn't run out to bray, "See there? Little Brother, the Lord is sure trying to tell you something!"

I got the blamed engine cranked. It was New Year's Day, 1946, and rationing ended for car and truck tires; therefore, I didn't worry about saving rubber, I spun the wheels to get away. But before I got the window rolled up as I sped off, I heard her yell, "Lord knows . . . you're awful, but I'll be praying for you."

Howard was home with a medical discharge, and I visited him and Cora Ann and all my relatives who lived in Memphis.

When in port at Charleston, the time I went to visit Howard while he was in the Oliver General Hospital at Augusta, Georgia, I learned he was quick to tell others his neck was broken on Saipan when he rammed an enemy tank to kill it after his tank ran out of ammo. This tall tale always got him free beer in bars despite the fact he had never left the USA. He broke his neck by diving into shallow water while swimming for recreation!

There were quite a few old boys like Howard, who were "over there" as "quartermaster commandoes," clerks, truck drivers, etc, behind the lines, but they had been "over there" and they "didn't want to talk about it," according to folks back home.

Of course they too functioned as a vital part of the overall war effort, but they were called "homemade" heroes by combat soldiers.

Howard had not even been over there but he would "talk about it"; he would fabricate any far-out hero tale he thought one might like to hear, then bystanders argued about who would buy him the next beer.

Cora had written a warm letter telling me how thoughtful I had been to visit Howard in Augusta. Yet, her letters continued to have the kid-stuff flavor regarding me. Nonetheless, seeing her again was a joy, although she had taken on a much greater grown-uppish air. She didn't have one word to say about her high school prom! But referring to me as a kid didn't set too well. I wanted to tell her to wise up.

I had just turned nineteen and was tempted to tell her that the kid had already seen, firsthand, more misery, sacrifice, and humiliation suffered by fellow humans, the likes of which she could never see in movie newsreels. I wanted to tell her I had seen a war-torn land where pretty girls like her were selling their virgin bodies for a pitiful nickel, a mere pack of cigarettes, so they could barter with farmers for a few potatoes in order to provide food for their families.

But I didn't, because folks at home didn't want to hear about what ordinary citizens suffered "over there" in the war; instead, folks at home wanted to identify with heroes like all those they saw in the propaganda war movies. And even with that in mind, unless a soldier was someone who caught the enemy coming through a pass and had mowed down twenty-five or thirty with a machine gun, few folks at home really wanted to hear about the war; not even from those battle-scarred dogface soldiers who had sloshed through the muck, ice, and snow, with frostbitten and frozen feet just slugging it out as everyday, hard-knocking fighting soldiers. And folks at home darn sure didn't want to hear any secondhand accounts from a young man who merely helped haul the real fighters back home; Cora and the folks at home had seen all the war movies, and they knew what a hero was.

No matter, the war was over, our side won, and everyone at home was of good cheer. . . . Now that tire rationing had ended, folks were overjoyed. They could now wheel about all they pleased.

I soon became restless while on leave. Things sure had changed in such a short period of time. In some ways, it was as though I were a stranger at home. Indeed, even to ole Bob, my cherished pony. Without the least sign of warning, the rascal tossed me headfirst to plow up loose gravel with my forearms and elbows when I took him out for a ride. And, dammit, I hadn't done a darned thing to aggravate him! Mom chuckled about it, saying it was just my pony's way of letting me know he missed me. Listening to Cora go on about her knowledge of hit records which she sold at a music shop, I thought she acted like popular music was the most important aspect of life. But, she never once had praise for any recording by ole Roy Acuff or Ernest Tubbs. She and I just didn't connect, and I decided that she would never learn to milk a cow and never want to ride a mule from the cotton fields, bucking or otherwise.

But Mom was overjoyed to have me home. She fussed over me and cooked all my favorite foods. Even hominy and also grits—to me the two are not synonymous.

However, Dad was Dad. He was happy to see me, but immediately he took me to task.

Eager to tell him about my experiences and what I was learning, I told him about problems we had trying to keep water in the boilers during the hurricane, with vapor-locked feedpumps taking suction from the overheated hotwell at 212 degrees.

"Hold it, hold it, right there," he insisted. "I might not have got to New York City or to any France, but your pappi's got sense enough to know that water boils at 212 degrees Fahrenheit. Now, if you already had steam in that hotwell-what's-you-call-it, why in the blazes did you need to try to pump it into them boilers? Who ever heard of pumping steam, anyway?"

Thinking I had a chance to show off some of the tidbits I had learned, I hastened to explain *latent heat of evaporation* to him; explaining that the hotwell merely had 212-degree hot water, and I made the point that while it took only one BTU per degree to raise the temperature of a pound of water to 212 degrees at sea level, it then took about 970 additional BTUs of heat to evaporate the pound of 212-degree water into steam.

I added, "Don't you see, Dad, containing all the heat that makes it expand from water is why steam packs so much power."

He grumbled that as far as he was concerned 212 degrees was 212 degrees no matter where it was at; in a hotwell, at sea level, or on top of a Smokey Mountain in Tennessee.

I should have left his remarks alone, but I just had to show off to my dad. I corrected him by pointing out that water would boil at less than 212 degrees on top of a mountain.

He frowned, snorted, and snapped, "What difference does it make? Who in the devil wants to climb way up a blooming mountain to boil water, anyhow?" He gave me that old familiar perplexed look, then mumbled, "Boy, I just don't know about you. I declare, I wonder sometimes if you'll ever make it."

He continued to grumble, and declared that as far as he was concerned X-unknown numbers and latent heat of confusion stuff were all stuck in the same muddy puddle.

I felt a twinge of sadness during my whole visit. I was back home, yet, I knew then that, indeed, Thomas Wolfe was right: "You can't go home again." I became extremely restless and was anxious to get back to my ship; it seemed the world was passing me by, and I felt the urgent need to get back out and make a grab for, at least, the tip of its tail. Biding farewell to the folks, I rode the bus to Memphis.

Howard and Cora saw me off at Union Station. At 8 P.M., January 20, 1946, I boarded the *Tennessean* and as the crack streamliner rolled into the night, I waved good-bye to Cora. A day and a half later, at 1:40 in the morning, January 22, the hourly train shuttle between Washington, D.C., and New York arrived at Penn Station in Manhattan.

I hastened over to Hoboken, New Jersey, where my ship was, and when I approached her in the shipyard, I was astonished to see that the old lady's once gleaming white hull had been covered with a dull marine gray. Gone also were the big red crosses on each side of her stack and her hull, and from the boat deck. Her bow wore the name: United States Army Transport *Bridgeport*.

I was promoted to assistant plumber. Wow, I would make $169 per month! I was really getting in high cotton. . . . Maybe I could keep on until I got be somebody, sure 'nough, I thought. January 26, 1946, we put to sea, taking the Northern Route. It was the shortest way across but usually the roughest. However, we had fairly smooth sailing—for the Northern Route. Few passengers were aboard, and I thought the assistant plumber's job was going to be a snap.

February 7, 1946, in weather cold and dreary, we plodded some twenty miles from the English Channel, passed the Isle of Wight, and anchored out at Southampton, England. I saw masts and stacks sticking out of the water from sunken oil tankers which were scattered along the inlet to Southampton. But I was surprised that the war caused little other damage there.

Early on the morning of the ninth we moved to the dock. One of my duties was to hit the beach first thing, hook a big hose to the shore supply, and start taking on fresh water. It takes a long time to fill a passenger ship's freshwater tanks, and I got no shore leave that night.

In fact, hardly a single crew member went ashore that night in Southampton, England. That afternoon over nine hundred war brides were ushered on board, filling the ship's passenger capacity.

I was bewildered. Especially when Woodie, the chief plumber, nudged me in the ribs, and with a devilish wink, said, "Now, Mac, I want you to stay on the ball. Son, we're going to give the best service in the fleet . . . when one of these broads squalls, you hitch your pants and come running."

I was indeed anxious to give the best service I could to nearly one thousand women each trip crossing the North Atlantic. And although my baling-wire, country-plumbing methods worked at times, there were other times when they were not very effective. We had a few "tough cookies" as passengers each trip, and they made me pay dearly when I often goofed up.

LINER AT LANDING STAGE, LIVERPOOL.   69418

THAT FIRST LOAD OF WAR BRIDES WAS CHEERFULLY welcomed aboard. They twittered with giddy excitement, and wanted to hear what we could tell them about America; particularly they wanted to know about the city or area to where they were going.

WACs replaced most enlisted men who had served as hospital-ship orderlies. Also, most army doctors and nurses were gone, except a few who remained aboard transport *Bridgeport* to care for bellyaches and seasickness, and seasickness, and seasickness.

Quarters were assigned in a pecking order; the higher her husband's rank, the better were the quarters a bride received. A few had private rooms, others shared a room, and enlisted men's wives were quartered in what had been wards, which were still numbered and called wards although the ship was no longer a hospital ship.

While we were still in port, the happy women were fed an enormous meal at evening chow. The quality and variety would have delighted the guests at any fine restaurant.

The dear ladies stuffed—we in America perhaps didn't fully realize just how bare the food situation was for the tenacious people of Britain during that war. After a hearty meal, the wives milled about in the foyers and out on deck, caressing an orange to their bosoms. When I made service calls, brides commented to me that the only fresh fruit they had seen, like an orange or banana, was in pictures.

Early morning, February 10, 1946, the USAT *Bridgeport* eased from the quay and got underway with the first load of happy women of a foreign land who had captured the hearts of warriors from America.

The hanky-panky actually started while we were still in port the previous night. And all the way to New York, it continued to outwit a vigilant Army Transport Commander and a pompous chaplain. Yet, considering the number of lady passengers in such close confinement, and the romantic effect long days and nights at sea seemed to have on some, there were relatively few sweets stolen from sugar bowls belonging to others.

However, such incidents that did occur made me wonder if girls were, after all, a lot like ole boys in many ways. It caused my thoughts to drift back and I mused that it was ironic that Prissy Fay Bean had slapped my jaws so many times!

With over nine hundred women aboard trip after trip, it was an eye-opening experience, to me, about human behavior.

There were the timid, drooling wannabe crew members, but there were also a few studs every trip who hunted with abandon.

Additional rules and regulations for all ships hauling war brides were immediately put into effect after the *Bridgeport* brought this first load of war brides to America.

◆—◆ ⊨◊⊨ ◆—◆

A pause here is in order to stress that, despite references that I've read in various articles down through the years which left the impression that most war brides were brought to America on such ships as the liner *Queen Elizabeth*, the fact is that the very *first* load—over nine hundred—of war brides who came to the

United States of America were transported in the United States Army Transport *Bridgeport*. And although a lesser number later came over on such passenger liners as the *Elizabeth*, most by far were hauled to America in U.S. Army Transport ships. It's on record; in fact, there was a big celebration—like no other—in New York City, welcoming this *first* load of brides aboard the *Bridgeport*. All New York newspapers, and many other newspapers across the land, carried big front-page stories about that event on February 22, 1946.

Anyway, whether or not the studs thought the sweets were worth the risk, some of them got caught and finished the trip confined to quarters and logged for all their pay. Also, the scuttlebutt was that these crewmen were blackballed from ever again serving aboard an Army ship.

And, too, there were those aboard various war-bride ships who didn't get caught, but "headed for the hills" when some of the wives, apparently suffering pangs of guilt when reaching their new homes, confessed their ship-board infidelity to their husbands, naming the crewmen who furnished service. These confessions by wives transported by dozens of war-bride ships, and the rage by their husbands, some who were high-ranking army officers, caused quite a stir even though efforts were made to keep such incidents quiet.

Although the roaming passion boys were few compared to the total number of crew members, it seemed that every merchant marine serving in the *Bridgeport* was suspect in the eyes of the transport commander and chaplain.

I soon formed the opinion that the good chaplain spent too much time sticking his nose in the crew's efforts to operate the ship and thus he had little time left to save any souls. And I also thought he was a pompous hypocrite.

For example, a buxom bride with a private room, who kept having me paged to take care of her plumbing, told me that the crew's business was not the only place the two army captains had been sticking their noses. Whether true or not, it was interesting and, indeed, educational for me to discover that there were also a few women who seemed prone to boast about whom and the numbers they had conquered.

Before we made it into the English Channel proper, women all over the ship started to heave. Throughout the ship, tall containers were spaced on each deck for quick access for seasick passengers to stick their heads into. But I saw passengers only a couple of steps away from a container who let go on the spot, puking that rich food to splatter all over the decks. The ship stunk like a fermenting slop bucket before we reached the Atlantic; it smelled worse than the paper mill at Panama City.

Lieutenant Swartz, the adjutant to the so-called transport commander, chided me for fussing about the war "broads" stinking up the ship.

The lieutenant was my pal; she rescued me on a number of occasions. And she was a no-nonsense professional, a good decent human being. Others referred to our passengers as war broads, but the adjutant kept scolding me until I stopped mimicking the ole salts and referred to the women as brides or ladies.

Woodie, the chief plumber, a master plumber ashore before embarking on a life at sea, was patient and he taught me much, but he delegated the "Kotex jerking" and such to me.

Although the brides were provided with airtight self-closing containers in every head in which to discard sanitary pads, some women seemed to delight in seeing how many they could flush through the johns. For example, all commodes located on decks above the ship's water line emptied into master drain lines that discharged through the ship's hull. Each of these commodes was fitted with a clapper valve designed to close when air compressed and gushed up through drain pipes when the ship rolled. But a coat of salt crust from seventy-five pounds of sea water pressure, used to flush toilets, accumulated on these free-swinging brass flaps at times. And this often caused the clapper valves to stick partially closed; thus the sanitary pads would often clog the johns. Then I had to disconnect water pipes and remove the johns from the deck to jerk out the nasty little bales of cotton. I bitched about the distasteful task so much that my shipmates started calling me Kotex Jerker. Once I jerked nine of those little varmints out of just one john!

I gingerly coaxed the rascals into a little bucket and beat it over to Miss Swartz's office. It was located just aft of a door on the port side, which was midships, aft of the foyer, across from the big ward on C-deck, numbered D-1.

The WAC officer got accustomed to seeing me at her office door. With a curl of her nose, she took due note of my problem, then hastened to the bridge and the public address.

She had tried mild scolding before, and this time she got on the PA and her voice cracked loud and clear, "Attention, ladies. Now hear this: You simply cannot flush Kotex down the johns. Put them into the containers provided for disposal. I repeat: Don't—Flush—Kotex—Down—The—Johns!"

This helped for a few days, then the clapper-valve clogging would start again as usual.

It didn't matter whether we had French, Dutch, Belgian, or English brides aboard, there were always those who seemed determined to flush their disposables down the john. I soon concluded that some of those ladies knew no more about modern plumbing than did an outhouse boy from the country.

I would tell myself how glad I was that good ole American girls had more sense. But in that regard, I was to be disappointed later, when we started transporting wives and families of American Occupational Soldiers over to Europe.

The ship only had two plumbers, the chief and his assistant, therefore, I put in days as long, and sometimes longer, as any I had ever worked on the farm or anywhere. And because of the constant demand, it was like living in a daze.

I made seven trips hauling war brides. We made fast turn-arounds in New York. And recalling the experience of hauling those brides is like remembering one long eventful voyage, but that first unique trip stands out. For sure, many eye-opening incidents happened to me, a young man who had much to learn about many things in life. And, although exposure to some incidents caused me anguish because of my concept of woman's image, it was fascinating duty . . . little by little, it all slowly sank in, and I, at least, learned that women were human, also.

Of course, the reason the first war-bride trip that the *Bridgeport* made stands out is because it was such unusual duty, unlike any ever previously assigned to any ship on such a large scale. Therefore, as the first ship making the first such voyage, and because of the various activity and conduct on that trip, the many regulations and rules that were spawned to govern all war-bride ships were varied and many.

There was never a let up for service calls from all over the ship each trip. And, especially, the big D-1 ward took a lot of my time. Its connecting head contained partitions with nine showers, and partitions separating nine commodes, and it contained sixteen lavatories. That head also caused my biggest headache, by far (literally on one particular trip). If I wasn't jerking Kotex, I scraped crust off stuck-open clapper valves after someone squalled when the cold Atlantic smacked them in the rear with concussion when the ship rolled.

Also, sleepless seasick brides all over the ship complained about dripping showers, running commodes, or stuck vents.

Plowing the North Atlantic, it seemed things were always running hot or cold. We would be cruising along with heat blowing through air ducts, then suddenly the weather would turn warm, especially when taking the Southern Route back and when crossing the Gulf Stream. Then the women started crying for their vents to be closed. Or, when it turned cold, they wanted us to open their vents. The salty environment often caused rusty louvers in heating ducts to stick open, then we had to run around and oil them so that they could be closed.

I did my darnedest to keep my mind on my duty, but those ladies constantly teased and embarrassed the devil out of me. The long rectangular air ducts were secured to the overhead and ran throughout the ship. Ward D-1 contained sixty bunks, and in it the big air duct ran fore and aft, smack dab over a row of double-tier bunks. The very first war-bride trip, one lady who occupied a top bunk directly under a vent frequently had me paged to come and open or close it. She always gave me a hard time. On one such service call, I knocked on the door so that everyone could make sure they were dressed before I entered.

She, wearing only a little skimpy see-through undergarment, squirmed and twisted her curves about in her bunk, and grinned down at me like she eagerly waited for the show to start.

I shifted from one foot to the other, not sure just how I was going to handle the situation. "Uhm, uh, Ma'am," I stammered, "your vent gettin' a little too hot on you, is it?"

She flashed a devilish grin, and cooed, "Oh, yes, 'tis indeed, Doll. Would you be a good chap and come up 'ere and close the bloody thing, I fear it 'as already toasted me bum."

Waiting, I continued to fidget, thinking she would surely climb down so I would have room to work. She stayed put, twisting and wiggling, still grinning down on me like a pussy cat with a juicy mouse cornered. And, as always when I tried to do my job, I found there was an audience of brides looking on.

Finally, I pleaded, "Well, okay, Ma'am . . . um, uh, if only you will . . . " I waited for her to climb down from her bunk.

"Will? Will, what?" she squealed. "Blimey, get crackin', you little devil. Get up 'ere and do your bloody job before you 'ave a scorched biscuit on your bloody 'ands."

Frustrated and embarrassed, I got angry, and I thought to myself: Miss Twisty Butt, if you want to get oil squirted all over you, it won't be my fault. I climbed up on the bunk, and darned if she didn't scoot to her knees, brushing her healthy bumpers against my back, breathing warm on my neck, like she was keenly interested in watching what I was doing.

Woodie would chuckle at my fuming about the teasing and toying around with which a few of the brides pestered me. I raved that us ole boys were supposed to do the chasing and I didn't fancy a gal chasing me because it scared me.

He commented that they were merely a bunch of broads who felt safety in numbers and were having their fun. However, he added, "But, watch your step, Mac, don't get yourself into trouble. Some of them ain't kidding around. Women like young tender virgins too."

"Hey, man," I raved, "where you get off, calling me a virgin? Heckfire, I've worked in the blooming shipyard where there were plenty of girls."

"Sure, pal, sure . . . " he chuckled, wagging his head in amusement.

A good decent man was Woodie. I never once saw him try to put anyone down. Good-natured, a friend to all.

The former section-8 ward for mentally ill patients, in the stern on D-deck, had a deck drain on the portside which, for some reason, the shipyard had failed to install a trap into; thus, stinking fumes vented into the stuffy quarters from a sump tank in the ship's bottom. To combat such problems, we kept a supply of muriatic acid aboard; a bottle of it was great stuff to help clear clogged drains and also to combat bad odors.

I had a standing order to keep the stern-drain treated, which I did when I had slack moments. And on one occasion in the little ward, the eight occupants, like all the brides did, flooded me with questions. I chatted briefly with them before turning to my task of pouring acid into the drain, located in the portside corner of the compartment, under double-decked bunks, forward.

One of the brides had obviously married a soldier from a southern cotton farm. But she kept referring to him as a cowboy who lived in Mississippi on a ranch so big that it was a plantation. She was very excited, talking about how grand life must be to live on a ranch big enough to be a plantation. She asked if I knew anything about big ranches. I told her I didn't but that I knew a little dab about how things were on some big cotton plantations.

She looked puzzled, and I asked, "Ma'am, are you sure? Reckon your husband didn't tell you he was a plowboy on a cotton plantation in Miss'sippi?"

"Plowboy?" she snapped. "Plowboy, did you say? Blimey, 'ow did your bloody ears tell you a silly thing like th'ot? 'E's no bloody plowboy. 'E's a cowboy, 'e jolly well is. 'E told me as much 'is ownself, 'e did. 'E is a cowboy on a big ranch in Mississippi."

I had already heard of tall tales being told to fair ladies in foreign lands. I had taken them with a chuckle and a shrug. But there I was, getting an example firsthand. There would be more of the same flavor in trips to come, but none that would top this one.

I chuckled as I studied the defiant set of the lady's chin, stuck out, just daring me. I mused, "H'mmmm, then I betcha he is a 'nightfighter' or Chickasaw Indian, or such, ain't he."

She jabbed both hands to her hips and stood up right in my face. "No, 'e bloody well, ain't. 'E's no bloody chicken or anything of the sort. But 'e is an Indian. 'E's a big strong Uhhhhpatchee Indian, 'e is. Like 'is famous fathers before 'im, 'e is a fierce warrior, 'e is!"

I shrugged, willing to let her cherish a dream of what her future would be like. But as I dropped to the deck, preparing to belly under the bunk to reach the corner drain, she followed, determined to make sure that I had things straight about her husband in Mississippi.

She kept going, "And, Yank, 'twould do you well to know, too, 'e came over to 'elp my people just like 'is great grandfather jolly well came out of your West to fight the devils who made slaves out of people. 'Is grandfather was a great chief too, 'e was. And w'ot thanks did you Yanks give 'im? You sent 'im to suffer in a stockade in the bogs of your bloody South to live with giant crocs and poison snakes, that's w'ot."

She struck a nerve which compelled me to set her straight. I sat up and leaned back against the bunk. Shaking my head at her, I tried, "Now, Ma'am, first off; I ain't no blooming Yank. And second; if I was you, I wouldn't be going off down there in Miss'sippi talking about any folks being devils. And the next thing is, I don't give a tuft off a rabbit's hind end how big a cotton, uh, ranch your husband lives on. If you say he lives on a big ranch on a cotton-pickin' plantation in Miss'sippi, that's fine and dandy with me. And I sure hope yawl live happy ever after. Good luck to you. Okay, Ma'am?"

She tightened her lips thin and, with hands still on her hips, leaned down to my face. "Blimey!" she squealed, "are you daft! I neva' said anything about any bloody cotton picking—'e don't pick bloody cotton. I said, 'E—Lived—On—A—Bloody Ranch!"

She turned to the others, who were gathered around, and twirled a finger at her ear in the universal fashion to let them know I was, indeed, daft.

I shut up.

I didn't even meet her challenging eyes.

I wiggled on under the bunk, opened the bottle and poured acid into the drain and waited before adding more.

The others listened to our exchange with keen interest, without the least sound of a snicker or giggle.

I wondered if any of them had also married a cowboy on a ranch on a plantation in Mississippi. Or that maybe some of them had married ole boys who went around selling the Brooklyn Bridge.

I chuckled to myself and mused about how tough life must have been for them during the war, then marveled that they still had plenty of spunk left in them.

Cowboys on a plantation in Miss'sippi, I mused. My, what an ole boy won't run into, blundering along, trying to amount to something.

We took the Southern Route, and off Cape Hatteras we hit foul weather and very heavy seas. For two days, bitter cold, gale-force winds blew clouds of Atlantic spray back over the ship's superstructure as she tumbled on towards New York. After we crossed the Gulf Stream, several hours before we made port, thick lacy ice covered the outside decks and every inch of surface on the superstructure from bow to stern.

She eased up the river and was escorted by scores of police boats, fireboats, and pleasure craft, large and small, all blowing whistles and horns. Hundreds of ships docked in the vast port also joined in, blowing their loud whistles in greeting.

Excited brides waved from portholes to the boat people and many braved the icy weather to stand out on deck and wave from both sides of the top-heavy ship. It was well that they were equally balanced, because even under ideal conditions, passengers crowded on one side of a ship will make it list enough to cause great concern about capsizing.

Bundled up against the cold, I stood on the bow as we eased along amid the cheers of our escort, and my gaze swept back over the ship. From bow to stern, every inch of her surface was shrouded with ice so white it dazzled the eye, glittering like a sparkling bridal veil. A big, rough-looking longshoreman later told me that the ice-covered ship slowly loomed into the harbor like a carriage from heaven; and, indeed, I also mused in awe at the spectacular sight and thought that surely the Big Skipper had seen fit to dress the ancient lady so appropriately in honor of the occasion.

We docked at pier 84 in Manhattan. It was February 22, 1946. And the fact is, on that date, the first shipload of War II brides from a foreign land had indeed arrived in America. It caused much excitement, and the *Daily Mirror* and *Daily News* ran full front-page pictures of the ice-covered ship; all other New York newspapers also ran blown-up pictures and big write-ups about the unique event.

Some wives were met by their husbands, and witnessing their happy reunions caused a soft warm feeling that stirred an ache in the heart of a lonely young man such as I, who thought of the woman in his dreams, with whom he yearned to someday share his future. I didn't know where she was or how I would meet her, but deep inside, my longing was eased by a mysterious assurance that someday I would find her and, when I did, I would know who she was. The image of her beautiful face was registered firmly in my mind. Instead of the man in the moon, when I stood at the fantail at sea and looked long at a full moon on a clear night, I always saw the slightly turned face of my smiling woman, with long hair fluffing down on the left side in the bright moon's image maker.

It was a plus to dock at pier 84 in Manhattan; we didn't have to spend much precious shore leave time traveling to and from the glitter, as we had to do when docked on the Jersey side in places like Hoboken, or when we docked at the Army's piers in Staten Island, from where we had to ride a bus, South Ferry, then the subway to Times Square. At pier 84, we were already there, close to the glitter, within a short trolley ride or even a short walk, for a country boy.

This trip in, I continued to get a broader sense of what the great city was like and a feel for its people. And, indeed, some of the finest people I have ever met were New Yorkers. I soon got used to the abrupt brisk manner of some and found that underneath it all they had hearts of gold. I began to think that New York was the greatest city in the world.

Brooklyn and another shipmate from Alaska took me to the Crossroads across from the Times Building. Each had made a couple more trips than I, therefore they attempted to wear the demeanor of real salts.

Two classy-looking young women were at a nearby table, smoking cigarettes stuck in cigarette holders longer than any I had ever seen. It made it look like each woman had a whole row of tobacco between her lips.

My companions traded boy-girl wits back and forth with the women.

When the women got up to leave, one patted Brooklyn on his head, and said, "You're cute, sonny boy, but I don't think you can afford a date with me."

Brooklyn didn't take it too kindly. He half raised to his feet, and raved, "Ehhh, up yours, Toots." Then he stiffed the air with a finger and slapped the crook of his arm.

Soon, the management asked us to leave.

We took in Jack Dempsey's for a snort then drifted on to the Metropol. It had the longest bar I had ever seen.

After a few slugs of sko-cat we were feeling good, and Alaska got me to calling ducks through the hollow of my fist. He said I did great, sounded just like a wild mallard. But Brooklyn said I didn't sound like a duck. Told me that all the ducks in Central Park went quack, quack, quack. I explained that a wild mallard didn't exactly sound like quack, quack, quack.

He wanted to know why. Argued that a duck was a duck and, if the ducks in Central Park went quack, quack, quack, den dem ducks in dem pig trails of Arkansas oughta go quack, quack, quack, also.

I told him you couldn't find any wild mallards messing around any pig trails but you could find them in rice fields and pin oak flats.

He allowed that it didn't matter, that they should still go quack, quack, quack just like the ducks did in Central Park. Because a duck was a duck.

I explained that a bird was a bird but they didn't all sound alike, and that a jackass didn't sound like a mule even though lots of folks often called mules jackasses.

Brooklyn said that had nothing to do with it because a jackass didn't go quack, quack, quack, anyway.

I again blew loud through my fist to give him a better idea of how a wild mallard duck sounded while hailing other ducks flying over. Then I chattered to explain the feed call.

Brooklyn liked to hear me chatter. He urged me to show him how to chatter and blow the hail call.

Alaska joined in and we were just chattering and hail calling all over the high-class Metropol. Brooklyn attempted to join in, but he kept blowing, Pooooo, Pooooo, Pooooo!

Man o' man, we were really having fun.

Then two great big jokers in black suits locked hands and formed a drag with their arms then raked us out onto the street. Heck, they didn't even let me finish the slug of sko-cat I had just paid for. It cost me a whole seventy-five cents!

Brooklyn told me not to fret, that he was going to sea long enough to make enough money to buy a bar in Brooklyn and he would let me call ducks all I wanted to in it. Alaska agreed. Said he was saving his money and was going to sponsor enough Displaced Persons in Europe to bring to Alaska to start a whorehouse, and he assured me that I could also call ducks all I wanted to when he got it opened.

We pondered about what to do next.

I glanced across Times Square at the big Camel cigarette sign blowing steam, depicting smoke rings.

Then the Maxwell House Mayflower Coffee and Doughnut shop caught my eye. The depiction of a steaming cup of coffee and hot doughnut held my attention. Also, with the glittering neon display was a little epigram I have never forgotten: As You Travel On Down The Road, Brother, Whatever Might Be Your Goal, Keep Your Eye Upon The Doughnut And Not Upon The Hole.

I was amazed. It seemed that message was directed right at me; because it seemed like I kept grabbing a handful of hole even though I was desperately trying to grab hold of the world.

Having been thrown out of two places, we felt a little subdued and so we returned to ship.

This needs to be said: During the years of the World War II National Emergency, a merchant seamen could sail in just about any position aboard a ship for which that ship's chief engineer or other licensed officer deemed him qualified. It was known as sailing on a sponsoring officer's personal license. And it is largely to the honor and credit of these old professional sea dogs, because of their tremendous patience to teach green lubbers, that the United States had even the resemblance of a Merchant Marine sufficient to man the thousands of merchant ships needed during that war. In fact, it is well to point out here, had it not been for the old professional sea-going chief engineers, ship's captains, and other merchant marine officers, taking a chance with novice seamen, I believe America would have been forced to federalize the Merchant Marine, a private industry, and draft merchant seamen. As it was, the U.S. Maritime Service and private shipping companies and the Army Transport Service—all constantly trying to recruit U.S. citizens to serve aboard American Merchant Marine ships—failed to encourage enough volunteers to serve in the USA's Wartime Merchant Marine. Therefore, were it not for several thousand foreigners who volunteered to serve in the U.S. Merchant Marine, victory for the Allies would have been greatly jeopardized. For example, England pleaded for at least twenty ships per day delivering supplies to British ports in order for that nation to survive. And, by contrast as a further example, in just the month of June 1942, German submarines sunk over 170 allied supply ships, most in the Western Atlantic off the coast of America. Think about it. That many lost ships and supplies in *just* one month . . . ! But, for the whole of the first six months of 1942, the Germans only lost about twenty submarines, and they were being built and delivered at the rate of thirty per month to form the awesome German U-boat wolf packs!

One of that war's ironic twists was that Americans manned merchant marine ships on the "Murmansk Run" in the Arctic Ocean, some of which didn't even have the 20 MM Oerlikon anti-aircraft guns with which to combat the German torpedo planes that attacked them daily as they struggled to get supplies to Russia. The Oerlikon was a British gun, and perhaps it's the human trait of "taking care of your own," because the ships we gave England that were also in the Murmansk-Run convoys, such as American made Liberty ships, all had the popular 20 MM guns.

Another little known and interesting fact: with the exception of U.S. Army-Transport Merchant Seamen—Civil Service Status—when a U.S. Merchant Marine's ship was sunk, that seaman's pay stopped! And so, the old timers—the professional seamen—who just happened to be caught up in a terrible war as they earned a living plowing the oceans of the world, are among the unsung heroes of War II, if there is such a thing as a live hero; the same is true about those landlubbers who *volunteered* to go down to the sea when their country needed them, who were sunk time and again but kept going back to serve aboard slow cargo ships, many of which were like sitting ducks for enemy submarines and torpedo planes.

March 6, 1946, we got underway for Southampton again. It was my sixth trip.

Mr. Voorhees had signed off for a visit home. And while in Florida, he would go to Miami and pass the examination for his First Engineer's License. But before he signed off the *Bridgeport*, I was pleasantly surprised when he presented me with a brand spanking new *Modern Marine Engineer's Manual*, by Audel, and he demanded that I keep digging in it. There was a lot of digging to do in the four-inch thick superb reference book.

We anchored out at Southampton, March 19, and docked early the morning of the 21st. The *Aquatania*, a sister ship to the ill-fated

England's passenger liner Aquatania *at dock in Liverpool, England. The* Aquatania *hauled troops in World War II. She was a sister ship to the* Lusitania. *May 7, 1915, a German submarine sank the* Lusitania *in sight of the Irish Coast. Many Americans were aboard. This attack on a passenger ship was said to be the cause of the United States entering World War I.*

Lusitania was in port there, and also I got my first good look at the *Queen Elizabeth*, which was docked across the way, getting refurbished from service as a troop ship to service as a passenger liner. More than a year and a half later, my ship, the USAT *Charles A. Stafford* (former passenger liner *Siboney*), would beat the great ocean liner to the rescue of over thirty seamen aboard the *Maria Carlota*, a Portuguese fishing schooner that was sinking in heavy seas a few hundred miles off Newfoundland . . . they had been desperately hand-pumping water all night, and we got to their rescue just in the nick of time.

I enjoyed my trip into Southampton this time; a view of what the world was like opened up a bit more . . . I found our English friends and a few of their customs interesting. I couldn't get the hang of drinking hot tea or the taste of Scotch though. Tea tasted too much like the awful senna leaf tea Mom used to either pour or cram down me for a purgative, until I learned not to ever forget around her. If any of her children ever let a stinker around Mom, she would cram a heaping tablespoon full of that dry senna leaf powder into our mouths, right then and there. I have gagged, spit, and sputtered with that crummy stuff stuck to the roof of my mouth until I nearly choked . . . it would take hours to get the taste out, or a big chaw of Days Work.

And Scotch whisky tasted to me like stump water with which I wet my mouth a few times when Dad and I ran out of drinking water in the log woods. Aside from the kick, I could tell little difference in the flavor. Scotch was severely rationed in Southampton anyway; Scuttlebutt had it that an American with powerful political clout had a lock on all the Scotch made, thus exporting most of it to America.

There were only two places in the fair-sized city that sold spirits. One we thought was a dump, and the other was a nice hotel, the Court Royal. Some of the patrons who hung out at the dumpy place were rather seedy looking; therefore, my shipmates and I patronized the Court Royal. It had a big ballroom and a great band that played our favorite music until 2 A.M.

By way of rationing spirits, Scotch could only be sold for an eight-hour period each day; therefore, the dispensing cove at the Court Royal closed at midnight. However, for little more than four pounds sterling, about twenty U.S. dollars (the legal rate of exchange was then around $4.80 for an English pound note; on the black market, it was only $4), one could buy enough of the little English jiggers to fill a small water glass, to have to sip on after the cutoff time. A dollar's worth was plenty for me. I simply was unable to savor the taste of stump water, either working in the log woods at home or in the merry atmosphere of the Court Royal Ballroom in jolly ol' England.

On this trip in, before visiting the ballroom, three shipmates and I went to a restaurant near a movie theater; I found it amusing that the British didn't go to a picture show to see a movie but, instead, they went to a cinema to see a flick.

Looking at the menu and food served to others, I sensed there was little choice; it was either fish and chips or Salisbury steak and peas. I wearily sighed, then to the waitress said, "Well, since we had fish and potatoes to eat a day or so ago, guess I'll have the hamburger steak and English peas."

The friendly smile flamed off the young lady's pretty face, her lips stretched thin, and she hissed, "Well, blimey. We m'ought not 'ave as much to eat as you bloody Yanks, but we jolly well don't 'ave to listen to you make fun abouuu-tit!"

She stomped off, and I hailed after her, "Hold on, Little Lady, what did I say? I wasn't making fun of anybody. . . ."

An older woman rushed to our table and took over. I should have merely told her that I wanted some peas and meat then let it ride. But I was truly baffled. I didn't want the young waitress peeved at me, but I knew not what to apologize for.

The older woman was no help, when she piped, "I would wager you are a fine lad who is a rebel from the South, are you not?"

I fumed. Wagging my head, I said, "Nope, I ain't no rebel, no yank or no nothing. I'm just plain ol' Mac."

I asked her what the young girl got so hot about, and she informed me that in England the peas were called green peas.

Of course that made sense, because indeed they sure were green. I should have let the whole matter drop, but I opened my mouth again to explain that back home Mom and everyone called the little boogers English peas, and I always figured that was to honor the good English folks for perhaps finding that they were good to eat. And I offered as a further example of the goodwill I wished to convey, that I had also figured out that the reason Limeys were called Limeys might be because everyone back home called lima beans, limey beans. And I guessed the reason they sometimes called the British, Limeys, was to honor them for discovering limey beans were also good to eat.

Her face sparkled with laughter, and she informed me that the term "limey" came about in the old sailing ship days when scurvy was a problem until it was learned that limes in sailors' diets prevented the scourge. But she hastened to advise me in a serious tone not to ever call an Englishman a Limey, not to his face, anyway.

After dining, we eventually got one of the scarce little taxis and went to the Court Royal Hotel.

There I met an attractive girl also named Lee; it seemed like I was often running into others who were named Lee, male and female. I felt at ease with her and we hit it off fine. But comments and hints she made from time to time caused alarm bells to go off. For no reason that I could understand, at first, she was quick to declare she was not going to marry an Englishman. I admired the British soldier, and her attitude caused a flash of disappointment about her, but I let it ride.

Lee was a very pretty girl. She was gleeful and a lot of fun, and I could hug her all the way around. But, although she was a decent girl to be with when we made port there, I knew she wasn't my girl in the moon. I felt sad and a sense of despair; it seemed that finding the girl to match the image of my dream girl was going to be very difficult, if not impossible.

One entered the ballroom from the side and faced the large seating area with tables. To the right of this area was a wide dance floor. The bandstand was beyond it. Left of the dance floor was a door to a spacious glassed-in patio. Above the door was the warning: If You Must Jitterbug You Will Go Outside.

Each night that I visited the Court Royal Ballroom, someone always challenged the sign, two or three times some nights. And each time, a tall man with the air of a gentleman would suddenly appear and march across the dance floor and firmly grasp the arms of would-be jitterbug couples, then, without uttering a word, shuffle them out the patio door. With mission completed, he would pause to give his jacket sleeves a tug. Then with a stiff back, chin in the air, march back across the floor to disappear.

Someone requested the band to play their version of Tommy Dorsey's "Boogie Woogie"—a phenomenal favorite everywhere.

I had progressed to where I could do a hop-a-long effort at jitterbugging, and I suddenly felt the urge. Lee and I got out on the floor but never got to do more than just a little jit. Out briskly marched the patio escort.

I suspected it might happen, still it was a shock when he poked us into the patio. Thus we stood, out there on shadowy display by the lights from the ballroom. I flashed a look inside, and the whole ballroom full of folks were laughing at us.

Then the band did something I had never heard it do before; it switched from Dorsey's "Boogie" to "Hold That Tiger" (the "Tiger Rag"). Then the crowd really roared with laughter.

I thought: What the heck, what's done is done. I grabbed Lee and tried to jig the Tiger but couldn't do much with it.

Another fascinating custom to me was, as Lee told me, no English woman, decent or otherwise, would be caught smoking in public.

Discovering such a strict custom in a foreign country was interesting; I remembered a time as a small boy in my part of America when no self-respecting woman would dare be seen smoking a cigarette or wearing anything but a dress in public. Any woman who did was frowned upon by other women and men as being a loose woman with no morals or self-respect.

My sisters did not smoke, and they would never think of wearing pants. After we moved to the farm, they were permitted to wear old overalls in the fields to hoe cotton, but they dared not wear shorts or slacks.

When I was just a little tot, one day near Beale Street in downtown Memphis, I stared at a woman's buttocks playing see-saw at the sidewalk as she twisted along in bright red britches. They looked too small for her, and I merely thought that because they were so tight was the reason her butt was acting so funny. Mom caught me staring bug-eyed and she shook me to get my attention, then warned that the old devil would get little five-year-old boys who looked at girls like that.

The day before we got underway, we took on another load of brides. They were also allowed to stuff on rich food at supper and breakfast chow, most of which they also would vomit in their bunks or all over the decks. Many of the dear women would get so seasick they did not, or could not, move; they moaned and groaned in their bunks and wallowed in puke.

Early next morning, March 24, we got underway. But other than the seasick women and a stinking ship, we had a relatively smooth trip back. With strong tailwinds and running currents and no hot bearings to slow us down, we made great time—for the *Bridgeport*. We dropped anchor in the harbor April 5, and docked at pier 84 early next morning.

The dismal hulk of the once proud ocean queen for France, the *Normandie*, was still at pier 86. The ship had been taken over by the

U.S. Navy and was in the process of being converted to the troop transport *Lafayette* when she mysteriously caught fire February 9, 1942. She capsized at the pier the next morning, and was later refloated.

After she was refloated, movie newsreels and banner newspaper headlines proclaimed how great it was that the former ocean queen would soon be back in service for the benefit of peace-loving people.

Millions were spent on her but she never went back to sea. Coming in to port as the years passed, we saw her ghostly hulk being towed about to be docked at different places in the great harbor. And mariners often wondered aloud to one another what would eventually be done with the ruined vessel. When we later found out, we were extremely disgusted.

CHAPTER 11

LINER AT LANDING STAGE, LIVERPOOL.   69418

AFTER OUR USUAL VISIT TO THE SHIPYARD TO TAKE CARE
of the old lady's frequent aches and pains, we took her to sea again
with the evening tide on April 17. I read a small news article which
stated that over eighteen thousand B-24 Liberator bombers had
been built during War II, and I remember musing to myself about
what it would be like to fly over the rough-ass Atlantic in one of
them at three hundred miles an hour instead of getting jarred day
in and day out while plowing along at less than ten knots in an old
ship. I crossed the North Atlantic over seventy times, over and
back, and I can only remember one crossing when we had smooth
sailing with calm seas all the way across.

Easter Sunday, April 21, 1946, we were outbound about one
thousand miles from New York when a ring on the second intermediate piston broke in the starboard engine. No sending
something down the street to a machine shop for repairs here;
engine crewmen in a ship at sea find a way to fix it, or improvise
to make it on into port. To have to be towed with a seagoing tug is
a horror no self-respecting salt in the blackgang would even think

about. Especially one like Chief Engineer Hunt, who claimed that after the sailing ships were gone, all the *real* sailors moved below to the engine room in steamships. He often called the skipper, deck officers, and deckhands department store clerks—to their faces— he was the sure enough embodiment of a bona fide old salt without fear!

Anyway, without the heavy duty tools needed, we worked for thirty-two hours, trying without success to remove the massive follower plate on the huge piston. Finally the chief engineer ordered us to disconnect that piston's leg. We bypassed the second IP cylinder's intake and exhaust ports, and plowed on with only the high pressure cylinder, first intermediate cylinder, and the low pressure cylinder working on the quadruple expansion engine.

Walter K. Hunt, Brooklyn sea dog, tough, fearless, and who made the previous trip as First, was now the chief engineer.

Mr. Mallard had moved to the *General Ballou*, the first of several C-4 ships transferred from the Navy to the Army Transportation Corp, Water Division, as we were now known instead of ATS. The C-4s were converted to passenger transports to serve in the Army Fleet, which was the largest fleet of deep water ships ever assembled in the history of mankind—the U.S. Army had more ships than did the U.S. Navy!

I would sail with and under the command of some colorful characters before my tenure at sea came to an end, but none who was more the all-around, salty, no-holds barred, professional seafarer as was Chief Hunt. And no matter what country in which we made port, he knew someone of authority. Sometimes they would be relatives who were also professional seafarers.

Even though he was tough and rough, he was fair; he would give one a second chance but not a third, never.

May 2, 1946, we tied up at Le Havre to a long pontoon that served as a dock, which substituted for all the docks destroyed in the war. There we took aboard a mixed load of war brides— French, Dutch, and Belgian. The ship then moved to anchorage, making space for a supply ship to dock.

We lay at anchor for five days while trying to secure repairs to the starboard engine. Again, as in Cherbourg, the Germans had left no heavy duty tools or steel with which to make a ring for the big cylinder. Chief Hunt merely shrugged about it, and he scoffed at the idea of crossing over to Southampton, England, for repairs, and gave assurance that he could pet "his" engines to "screw" us back to New York. We got underway May 7.

Running about the ship taking care of plumbing problems while still at anchor, Woodie and I had noticed considerable grumbling and cat-spitting between several of the passengers. I was puzzled that they were so hateful to one another. While I realized they had suffered through a terrible war, I still couldn't understand why some were not of good cheer like those happy English ladies we had already carried to America.

No sooner had we gotten underway, all hell broke loose. But no one had any reason to suspect that women would fight the blasted war over again among themselves. That is, with the French on one side battling the Belgian and Dutch brides joined on the other. At the mere drop of a hairpin they would tear at each other throughout the ship!

Within hours, haste was made to reassign the Dutch and Belgian together in one section of the ship and put the French brides in the other, with guards in between.

However, that did not stop the war on the Atlantic aboard the old *Bridgeport*. The fights raged on—raw, hair-pulling, haymaker, knockdown humdingers. The ship's masters-at-arms and army personnel darted from one battle to the next, running all over the ship trying to be peacemakers. But they were far out numbered by the skirmishes, and by the numbers of combatants.

For example, there was a large self-service mess on D-deck where over two hundred could eat chow at each sitting. Therein, heavy duty GI stainless steel food trays often made music as the ladies whacked each other on the head. Dozens would be drawn into the fray, and sometimes there was more than one head-banging going on at anytime in chow lines.

I was adjusting the long conveyor of the dishwashing machine in the D-deck mess during chow one evening. The chow line passed close by, and suddenly so many trays started whipping the air, banging heads, I shut the machine off and crawled up inside its tunnel to keep my noggin safe. Thus, while hunkered down peeking out of a dripping dishwasher, my education continued.

It soon became apparent that the brides had to also be separated into groups even when they had chow.

Because it was the Southern Route, after a couple of days the weather was nice and sea calm. Corporal "Flick," an army lab technician who also ran the movie projector, was a jovial accommodating person. Since the weather was so nice, Flick ran a movie outside on C-deck, aft, displayed on the cabin superstructure.

It was one of the typical war movies, and hardly had it flashed on the white superstructure when a real war started on the fantail of the *Bridgeport*. The ladies shouted obscenities and insults at one group and the other; brides from Holland and Belgium were united in blaming the French for the German occupation of their countries, and ridiculed them about France's supposedly impenetrable Maginot Line of defense. Curiously they all shrieked in English, which fascinated me. I surmised that they probably used English to make sure everyone aboard understood their views.

The French shot back to remind them that Belgium and Holland fell to the German juggernaut before France did.

The Belgian and Netherlands gals fired a broadside, claiming that General Gamelin hid behind his precious Maginot Line and let the German Army take over their countries. Then the Belgian and Tulip brides poured on salt by screaming that the Germans had slithered around and over the Maginot Line like snakes after a bunch of frogs.

The French ladies surged to their feet en masse, shrieking that the Yanks were to blame for the whole matter because America didn't get into the war sooner.

(I also got an earful of that charge. I was taken to task while fixing plumbing problems in their quarters when French brides gathered around tossing such barbs as: "You Yanks waited to come over so you could strut and take credit. You Yanks think you're hot stuff. . . ." In self-defense, I replied, "I ain't no damned Yank! Anyway, why did so many of you, uh, ladies marry a Yank?")

While images of American soldiers battling the enemy flashed in silver on the aft bulkhead, the movie's lights reflected upon battling brides slugging it out in a real live brawl. It erupted so suddenly it was as though *Davey Jones* had called out from below,

"Ladies o'er the deep, let the hair pulling begin!" Then while the sound of guns blasted away in the movie, the ladies from afar fought their own war. With their shrieks and screams wailing abaft the beam, they pulled hair and lashed out with haymakers at one another with such violence like none that a boy from the cotton fields had ever seen from ladies.

While the old ship eased along over smooth-running swells, continuing into the night over waters on which other fierce battles had been fought not many months before, the melee seemed to intensify, with our big chief master-at-arms, his two assistants, and army enlisted men and WACs, trying their best to break it up.

Suddenly, screams of terror at the stern shrilled over the battle-rage. A sergeant and the chief master-at-arms rushed around the little aft deckhouse. Although the French ladies far outnumbered them, the Dutch and Belgian gals gave no quarter. However, two French brides had a Zudder Zee lady heisted halfway over the stern rail. The MA and sergeant rescued the Dutch lady in the nick of time. Finally, enough GIs and seamen pitched in to get the battling brides bottled up in their quarters.

That incident had a disturbing effect on me. For days I thought about it. I tried to think it out to some sensible conclusion. They were all good people, I was sure. But why they got so vicious towards one another about something already over and done with, really puzzled me.

The ship's heart throbbed on, and after what seemed like endless days we again tied up at pier 84, May 20, 1946, and quickly off-loaded the passengers.

It had been a hard crossing for both Woodie and me. We had been on call constantly. And with our disgruntled passengers buzzing in their quarters, one was reminded of an enormous swarm of hornets ready to pop anyone who shook their nest. I shuddered with dread when having to enter some quarters on service calls.

The vast majority, by far, conducted themselves like ladies and devoted wives, and they expressed their disgust for the actions of the brawling brides. But out of more than nine hundred in such confinement for several days, a few dozen rowdy wolverines made it seem like they were three or four battalions.

———•——— ✠ ———•———

With our engine repaired, in two weeks we headed for Le Havre again. June 16 we docked there around 9 A.M., unloaded 250 WAC passengers who went over to serve in occupational duty, then we again took aboard French, Dutch, and Belgian brides—this trip they had separate quarters and were separated at chow time.

We had only half a shipload, and we crossed the Channel to take on British brides. In Southampton, we docked around 4 P.M.

The English brides were waiting on the dock and were quickly brought aboard in short order. The Army transport commander was in a frenzy to get underway for New York that evening. Unloading passengers in Le Havre, taking on war brides, crossing the English Channel and taking on an additional four or five hundred brides, all in one day, and then having a hissy to also sail for New York, without the chance to fill our freshwater tanks . . . !

A TC with merely the Army Reserve rank of captain, with a short service tenure, was about to lock horns with a professional sea dog with over forty years at sea who knew the "rules of the road" concerning international laws governing the operation of seagoing ships. In fact, I saw the old chief physically throw the astonished TC out of the chief engineer's office, with the ship's skipper standing by, looking on, meekly.

For sure, the crew loved Southampton as a liberty port. Even the Army permanent crew, who had remained aboard since we had operated as a hospital ship, griped and howled like the rest of us when we learned that the Army transport commander was going to be the cause of no shore leave in Southampton this trip.

It appeared the ship's skipper was not going to buck the TC, and, through the mystic medium aboard a ship, word spread quickly that Chief Engineer Hunt was the man to see. Thus a steady flow of unhappy crew members, both army and merchant marine, rushed in and out the chief's office, which was on D-deck across the starboard passageway from a door in the engine room casing.

Woodie and I had been called to Mr. Hunt's office, and after we watched him remove the TC, we looked on while the salty chief consoled unhappy seafarers as they stomped in and out.

He sat twisting at a bushy eyebrow with chuckling growls rumbling from his barrel belly as he listened. His Camel cigarette dangled, burning nearly to his lips. I watched in fascination, waiting. Finally the long ash dropped. He unconsciously wiped at his barrel belly without looking, as though he intended to brush the ash off. Instead, it was absentmindedly rubbed into his chambray shirt. With a disdainful flip of his hamlike hand he acted as though he could not understand why the disgruntled visitors were so alarmed. He told each not to worry, that they should make ready to go ashore.

He had already sent one of our two boiler feedwater pumps ashore for repairs(?). And he had informed the skipper he would not raise steam to sail unless he, the ship's master, signed into the engine room log that he would take full responsibility for the safe operation of the fire room, and also take full responsibility in the event of a fire. The skipper declined to sign such an order into the engine room log; because in an emergency, either of the two boiler feed pumps could be converted into use as part of the fire fighting apparatus.

We did not sail that night, and the crew got shore leave.

A watch engineer learned to his sorrow that he should not have challenged the chief's no-third-chance policy; he had bucked the chief a second time with insubordination. The second engineer was busted, confined to his quarters, and he rode out the remainder of the trip without pay. A third was pushed up to act as second engineer and a junior third was pushed up to run a watch in the engine room, and Woodie was promoted to junior third engineer for a watch in the freshwater evaporator and refrigeration flat.

Mr. Hunt promoted me to chief plumber. I thought: Hot dog, chief plumber on an everlovin' war-bride ship. The very first war-bride ship . . . Man o' man, ain't that something. . . .

Woodie left to make ready to go ashore. However, the chief had me remain in his office to offer suggestions about whom to make my assistant, and to remain aboard until all the freshwater tanks were filled.

The old-timer sat sprawled back in a swivel chair at his desk, which was secured to the office's forward bulkhead, right of the starboard passageway door. He yawned, then raised to pull a bottle from a drawer. He gulped a slug of Scotch, then half filled a glass with the booze and swallowed another jolt, chasing it with a mix of equal parts of grapefruit juice and grape juice.

My nose curled as I looked on.

He caught me frowning and grunted, "Humph."

Chuckling to himself, he snatched another glass from a rack attached to the bulkhead over the desk, and dashed an inch-depth of Scotch into it. Flashing me a devilish grin, he poured equal parts of the juices from quart cans into another glass. Still grinning as if he were privately entertaining himself, he mixed the juices with his oil-stained finger, then shoved both glasses before me, where I sat frowning with my chin in hand, propped by an elbow on the starboard end of his desk.

I offered a weak grin, shaking my head. "Uh, thanks just the same, Chief. But I just can't get the hang of that stuff, and if you don't mind, I'll pass."

He jerked back and stared at me, then howled, "Nuttin' doing. Dammit, I'm not asking youz to kiss my salty ass; like it or not, youz chief is asking youz to have a drink wit' him."

"But, Chief, don't you see, it's like, uh . . . I don't like stump—uh, dad-gum-it, I got work to do. What's you want me to be drinking that danged stump water for—uh, I mean, uh, yeah . . . what I mean is, when I was a young'n' helping Dad in the log woods in hot summer time, and sometimes we might break or tip over the water jug and run out of water in those steamy woods and all, then, well, we'd cup a hand full of rainwater out of ole hollow maple stumps just to sort of wet our tongues, don't you see. Now, it's not like I'm trying to not be social, but. . . ."

"But, hell," he stormed. "Just hold it. Hold it, right there. Jeez," he exclaimed, slinging his head then brushing at the bushy brow. Leaning to nurse his chin in the crook of an arm curled on the desk, he sat squinting at me. "Jeez," he again grumbled, "Boy, I don't know about youz. Youz think youz ever goina make it . . . ?"

That nearly decked me. Though they were miles and customs apart, that old sea dog had mannerisms just like some of Dad's! As he sat there resting his chin on his arm, lazily blinking his eyes, just looking at me, I wondered how the devil he ever picked up on Dad's often-used expression.

I ducked my face and pushed my cap over my forehead to scratch at the back of my head, and nervously laughed. "I don't know, Mister Hunt, but I'm trying. Maybe I'll get to be somebody one of these days."

"Somebody . . . ?" He jerked erect. "One of these days? Maybe? Hell, Mac, what's with this somebody bilge. Jeez, we're all somebody. Here, Somebody!" He shoved the Scotch at me again, and growled, "I don't know nuttin' 'bout non' dem hollow stumps or non' dem woods but, dammit, youz goina have a drink wit' old Hunt."

I took a sip of Scotch and held it until I also sucked a big gulp of the mixed juices, then I swallowed. Amazing! To my great surprise it did not taste at all like stump water.

Apparently "repairs" on the pump were slow because we didn't sail until two days later.

The crew was happy.

There are few secrets aboard a ship, and both army personnel and merchant crew, praised the old chief for making shore leave possible.

Chief Hunt was also pleased, I am sure. He would growl to us from time to time, "The noirv of dem guys . . . keep a crew for days around joints like Le Havre wit' nuttin' to do but shack up and catch da clap . . . den when we make a port of joy, dey want to shove off wit'out any shore leave."

Although the crew was happy, there were several French war brides who, having been cooped up for days, started an angry buzz that grew. I, at first, thought all the brides this trip were going to be nice and peaceful. Most were but, again, we had a few dozen aboard who were like tigresses.

After a couple days back at sea, we hit rough waters. And, as always, when the sea tossed the ship about, crud dislodged from traps in the pipes and clogged drain lines.

The big head in D-1 had a deck drain in its aft/port corner and it was a frequent problem. After 10 P.M. curfew one night I was called up to unstop the drain. Lieutenant Swartz met me and knocked on the door of the big head and told those inside to get decent because a man was coming in.

I was greeted with squealing and giggling from inside, and loud, "*Oui, oui, entree, entree.*"

I entered, and did a double take; French ladies stood all around the lavatories washing their fancy delicates. A few wore panties but most were stark naked. They giggled to one another, and a few winked and pursed their lips, teasing me with come-hither looks. But for the most part, they acted like they didn't care that a man was looking on, as though they had nothing unusual for him to look at.

I realized the war had left them with few fancy panties and such, and reasoned that they were going to wash what they had, come hell or high water, and it didn't matter who was around.

The water was, indeed, getting higher as it sloshed about over the deck. I could hear all nine showers gushing and splattering. Also, dirty water from all the lavatories was backing up across the white tiled deck because of the clogged main drain. Water was already an inch deep.

I connected a heavy duty inch-and-a-half hose to the sanitary waterline and secured the other end into the deck drain by tamping a small towel around it. Then I opened a valve to let the North Atlantic jar the clogged main drain open, I hoped. But shortly the hose stiffened as the blocked pressure raised it from the deck. I thought: Dad-gum-it, don't look like it's going to work this time.

All over the deck the filthy water was sloshing, and the naked brides were chattering and joshing.

Suddenly my hose went limp, then I felt it vibrate as I heard the Atlantic Ocean gushing through it.

Sighing with relief, I mused I wouldn't need to go below and clean out the messy trap in the four-inch main drain pipe. But my thoughts were shattered by a shrill scream behind me. I jumped up from my squatting position and looked with alarm. A big solid stream of the ocean was smacking the overhead directly above the john in the farthest enclosure. I knew then that the darn clapper valve in the john was stuck partly open.

A lady had been sitting there all along playing 'possum behind the partition. When the ocean filled the four-inch drain it took the path of least resistance and blew her off the john.

I wondered if maybe she was sitting there, feeling all secluded and cozy, dreaming about life in America, when that solid inch-and-a-half stream of cold salt water driven by seventy-five pounds pressure smacked her setter.

Anyway, she was wide awake. The wild-eyed lady came charging at me with a big wet towel and whipped it across my face.

I'd bet that she didn't weigh one hundred pounds soaking wet. But that was enough, because when the towel wrapped around my face, she gave it a hefty jerk with her feet planted. Down I went in all that toilet water sloshing over the deck.

Before I could gain my feet, others joined in. They came pouring out of the showers and, as I got to my knees, a lady snatched my hair from behind and sprawled me across the deck on my back. Then with her claws full of my hair, she banged my aching head on the deck, splashing nasty water with every bang.

I bellered like a scared bull calf but it didn't stop the mauling I was getting.

The woman hung onto my hair while another stout lady with a butt shining like a wet hippo dropped it astraddle my belly, squashing the air out of me. Then she boxed my jaws.

I squirmed, twisted, and humped with all my strength, but the big woman stayed astride like she was riding a bucking bronc. I got angry and poked a thumb in her ribs. She howled. It was in French but I was sure that she cussed me as she took a belly flop in the cruddy water sweeping the deck.

Again, struggling to my knees, I reached back for the woman pulling my hair. I just grabbed for whatever and got a short handful of whatever. She screamed and nearly ruptured my ears while boxing my jaws.

But she let go of my hair.

I bolted out the door with screeching women chasing and whopping me with those heavy wet towels; they felt like sacks filled with liquid lead. The little lady who got her buttocks sand-papered by the cold salty ocean followed all the way as I sloshed down the wide stairs.

The landing on D-deck was at an entrance to the starboard passageway, at a point where it served the engineer-officers' quarters. Just inside the passageway, a step to the right, aft, through the watertight door in the bulkhead, put one at the chief engineer's office. Chief Hunt's puzzled bulldog face stuck out the door.

Miss Swartz hopped down the stairs after the woman who was horse whipping me, and she marched the raving briny-bottomed bride back up to D-1, trying to calm her down.

The chief stepped over the hatchway and stood squinting at me while he twisted at his busy eyebrow. "Jeez, Mac," he chuckled, "wha'd youz do to dem broads this time?"

I stood there like a rooster in a rainstorm, with sloppy water running out of my hair, down the back of my neck, making a puddle on the deck as it streamed from my khaki pants.

"Nothing," I yelped, "but those crazy wildcats danged near cracked my head and drowned me in their pissy water! All due respect, Chief, but I ain't ever going back into that D-1 without somebody—two somebodies riding shotgun to guard me!"

"Yeah, but, jeez, Mac, youz ain't goina tell me youz didn't do nuttin' to dem broads. Jeez, just listen to 'em up there, they're still bitching. What happened?"

I explained it to him while he just stood there running his tongue through the gap of a missing jaw tooth, chuckling at my soggy disposition. Wagging his head, he started back to his office, then turned. "Bejezus, youz best stop wiping everybody's ass with that saltwater stunt, they goina t'row youz overboard."

He was referring to the chief radio operator.

On the trip over, the PX storeroom flooded with water backed up from a clogged drain. Big boxes containing cigarettes, candy bars, Sweetheart soap, and the like were getting soaked. The store-room was centered forward of the midships foyer on C-deck, and its deck drain also tied in with a common drain that dropped down from the ship's officers' quarters above, on the starboard. When trying to blow out the PX drain, I could hear water running through but the drain still didn't drain. I left the seventy-five pounds pressure gushing while I went topside to check all the rooms. I knocked on the door to the chief radio operator's room and got no answer, but when I entered then opened the door to his head, there he was, all bent over, gasping, "Ooooh, Ooooh."

A stiff stream shooting through the john had already lifted him off the seat, then it smacked the overhead, giving him a cold water shower.

A naked woman floated about in front of the commode on a smut magazine cover. The radio operator, all bent over, turned his pained face to me with pleading eyes, and shivered, "Ooooo, Mac, will you please shut off that cold-ass ocean and get me some dry towels?"

He was a good sport about the incident. But when trying to convince Chief Hunt that I had not done it on purpose, that it was merely all part of blowing out a clogged drain, he just looked at me while wagging his bulldog face, then growled, "Boy, I don't know about youz . . . think youz ever goina make it?"

The trip back was hectic and eventful. Days and nights for the whole trip blended in as one long continuous period. Never once did I sleep between the sheets in my bunk.

I shared a room with the chief refrigeration engineer, and we had wide bunks with comfortable innerspring mattresses, but I only got to use mine for napping. Each evening, after a shower and a change into fresh clothes, I would simply sprawl across the top of my bunk fully clothed and doze, waiting for the next service call. Sometimes I would get seven or eight within the same hour; often three or four at one time. During the day, calls came over the PA for a plumber to report to this deck or that deck, but at night, a firewatch patrol or an MA frequently shook me awake from short fuzzy naps to make service calls.

My assistant helped during the day, but new regulations restricting access to passengers' quarters after 10 P.M. curfew permitted only the so-called chiefs in the restricted areas.

Indeed I hustled, even though most calls were minor: a shower dripping and getting on the nerves of sleepless brides who lay moaning in vomit, too seasick to move, even to tighten the faucet in a dripping shower; or a flushometer handle that merely needed jiggling to stop the noise of running water in a john.

After making port, July 3, 1946, I didn't go ashore much. I only ventured from the ship to catch up on the latest movies and news-reels, and to get a Memphis newspaper—thus I learned that the U.S. gave independence to the Philippines July 4, 1946.

The ship was moved about from Staten Island, to Prospect Basin, to Erie Basin, and to the Brooklyn Army Base, getting various repairs and taking on supplies. All the while, I was content to stay aboard and read and also study; Audel's *Modern Marine Engineers Manual* was a gift from Mr. Voorhees that I cherished and felt compelled to study often.

We sailed again July 20, 1946. I had been in the ship a few days more than a year, and this was my ninth voyage.

After about thirteen days we picked up a North Sea pilot at Dover, England. The sheer White Cliffs of Dover fascinated me, and while gazing at them in awe as we plowed on into the North Sea, I mused, "Schools all over the world should never run out of chalk for blackboards."

All along our course in the shallow sea we passed masts of sunken ships, one after the other, sticking far out of the water. The pale masts and their rigging reminded me of dead tree tops sticking from the water of a vast imaginary flooded plain.

There was concern about uncharted and wandering mines, and extra lookouts were posted.

The next morning, around nine, August 3, 1946, we docked at Columbus Quay on the River Wesser in Bremerhaven, Germany. After a fourteen-and-one-half day crossing, the old ship had returned to the place of her birth, forty-six years in the past. In World War I, she departed as a Man of War; now she returned on a mission of mercy. In addition to war brides from Holland and Belgium, we would also bring back a few sick soldiers.

The famous German passenger liner *Europa* had been scuttled at War II's end, blocking the harbor to Banana Quay for big ships, and it had been refloated only recently. (It was destined to become the property of France, renamed the *Liberte*, as a part of to-the-victor-go-the-spoils; a generous gesture which the actual conquerors extended

a people who were defeated by the Germans within a few weeks.)
I was gripped with an erie feeling while looking out over the
low country when we glided up the River Wesser to tie up at the
quay. Every man, woman, and child in America, with few exceptions, thought that Germany had been a devil running amuck on
this earth, intent on becoming its master. I sensed the chilled feeling
one had back then—I still can, sharp and vivid, with flashes of
memory like it was only yesterday. At the beginning of it all, many
of us who were stuck back in such remote places as the cotton and
cornfields of Arkansas gave little thought about where Germany
was or what Germans looked like. Most of us had never even been
as far away as Little Rock. But by news from our weekly *Kansas City
Star* newspaper, listening to our radio, or listening to the gossip
around the old potbelly stove in the general store at Cottonbelt
Junction, we all quickly became convinced that Germans were not
people; they were demons from hell who spewed fire from their

Just before World War II, German luxury liner Bremen *in River Wesser coming into port at
Bremerhaven. Her sister ship, luxury liner* Europa, *was already docked at Columbus Quay.
The* Europa *was scuttled just as War II ended, blocking the harbor to Banana Quay in
Bremerhaven. She was raised by the USA and given to France. She returned to service as a
passenger liner as the* Liberte, *flying the French flag.*

nostrils at little babies and children. According to some old folks and hellfire and brimstone preachers, Germans were the *Beast*, and they were out to mark the foreheads of everyone with the crooked cross, and woe unto those who refused to be *marked*, for they would be spewed with fire and gobbled up by the *Beast*.

Or even worse, according to old Lady Darrow—our neighbor who lived down the road and who often unctuously proclaimed that she was God's Saintly Child who could speak in Sacred Tongues and that God, making Himself visible, talked directly to her—Hitler and Mussolini would force all Americans to have an identification ring clamped in our noses; like those rings used on hogs' snoots to keep them from rooting out from under a fence. Then, according to her, we would all be herded into the enclosure of the pope in Rome. In her low, squatty log house, gathered around a stove on a cold winter's night, in the flickering shadows cast by the dull glow of a coal oil lamp, she made us youngsters shiver with her tales of how evil the pope would be to those who dared to "keep the faith and walk the True Path to Heaven."

But such expressions were, I believe, merely a spinoff of the one major fear that gripped the country, which united most Americans in a common cause like never before in our history: no one wanted the demon coming to our shores, spreading death and destruction. Such was unthinkable. The right thing to do, as over 98 percent of us were eventually convinced by the nothing-to-fear-but-fear-itself wheelchair commando, President Roosevelt, was to go "over there" and destroy the demon, and keep our homeland intact and safe from destruction, plunder, and rape.

After my ship docked in Bremerhaven, there was nothing moving; no vehicle, no person, nothing stirred as far as I could see all around. The demon was dead, and we sat there looking into its mouth. Goose pimples pricked my skin.

I, ole Mac, a nobody from the sticks, was breathing the air, seeing, living right there in a general area of our earth where, not too many months past, Americans who were just like me had fought and died while destroying the demon. I felt very solemn and reverent on that day.

Completed agreements to all the official terms of surrender had not yet been signed by all nations; therefore, America's National

Emergency hadn't been declared over. Thus, in Bremerhaven, strict nonfraternization rules were still enforced by the U.S. Army of Occupation.

Germany was divided into four occupation zones, each governed by one of the four powers: USA, England, France, and the USSR. Actually, Bremerhaven was in the British Zone but relinquished to furnish us a convenient deepwater port for many American ships that would be coming to Germany in years to come.

There was little to do in Bremerhaven but browse around and look at a part of the world I had never seen before. Or we seamen could visit the Special Services Canteen and get a soft drink for ten cents. Or we could go to Hotel Norddeutcher, facing the corners of Kaiser Wilhelmstrass and Hafenstrass, in which the United Seamen's Club was located, and get a big mug of German beer for a nickel. Merchant crewmen while on duty aboard ship loaned their seaman's ID to soldier-shipmates so that they, too, could go to the Seamen's Club dressed in civvies and gain admission to guzzle beer—for many months, except for the military officers at their hurriedly established officers' club, this was the only way in Bremerhaven that our shipboard noncom soldier friends could quench a thirst for beer.

I did a lot of strolling about the city, looking and meditating. There was no damage to any of the docks, neither inside the locks at numerous piers known as Banana Quay nor outside on the River Wesser known as Columbus Quay. I heard comments that the Canadian Air Force knew their stuff, careful not to destroy any of the dock area; Scuttlebutt was that they had made just one massive seventeen-minute blitz over Bremerhaven.

But it was effective; the industrial section, located in the southern part of Bremerhaven, was nothing but piles of twisted steel and rubble, for city block after city block. Many blocks were pulverized, not a single building left standing. Nothing.

There was a strong putrid stench in the air. I was told it came from bodies of animals and people still buried in the rubble. However, the local citizens were busy everywhere digging useable bricks from the ruins and stacking them in neat rows along the sides of strasses, with which to rebuild.

American Seamen's Club in Bremerhaven, Germany. Entrance to the recreation area of the seamen's club at far right. Barefoot children aged eight, nine, and ten years of age stood outside this entrance in the bitter cold, begging for cigarette butts. First entrance was to upper floors of hotel.

The main part of town was left intact, except here and there, throughout the city, a bombed-out building could be seen. And it also looked like all buildings in the heart of the city were marked with heavy strafing from war planes. Months later, after fraternizing was permitted, I met a German family who had close relatives living in the Bronx of New York, for whom I acted as a messenger. The Bremerhaven family expressed bitterness for the Canadian Air Force. They claimed the planes flew up and down over strasses, strafing buildings and any person in sight. Marian, the seventeen-year-old daughter, told me that once she was working in nearby fields with other youths when they were strafed, and a friend near her was killed.

I had seen most of the war movies and I would not have believed such accounts had I not seen the strafed buildings. The propaganda war movies I had seen didn't show such acts towards civilians by Allies; it was only the enemy who did this. I could only comment to the German family that war sure was hell.

Going into Bremerhaven that trip gave me the feeling that I had come full circle regarding the affect the war had on me. I began to form a personal notion about what all of us were like. From the depths of my subconscious, bits and pieces fixed the thought in my mind: that despite the fact that people, enemy and ally, had various attitudes, in reality, we did what we were told to do by old men too old to fight. All of us, right or wrong. While it may be argued that such a truth is a foregone conclusion and is taken for granted, I had not previously faced the raw, naked meaning of this fact.

Anyway, I had held the preconceived notion that the German people perhaps had horns. However, when I looked upon those beaten, empty-faced people, I thought, why, they look just like a lot of us Americans. It was sad, seeing a defeated people going about their drab daily lives amidst the rubble they had caused to be brought upon their land. Because, right or wrong, humans were still humans. The German people were humans; I was a human.

I would stand for a long time, scanning block after block of nothing but piles of ruin which once had been buildings where humans had lived and worked. Humans who looked just like me. Surely, many of them were also Christians or believers in God, and believed in His mercy. . . .

Memphis, with its tall Sterrick Building, came to mind, and I tried to picture that pretty city, perched on the Chickasaw Bluffs of the Mississippi River, as a pile of rubble like that I gazed upon in Germany. But no! Memphis was home—it was America—we are the good guys, and I should not have such thoughts; it was sinful!

Yet, it was spellbinding to stand at the very spot, a tiny bit of this earth, where people had their last thoughts in those seventeen terrorizing moments when it all came crashing down.

I asked myself was it not right for me, another human, who still lived and breathed just like they once did, to spend a few moments thinking about the fate of other humans whether friend or foe? Women, children, babies, young and old, whole families wiped out in the time span of only a few minutes. Indeed, I realized they had been the enemy; their sons had killed our sons. But, nonetheless, they were God's creatures, I was a creature of God, and there I stood at the very spot where life had ended for those other hundreds . . . thousands, only a short while ago. . . .

It was a sobering experience for a young man trying to figure out what human life was really all about. There was I, who only a short while past had been plowing cotton, hustling cotton pickers, just living day by day in the tranquil routine of farm life. Yet, as if by something sinister and magic, I had suddenly been removed from a landscape of orderly corn and cotton fields to stand there in the midst of cold, stark rubble where human lives had been snuffed out.

To fully grasp the scope of it all, a time frame came to mind and my thoughts drifted back to when it all started. Within the span of time that youngsters were getting a college degree, a great war had been fought. Those youngsters who had only started college a few months after America entered the war, now had just graduated a few months past. And I thought about what I was doing and thinking about back in December 1941.

In September 1940, our first peacetime draft was approved. Then, indeed, a little more than a year later, the United States and Germany declared war on each other.

The next day, I rode my pony the two miles to Cottonbelt Junction for salt. We had butchered hogs and Dad needed another bag to preserve it in our big meat box. All the talk around the potbelly stove in the general store was about the war. Emotions were high; everyone actually acted giddy as each hastened to express his views. Some grown-ups declared that we would make short work of the war now that we were in it. Others who had been in World War I argued that America was in for a long haul. All agreed it would be a big help to the price of cotton.

Carl, my baby brother, was barely a year old then, and I worried day after day about the war lasting long enough for him to get killed. But Dad assured us that the war would be over in no time, that President Roosevelt knew what he was doing.

I remembered telling Dad that I was bumfuzzled because in President Roosevelt's "fireside chats" over the radio he had promised the whole nation that no American soldier boys would be sent to fight in any war overseas. I kept pointing this out to Dad, seeking an answer to something that baffled me, and was further confused when he flew into a rage.

His reaction left me dangling. I came close to getting a tenderizing with his razor strap when I pressed for an answer; for acting too big for my britches, as he called it. Instead, he closed the subject with his familiar grumble, "Boy, sometimes I just don't know about you."

The past year had been one in which I had only been exposed to the surface of many aspects regarding the terror and tragedy of war. I realized that. Yet, I had seen enough crippled young American soldiers, hunger and misery of the defeated, to hear that voice within, wailing, "Why did it all happen?"

Having concluded that it was because people did what they were told to do merely caused an innocent young man like me to ponder further; I sighed, convinced that folks had to somehow find a way to keep their national leaders from getting pissed off at one another, and thus stop getting lots of folks killed in wars. I made myself believe that some day they would find a way for lasting peace. I sighed again. Then I felt better.

After a few days in Bremerhaven we sailed and stopped at Southampton. I saw Lee every evening. She was by then coming on strong, hinting about loving little babies, getting married, and going to America. I became more gun-shy.

After four days in Southampton we took on a mixed variety of passengers, made up of war brides, USO entertainers, Red Cross people, patients, and a few soldiers and sailors going home on furlough. Then we made Liverpool and finished loading the ship with similar passengers.

When we got underway for New York, there was another shift in engine department crew and I was promoted to junior third assistant engineer. Hot dog! I was a ship's officer! But I knew I couldn't hold the position after the National Emergency was declared over, at which time peacetime rules would be in effect and an engineer's license would be required.

Scuttlebutt was that the Axis Partners were about to sign final surrender terms, and qualified sea time would go back to three-years peacetime requirement before one could take an examination for an original engineer's license. I harbored considerable doubts about having enough gumption to pass such a test but nonetheless it was a goal to aim for; I was convinced it would mean I was really making headway in life if I achieved it.

Mr. Voorhees was aboard the Hospital Ship *Charles A. Stafford*, later to be recommissioned simply as passenger transport *Charles A. Stafford*. She was the former Ward Line's Passenger Liner *Siboney*, twin screw, driven with two low pressure 225 pounds saturated-steam pressure, turbine units. Mr. Voorhees was then her first engineer and he offered me the chief plumber's job. Although it meant a much higher salary, I turned it down and took an oiler's berth to gain the experience in the engine room with the turbines. Thus I signed aboard the *Stafford* to once again sail under the command of my old mentor.

The *Bridgeport* had repairs costing three million dollars, I was told after I signed off, and she made only one more trip to Europe and was then retired from service.

Along about this time, I happened to read in the back pages of a New York newspaper an article that stated the United States would give France three million dollars for the scrap of the *Normandie*. And that payment would be made in the form of Liberty ships priced to France at twenty thousand dollars each; 150 cargo ships for a floating pile of scrap. . . .

Professional seamen and also seamen like myself were enraged and disgusted; we knew of no American seaman or any other American who could buy a new Liberty ship, as some were, for twenty thousand dollars.

Also, Greeks in the "know" of Americans with political clout could buy on credit multimillion-dollar T-2 tankers with modern turbo-electric power plants from Uncle Sam for scrap-iron prices and become world renown playboy shipping tycoons overnight. In later years, one would marry the widow of a president.

With American-made ships, we would rebuild the merchant fleet of France, a nation which would later refuse to take on supplies in these same ships in New Orleans to provide aid to Americans fighting and dying in another conflict in Southeast Asia. I happened to be in New Orleans at the time.

But life aboard the *Stafford* was relaxed and easygoing. She was the only hospital ship left operating in the North Atlantic, which was for the benefit of American occupational personnel in Europe. We crossed every thirty days and less, making routine trips to Bremerhaven, with an occasional stop in England on our return. Often we only had a hundred or so patients and a few hundred war brides coming back. Some trips we had more dogs than humans as passengers. We made so many trips to Bremerhaven, we joked that "we didn't need a navigator, just get her out of the harbor and the *Stafford* would find her own way to Germany."

The Army Transport *Alexander*, formerly the United States Line's passenger liner *America*, struck a mine in the North Sea and was stuck in Bremerhaven for months. Each trip we were hounded by members of her crew who wanted to switch berths.

One particular oiler in the *Alexander* dogged me each time I visited the Seamen's Club. He was tired of Bremerhaven. Said he was sated with free love and wanted to get home and rest. He said that he had a wife and young baby daughter back in the States and they needed to see him. I didn't switch berths with him. I saw no need to get stuck in Bremerhaven for months merely to accommodate someone who ran out of fuel for his burner after firing all the furnaces he could in Bremerhaven.

But mostly we were pressured to bring cigarettes over for the *Alexander*'s crew to give to their shack-ups for bartering. An egg could be purchased for one pack of cigarettes. But a half ton of coal could be obtained in exchange for a carton of American cigarettes. Cigarettes were worth more than gold.

Small children in filthy ragged clothing stood with bare feet outside the Seaman's Club in bitter cold, begging just for cigarette stubs. Some suffered the cold with tears streaking their dirty anxious faces; there was little or no soap for washing clothes or bodies in Bremerhaven. The children said they took the cigarette stubs home for their fathers to smoke in pipes. But one knew that the tobacco was accumulated then swapped to farmers for morsels of food.

I had lived a meager life as a child, felt hunger pangs a few times, and was no softy, but I was stunned to see seven- and eight-year-old children fight over mere cigarette butts tossed away by seamen. More appalling was to see a few American seamen intentionally toss cigarettes among the urchins then stand back and laugh when they fought over them.

One bitter cold evening, I blurted to a shipmate that he should hang his head in shame. He was an older man, standing just outside the entrance to the Seamen's Club, breaking cigarettes in half and tossing them among the children. He then stood back and roared with laughter. I didn't see them as children whose parents were recent enemies; instead I pictured my own little brother and sisters there fighting for mere cigarette butts. They were innocent little boys and girls. And so, on impulse, I called his hand.

No big show, just simply one of those times in life when a person feels he has to say something in protest.

Without warning, he bent my flesh, snarling that I had better mind my own damned business.

I jumped up off the "deck" and charged back.

No big deal. Other shipmates broke us up.

The man had been torpedoed on the *Murmansk Run* in the frigid Arctic Ocean, then he suffered dire conditions while stuck in Russia for many weeks, and he often expressed dislike for Russians and his hate for Germans.

Even so, the sight of those ragged, shoeless children fighting like dogs over a mere cigarette stub, and a fellow American finding it entertaining caused me to cringe.

Perhaps without fully realizing it, I was rapidly becoming a man. And, after those past few years meeting different people and experiencing new places, sights, and sounds, farm life seemed very remote and faraway. Thinking about home, like it used to be, was like recalling a dream.

However, I kept trying to grab the world by the tail, and I clung to my fervent hope of finding my dream girl. God . . . ! How I longed to find "that" girl . . . not just any girl . . . not a bunch of girls, but *the* girl!

But just when I thought I might have a grip on the tip of the world's tail, the darn thing switched again.

CHAPTER 12

LINER AT LANDING STAGE, LIVERPOOL. 69418

AFTER SPENDING CHRISTMAS OF 1946 AT SEA, WE MADE Bremerhaven, then made anchor at New York, January 16, 1947. We tied up the next day at pier 11 in Staten Island.

Because of our fast turnarounds, mail which missed the ship the previous trip finally caught up with us. I eagerly read and reread my letters from home. Some were written well before Christmas; all the folks expressed hope that I would be home for those holidays.

Dad had gotten the "call" to become a preacher and he went all out to do it right; he enrolled at the Southern Baptist College at Walnut Ridge in north/central Arkansas.

Time was running out and I didn't yet have enough qualified engine-room sea time to take the engineer's examination.

On another trip we carried undertakers over who would scatter across the battlefields and prepare fallen American soldiers to be shipped back for reburial at home. Several trips going over we hauled "grave diggers," so-called. After a long stay in Bremerhaven, with brief stops at Southampton and Liverpool,

England, we again made port in New York. More than a year had passed and a lot of water had rolled under my feet since we docked with the first load of war brides.

I learned the deadline was near, and I had only seventeen months and thirteen days of qualified engine room sea time, and there was not enough time before the deadline to make another voyage to get the additional seventeen days that were required.

I fumed and fretted and was convinced it was just my rotten luck that I would have to put in another eighteen months at sea before I could meet the peacetime requirements that were about to go into effect. I mused that the Lord was probably displeased with me because I spent too much time studying the engineer's manual instead of the Bible like Sis kept insisting. Overall, I had doubts about whether I had enough smart top-side to pass the rigid examination; I seriously entertained thoughts that it just was not in the cards for an ignorant boy from the backwoods of Arkansas to become an engineer or anything else to earn a decent station in life.

America was on the move. Everywhere it was hustle and bustle. Young men and women who had been in military service were going to college on the GI Bill to become teachers, doctors, lawyers, and engineers—to be useful members of society. Even friends back home, who did get to go to town on Saturdays and attend school regularly, were going to college because now there was money from high-priced cotton, and jobs for everyone.

Poor ole me . . . I was being left at the starting gate . . . the world didn't care about me. . . .

But fate was good to me, and I had little time to fret and wallow in self-pity. I ran into Mr. Hunt, the man who knew everyone, at the Brooklyn Army Base. He was waiting around for a little ship being converted to furnish living quarters for Americans while they built the United States Strategic Base in Thule, Greenland, where the ship would be stationed.

He listened to me explain my dilemma. Then he gave me that look, running his tongue through the gap of his missing tooth. "Humph," he grunted. "Jeez, Mac, youz are really serious. Youz just might make it yet. Don't worry, I think I can help youz."

U.S. Army Transport Service Joseph V. Connolly *Liberty cargo ship in early 1948, docked astern the* Stafford *at Army Piers. Two months before she caught fire and met her fate in the North Atlantic, about one thousand miles out of New York on her way to Belgium with a load of empty coffins in which War II warriors were to be returned home. As a welder, the author helped build the* Connolly *in the Wainwright shipyard. Captain Bostleman, who was the first skipper I ever sailed under—aboard the* Larkspur*—was master of the ill-fated* Connolly. *Author also served seventeen days as an oiler on the* Connolly *while it was at anchor under steam in New York harbor.*

A day or so later, Chief Hunt advised me to contact Coast Guard Commander Fox, the officer in charge of approving sea time and giving tests for merchant marine officers in the port of New York. I did, and Commander Fox gave me assurance that he would approve my application to take the exam, if I could find a berth for seventeen days in a ship at anchor under steam.

I signed off the *Stafford*, and February 28, 1947, Mr. Toff, recruiting officer at the Brooklyn Army Base, assigned me as oiler in a Liberty ship at anchor out in the bay, with one boiler under steam to service the ship. She was the *Joseph V. Connolly*, one of the last Liberty ships I helped build in Panama City. What a small world, I thought.

With exactly eighteen months qualified engine-room time, my application was approved, after which the deadline didn't matter. I attended a 120–hour U.S. Maritime Service Pre-license Merchant

Marine Officer School at Sheepshead Bay, where I anxiously studied marine engineers manuals day and night for four weeks, cramming for my license examination.

Professional mariners claimed that New York was the roughest port in the world at which to take an examination for a mate's or an engineer's license, because one was merely a number to the busy inspectors. And one like myself, with limited experience, was urged by shipmates and friends to go to some smaller port like Providence, Rhode Island, or even the Panama Canal Zone.

It was widely rumored that one could go to the Zone with a couple hundred dollars and be assured of passing the examination.

When I sought Mr. Hunt's advice about taking the examination elsewhere he threw a Hunt fit. He raved, "Nuttin doing! Youz goina set for it in New York or bejezus I'll request Commander Fox to revoke your application. Wit'a license issued in the port of New York, youz can always get a ship."

He remembered the depression days when engineers sailed as oilers or watertenders and the like, and were glad to get a ship in order to feed their families.

But everyone was right. In New York, a big port where thousands of seamen made port and where many took examinations, one was little more than a number to the old salty Coast Guard commanders waiting to retire, who sat at the head of each row of desks. There were seven desks per inspector, and those old sea dogs kept a sharp eye to make sure there was no cheating.

April 11, 1947, Jackie Robinson joined the Brooklyn Dodgers as the first black man to break the color barrier in major league baseball. I mused that he surely felt like he was all alone in tackling the "impossible." I know that I felt all alone that day; I started taking my marine engineer's examination.

We each were given only one sheet of paper at a time during our seven-day examination; any scrap sheets, or sheets used to figure mathematical problems, had to be returned to the inspector, who then furnished another single sheet. Stretching to look over another's shoulder would get one kicked out immediately. One would then have to wait another six months before being permitted a last and only chance to take the examination again.

After seven long agonizing days taking the examination, I managed to pass. When it was all over, I felt like I had awakened from a terrible dream. Had I really managed to pass?

It had been an extremely tense ordeal for me with my limited formal education. One had to make a minimum score of 70 percent on each phase of the exam. At the outset we had to solve ten math problems about engine horsepower, boiler bursting pressure, efficiency of various riveted, and welded seams, etc. And on math, we had to make 100 percent—if one flunked math, the test ended for him—failing any one phase, a person failed the entire examination.

I felt sorry for a personable young man who could not keep his voice from quivering when he told me that he was informed he had made an average score of 89, excluding the phase consisting of questions about marine boilers. He was said to be one of a dozen or so cadets from a Seamens Academy, and, as I recall, he scored 61 on that phase about boilers.

However, it had been stressed at the outset that there would be no exceptions, that we had to make a passing score on each phase. We were reminded of the old saw about the "weakest link in the chain."

I was in a daze and actually felt stunned. With the stress and anxiety suddenly lifted, my head spun and I felt dizzy. I had made an overall average of 84 percent; still I kept asking myself over and over if it was real. Had such an uneducated country hick as I really succeeded? My thoughts flashed back to the long miserable days in class near the end of my formal schooling. Sneers and remarks about being a dummy from a few of my classmates were still fresh in my memory.

During the seven days I spent writing the examination in daytime then probing manuals late at night, I felt like I was all alone, compressed inside a whirling chamber with my head throbbing from the pressure. Often my mind would go blank, causing a sense of panic. I had had some good teachers in mentors like Mr. Voorhees, Woodie, and Mr. Hunt who crammed knowledge into me, but, nonetheless, I knew that with my limited experience and self-study, I couldn't coast with my brain out of gear. With head aching and sleepy, I would rub my eyes and force myself to keep digging in those marine engineers manuals.

Gazing at the crisp new license, my thoughts broke through the haze, and pride swelled inside my chest. It was not a dream. There it was—I had been issued a license by Uncle Sam on crisp paper—it was the color of new money, it looked like new money, and it felt like new money. I read it over and over: "United States Merchant Marine Officer; Third Assistant Marine Engineer; Any Horsepower; Any Ship; Any Ocean."

Recalling a flash of the bitterness I felt when shipped out as a messman from the Maritime Base at St. Petersburg, Florida, I shrugged, thinking that Uncle Sam was a pretty good fellow after all.

Perhaps it would not have been such a big deal to someone with a well-rounded formal education. I don't know; although, some with college educations have failed the examination.

The tests were prepared individually in Washington, D.C., assigned a number, and sealed then sent to Coast Guard Inspection Offices. And in New York, you were indeed just a number. You either did pass or, if the tests revealed that there was a "weak link," you didn't pass. Indeed, I was fortunate to have sailed with some professional sea dogs who generously gave of themselves to teach and push young men like myself upward in life.

In short, it was a tremendous milestone in the life of a young man who had doubts about having enough gumption to find a rewarding place in life. It gave me a sudden surge of self-confidence, proving to me that a single-minded pursuit of a goal could be successful. What Dad and Mom meant about having sticka u-nus became crystal clear in those moments.

I floated along the sidewalk down in the Battery that day, hurrying to the South Ferry to go show off my new license to Mr. Voorhees, who was back in port at Staten Island. Time after time, I would feel that crisp license while reading it over and over. I would glance over my shoulder and look up at the Empire State Building, and I felt just as tall.

I do believe at those moments, had someone challenged, I would have bet I could pee a stream over the top of that building.

The country boy thought he finally had the world by the tail, but still wondered what he would do with it. Nonetheless, I was "right up there amongst them," really in tall cotton.

However, much of life's teaching process still awaited me; I was to learn that there were some intelligent people who were still so dissatisfied that they would jump overboard in the middle of the Atlantic, and that a human could get stomped to death over a mere dollar. . . .

CHAPTER 13

LINER AT LANDING STAGE, LIVERPOOL.   69418

SURELY, ANYONE'S OUTLOOK ON LIFE REACHES A HIGHER perspective when they feel they have achieved an important goal. I was no exception. And there was not so much intensity about being somebody. Rather, I concentrated on refining the somebody; I had self-confidence, now I wanted the polish.

I was assigned back aboard the *Stafford*, and Mr. Voorhees was a reassuring influence. He seemed to sense my apprehension when I went below to stand my first watch as an engineer in a ship where I had been an oiler only a few months past; a ship in which I had maybe goofed off a few times with my shipmates, but now I was back aboard as a ship's officer.

He patted me on the back and once again congratulated me, then got serious as he spoke, "Son, I know just how you feel. Doubt is tugging at you. You're thinking about how you'll run all this interconnected complex machinery by yourself. But you're not going to. You will utilize the performance of the men on your watch. All you must do is make sure that it is directed at the safe operation of this ship and its power plant."

Making so many trips over and back to Bremerhaven every month got monotonous. And there was not much quality time ashore, because we made quick turnarounds in New York.

But the U.S. Maritime Service provided correspondence courses covering a wide variety of general education subjects for merchant seamen, and I studied them. So, actually, day after day at sea passed rather quickly. I was still eager to learn, and felt more pleased with myself. No, I didn't feel stuck-up, I still felt rather humble and thankful. But, indeed, I was a proud young man. "Hot dog, not even twenty-one but I'm right up there amongst them . . . eating officers' chow and sleeping on a wide bunk complete with a comfortable innerspring mattress in my own room," were thoughts I marveled about. I felt it was tall cotton for a country boy, trying to measure up.

By contrast, I was baffled at times when I would see others who were well-educated and apparently intelligent, yet sometimes acted dissatisfied with themselves and life in general. For example, during a trip to Bremerhaven just before my twenty-first birthday, our chief refrigeration engineer lost his rudder. It had to do with an illiterate wiper in the blackgang who was from Rocky Mount, North Carolina. However, Rocky exhibited much common sense and he was a friendly, easygoing man. But one morning, midway across, just out of the blue, no provocation of any sort, the chief refrigeration engineer—called chief reefer—went berserk. He decked the wiper and violently banged his head on the hard steel, and actually tried to beat the devil out of him! Said anyone who was as ignorant as Rocky had to be possessed with the devil and he was going to exorcise him.

However, contrary to the reefer's claim, Rocky often expressed his belief in the Almighty. But, his battered face caused me to reflect on Mom's advice about turning the other cheek.

Instead of being locked in the brig, the reefer was confined to his room, with a master-at-arms stationed outside the door. But having been built as a passenger liner, the *Stafford* had extremely big round portholes, and the reefer simply bounded through the one in his room, took a step on the narrow starboard side deck, and leaped over the rail. Only two other rooms separated mine and the chief reefer's, and I heard passengers out on deck screaming, followed by shouts "man overboard" from alert deck hands.

As I rushed up to the boat deck, I felt the ship's bucking tremors, caused by propellers suddenly reversed to full astern. However, it takes considerable distance, sometimes as much as a mile or more, to slow a big heavy ship's headway and reverse its course. Thus, while the ship's speed was reduced, our emergency lifeboat crew charged up to the boat deck and dropped a boat in the water. They had almost rowed back to the overboard exorciser by the time the ship circled back.

There was little wind but broad slick swells with deep valleys rolled like smooth blue oil across the ocean. From our view high up on the boat deck we could see the reefer, and it looked like the devil was suddenly after him—he was swimming hard. Upon hitting the briny water, his sense of survival surely took over and he really clawed at that ocean.

A high rolling swell swept the lifeboat up to ride its crest, and the crew rowed hard towards the man, who frantically tried to stay afloat. Just when those of us who eagerly watched cried out with hope, the lifeboat soared down into a deep trough out of sight. This happened several times, and the reefer was carried farther and farther away by the cold relentless sea. I shuddered, picturing myself out there in the middle of the empty ocean desperately struggling in its hungry clutches, sweeping me on out into its vastness.

The bridge maneuvered the ship past the lifeboat and closed the gap. We were only about a hundred yards away when suddenly to our horror the frantic man was instantly sucked under. His stamina had been amazing.

Whether it was because he was an excellent swimmer or his renewed will to live gave him strength, he had struggled for twenty minutes or longer with the added weight and drag of his clothing, and he was still swimming hard, when, zap . . . we were close enough to see the terror in his face when he went under.

Everyone's excitement died into stunned silence. My feet were frozen to the boat deck as I stared at the empty sea. Mere seconds had passed since I had seen him . . . he was a live active human being. But in a split second he shot under. He was gone. The professional mariners all agreed a big fish had grabbed him. They insisted that those hungry monsters were indeed out there and were not always sharks, necessarily.

Of course witnessing the finality of such tragedy leaves one shaken, feeling drained and very sad.

This was the second incident I saw when a person thought he wanted to end his life by jumping overboard. While I was still in the *Larkspur/Bridgeport* we left New York early one evening with a full load of Germans who had been prisoners of war. It was wintertime and extremely cold. I was lulling about in the midships's spacious foyer on C-deck when a young German walked up the wide ladder from the big mess room on the deck below. The young blond-haired man merely strolled outside, stepped across the narrow side deck to the starboard rail, and jumped. He never broke his stride.

We had not yet dropped the harbor pilot as darkness fell, and the lights along the coast shone brightly as we eased towards the sea. After a matter of minutes, there was no hope of the man surviving in the icy water but, nonetheless, the skipper did his best to find him; he kept the ship searching the area for over two hours.

I stood out on deck with teeth chattering, watching the bright search lights scan the water's surface. Finally the old man broke off the search, and the ship got underway again.

It was disturbing to witness a young man throwing his life away, regardless of whether he had been a recent enemy. Those POWs who knew him claimed he could not endure the thought of returning home as a defeated German soldier.

For me, it was sadder still to see the refrigeration engineer throw his life away. I had laughed and talked with the man. I had dined with him. He seemed to have everything going for him. He was part of the close-knit shipboard community in which I lived. I tried to understand why, but, of course, could not; why he did it, perhaps only he and the Big Skipper knew.

It was a sobering tragedy. I thought about myself struggling to find a secure place in life, and there had been a man whom I thought already had it, but he just threw it away. He was well-liked, his knowledge was in considerable demand, whether aboard ships or on the beach, and, in mere seconds of time, it was all gone.

Later in life I hung desperately for years between life and death, and I thought about the jovial refrigeration engineer and continued to wonder why he wasted his life. But I could only sigh and conclude that perhaps mortals are at times more fragile than we sometimes realize, and the poor man simply snapped.

On our return, we tied up at the Army Docks in Staten Island December 17, 1947—I would be twenty-one years old the next day. I had not been home in a long time and had planned to sign off the *Stafford*, take a thirty-day leave, then get a berth in a modern ship with a high pressure superheated steam power plant.

However, many other merchant marines were signing off ships in our fleet and also going home for the holidays.

The *Wilson Victory* Army Transport cargo ship made port in New Orleans after eleven months in the Pacific. The *Wilson* was part of the East Coast Fleet and most of her crew were from the East Coast. They hit the beach and headed home for Christmas.

Mr. Toff, the recruiting officer, made the rounds, visiting ships in port at New York, requesting others and myself to help him out of a jam. He said the *Wilson* was due to sail before Christmas, and he had to get her a crew in a hurry.

I reminded myself that Mr. Toff had been helpful to me. Therefore, I became one of the *Wilson's* new engineers.

But, having saved an adequate bankroll with anticipation of taking a gala trip home in style with nice gifts for brothers, sisters, Mom and Dad, nieces, and nephews, I was disappointed because I would have to wait until another time.

I got to New Orleans and signed aboard, and the *Wilson* just laid there tied up in the harbor, going nowhere until well after the holidays. I dwelled for days in misery.

After my first eight-hour port watch ended at midnight, my oiler, who was a native of New Orleans, offered to show me the sights of Bourbon Street and the rest of the French Quarter. I didn't see much. A b-girl slipped a Mickey into my beer and rolled me for over a thousand dollars.

It was *not* a case of a "country boy come to town." Hell, they would roll anybody.

I had been all over Manhattan, Hoboken, Staten Island, Brooklyn, at times by myself, at all hours, and never once had I been rolled or even threatened. I have also been to several ports in different countries of the world, and Bourbon Street in New Orleans is not at the top of my list of fun spots. Of course, the French Quarter is very historical and it is still making history. But a young man messing around Bourbon Street's clip joints alone may well find his bankroll history.

After leaving port, we dropped down to Cuba to take on sugar for the hungry people in those zones of Europe occupied by U.S. Military Forces. We went from place to place, anchoring out, waiting for desk-jockey U.S. Army dispatchers to finally realize a fifteen-thousand-ton ship needs deep water to make it back out to sea after taking on cargo. The water was so shallow at a couple of places we couldn't have loaded ping pong balls.

We had several days of leisure fun though. One of our daily news bulletins stated Memphis, Tennessee, had a record-breaking twelve inches of snow, and there I was basking in beautiful sunshine and tropical weather. We were anchored in shallow water so clear we could see big turtles, shrimp, and lobsters crawling around on the sandy sea floor. The *Wilson* crew did a lot of diving off her fantail and swimming while we waited.

Eventually we tied up at a crude wooden pier near the town of Nuevitas on Cuba's northeastern coast. We were there more than a week as sacks of raw sugar were hand loaded with the aid of our ship's cargo booms.

Like most ports large or small, as I found in every country, Nuevitas had an American bar. It was a big place, typical with a long bar and a connecting large room. Therein, a long dance floor separated tables that filled the spaces along each side. A jukebox blared constantly on the east end. The north wall was lined with about a dozen doors to the little service rooms where a patron could get a shorttime tune-up for one American dollar or, after midnight, an all-night overhaul for twenty dollars. In the south wall of the big room there were wide archways to a tropical garden.

A Norwegian cargo ship was also docked at Nuevitas, and attracting the crews of both ships, the American bar really jumped at night.

My shipmates were all gathered as a group on the south side, and were eagerly diving in again. This time, instead of the ocean, it was rum and Co'Cola. The Norwegians were grouped at the tables on the north side, those who were not in line for shorttime service from the queen mechanic.

All of the prostitutes were pretty young girls. I was amazed, some were exceptionally beautiful. There were plenty to give all who wanted their engines cranked a quick jump-start. But it was early, and several of the Norwegian seamen seemed to think waiting in line for service from the queen, as she was actually called, was worth the trouble. Each of them didn't have long to wait. Apparently she did indeed give quick service, with one bang to the customer.

Finally, though, queen took a break. To my surprise, she made a beeline to the big table at which I sat with eight or ten shipmates. We had a middle-aged junior officer aboard who had premature white hair. He always wore a "high-pressure" uniform, gold braid and all. The queen plopped down in his lap, and he flashed us a go-to-hell grin, like he had conquered a real queen. I soon learned that the dude had already contracted with queen for an all-night overhaul, after she cranked as many engines as she could until midnight. Then, she was all his for the rest of the night, he kept telling us, again and again.

She was a very attractive young woman, with an uncanny resemblance to movie star Rita Hayworth. Her father was German and her mother Spanish, we were told. She talked without letting up, and proudly informed us that she was married to a U.S. Marine who was stationed at Guantanamo and that they would go to the States the following year.

I was astonished; she was so flippant and casual about it. I had to ask, "What if your husband learns about you banging around?"

She stuck out her tongue at me, cocked her shapely rear to pat it in defiance, then hastened to tell me that she did not bang around, that she merely made people happy, and, yes, her husband knew all about it. Then she thrust her chin at me and proudly declared that she was going to buy him a new Cadillac when he took her to the United States of America.

I had no doubt that she would soon have the means to buy it, because she stayed busy. With a gleeful air, she took on anyone. I knew the dude put her up to it when queen started pestering me about a shorttime quicky. Dude said he would even give her the dollar. Not wanting to insult her, I simply said I didn't enjoy taking a bath in water everyone else had used to bathe in.

She didn't quite understand and, with a puzzled frown, countered by saying that she wasn't about to waste time to take a bath with me unless I paid her at least ten dollars.

I hung around with our radio operator, and we snacked on Cuban Chili and sipped rum and Co'Cola, watching everyone mojo.

Around the middle of the evening, the gay clatter—and I don't mean queer—was shattered by shrieking from one of the little cubicles. Queen came bounding out along with one of the Norwegian sailors. It was shades of Lee Hi at the whorehouse in France all over again; she beat on the Norwegian as she raved.

Finally, he turned and struck her with his fist. She screamed and went down.

Instantly, through the portals, Cubans came charging out of the dark night. The image of a horde of enraged primates scampering out of the bush, flailing arms at an intruder, flashed to mind as the snarling mob rushed the Norwegian. There were so many raging Cubans stomping on him, I couldn't see the victim. They literally kicked and stomped the seaman to death. It was all over in a minute or two.

And just as quickly as they came, the defenders of womanhood disappeared out through the garden into the dark night.

Someone unplugged the jukebox and a hush of deadly silence filled the big room.

Strangely, not one of the victim's shipmates moved to help him. To a man, each of them just sat with a stoical stare only lifting a glass to gulp another drink. Not a word of protest, or hardly a pause in their pursuits of the evening.

Of course it happened in a flash, but still . . . it was eerie.

Sparks sighed and broke my stunned spell, growling, "Drink up, Mate . . . nothing we could do. 'Tis the code, son, the unwritten code. You never mix in another's affairs unless it's to help your own shipmates. But, Jeeee-Zus . . . " he hesitated, obviously affected also, "damned good thing she's not a Sunday School teacher or a nun, the whole crazy town would've wiped out the lot of them—us included!"

Sparks was a professional seaman of many years. He was seasoned and tough, but this brutal waste of a human life got to him also.

I never learned for certain what set it off. Scuttlebutt among our crew gave several accounts; some said the man would not pay her the dollar unless she also allowed him to stay all night; others said he clipped her for money she had stashed in the little room.

After about two weeks in Cuba, we eventually got underway with the *Wilson* riding very low in the sea—I soon realized that raw sugar was very heavy. Headed for Bremerhaven again, I wearily sighed but took it in stride.

Damp, rainy weather caused us to keep cargo holds sealed at times and it took two weeks to unload. But, we finally made it back to New York.

After offloading tanks and other war junk and pet dogs, we loaded supplies and made another run to Bremerhaven with vital supplies for those folks within the zones we occupied. The *Wilson* was recommissioned under the name of *Private Sadao S. Munemori* in honor of a War II hero.

America's ships stayed busy hauling supplies, about which I read a news article in the Paris edition of the *Stars & Strips* at the Seamen's Club one trip into Bremerhaven; in essence, it stated our Allies were bitterly complaining because we Americans were showing them up by busting our butts to flood supplies in to feed and clothe folks in the zones we occupied, showing them what great humanitarians we were.

April 1, 1948, the Russian blockade of West Berlin began, and we hustled shipload after shipload of supplies over to be airlifted to the besieged West Berliners.

We hauled back additional war junk and dogs—we had dog passengers coming from Germany nearly every trip. I wondered if any canine would be left in Europe after some Americans acquired all the pets that caught their eye.

I had planned to take my delayed thirty-day leave but got word that the ship was going to the Pacific and back. I had always wanted to make a trip to the Pacific. However, I didn't want my records transferred to the Army POE on the West Coast in order to do so, but since the *Wilson* would return to the East Coast, it presented a practical opportunity.

After getting off an eight-hour port watch at midnight one night, I strolled outside the gate to Bay Street in Staten Island and called my folks at the college. I informed them that I was making the trip to the Pacific and would have to once again delay coming home a little while longer.

Returning to the ship, I took a shortcut across freight platforms for boxcars and, while jumping off one in the darkness, twisted my foot after jamming it into the recess of train rails embedded in the pavement. Bones were fractured in the foot. After a few days in the Staten Island Marine Hospital, I was discharged: "Not fit for sea duty for two weeks."

My ship sailed, and I went home to heal.

My Mom would say that even though it was painful for me, the Lord sure worked in mysterious ways, sometimes for the best.

It was a leap year. I had a bum ankle. I couldn't run. And I found myself in a place where a beautiful angel didn't fear to trod.

Part Two

The Girl in the Moon

LINER AT LANDING STAGE, LIVERPOOL.

69418

DAD AND MOM MET MY TRAIN IN MEMPHIS AT 8 P.M. When Dad rented out the farm to attend preacher college, he purchased a new 1941 Chevrolet four-door sedan for $1,300. Some of the old folks said the price of a new Ford, Chevrolet, or Plymouth would eventually cost $2,000, but others scoffed at that and declared that no one in their right mind would ever pay $2,000 for a car.

From Memphis on this moonlit night late in May 1948, we motored the one hundred miles northwest to their apartment at the Southern Baptist College at Walnut Ridge, Arkansas.

The college was located on what had been one of the many little Army Air Corp bases that sprang up across America at the outset of World War II and later closed just as quickly. The little college spread over treeless flatland where, in addition to all administration buildings, there were neat rows of long military-style apartment buildings. Therein lived ex-service men who had gotten the "call" and were attending the preacher college on the GI

Bill. Country preachers and their families also lived in the apartments while attending school. Each long building contained four spacious apartments, and Dad and Mom had a center unit in their building.

We were late getting home, and I was a real sorehead when Mom persisted in getting me out of bed at sunrise the next morning. She had prepared a grand breakfast and was anxious to watch her son enjoy it.

I got up grumbling while taking a peek out the south bedroom window.

"Hhhhhhhod-damn," I howled, suddenly wide awake. "I know this is a religious place, but didn't know you had everlovin' angels prancing around here, too!"

Mom hurried from the kitchen, fussing, "Now, you hush up that kind of talk. I won't have no cussin' in my house, and just because you traipse around over them old oceans, that don't mean your mama can't still spank you, do you hear me? What are you braying about, anyway?" She followed my gaze out the window at a beautiful young lady briskly stepping along with her shoulders back, head up, and her long wavy brown hair fluffing in the early morning breeze.

"Good God, Mom," I gushed, my eyes still following the beautiful creature, "I have never seen anything or anybody as pretty as—she must be an angel! Who the heck is she?"

I can still picture Mom's pleased smile spreading over her warm face as she chortled, "Oh, that's Sylvia. She's the nice little daughter of the Watkinses, our neighbors here next door. She sure is a mighty fine little lady. The Lord sure works in mysterious ways . . . I've been praying you might get yourself home to meet her—but now, young man, don't you go to gettin' yourself to thinking you can play loose with her! Now, do you hear?"

I was mesmerized, watching Sylvia out of sight, and Mom repeated herself.

I finally responded, "H'mmmm? Uh, Oh yeah, sure, Mom, I hear you. Wouldn't think of it. But I darn sure want to meet that sweet chick."

Sylvia in July 1948, a few weeks after author first met her. Taken at Southern Baptist College apartments at Walnut Ridge, Arkansas. College was former Army Air Corp Base, during World War II.

Her face flashed alarm, and she warned, "Now, L. R., don't you talk that way about that young lady. Son, I'm serious! And I'm telling you, she's not one of your chicks as you say; that little lady is one of the finest young women you could possibly ever hope to meet."

I made the facetious comment that it was leap year and I had a broken foot and couldn't run, but that I sure wouldn't mind being chased by that pretty young doll. However, there was little chasing done by either.

Within a day or two, the family went on a picnic-fishing outing at a nearby lake. Sylvia was invited, and she and I were instantly drawn to each other. With her beautiful face, glittering hazel eyes, and her warm smile, all framed with her soft brown hair, her petite waist, and trim figure, she was my girl in the moon and I knew it. There was no "maybe so." She was it—the whole package—100 percent. For me, it was love at first sight, and she has told our children down through the years it was the same with her.

We were together often on simple dates. We went to movies, and went fishing and swimming, and we attended church with the folks, hers and mine.

One particular outing we will never forget; we went blackberry picking and got covered with red bugs. Those darn chiggers caused a solid ring of red whelps all around my belt line and were clustered in every crevice of my torso!

That night while attending a revival meeting at church, Sylvia and I both sat scratching. We could not stop.

Both of us scratched so much the preacher got distracted and started stammering and losing his place in the Scriptures. Folks all around turned their heads and frowned at us, and Sylvia's mother thrust us a scolding frown, nodding towards the door.

All alone under a beautiful moon on that summer night, with my arms all the way around my girl in the moon, the love bug gnawed me and I forgot all about chigger bites.

Our days of joy sped by, and I felt the need for more leave time. I told myself: One needs good feet and sea legs riding ships. Therefore, my foot needed to have plenty of time to heal good and proper. And, since I had several weeks of sick leave and annual leave accumulated, I merely made a telephone call to the Brooklyn Army Base and got my leave extended.

As most of us know, women and men have tried down through the ages to define love. From time immortal, countless wonderful stories have been told and written about true love, the kind that bonds one woman and one man together for life. Still, love remains undefinable. But this I do know beyond any doubt: Love is a very awesome force. Its power is overwhelming. We cannot see it, but we know it exists because when it strikes us we are jarred to the depths of our souls, and it hangs on and just will not let go.

Thus, love had me in its clutches, and I faced a lonely, agonizing dilemma when I returned to sea and the temptations in foreign ports of call.

CHAPTER 15

LINER AT LANDING STAGE, LIVERPOOL.   69418

ONCE MORE I BOARDED THE *TENNESSEAN* IN MEMPHIS, and as she rolled through the night I didn't relish the thought of signing aboard another ship and spending day after day at sea. But having gained self-confidence, I tentatively set a goal to achieve; that I would go to sea until I got a chief engineer's license, then come ashore for good and really take on the world.

I signed aboard the United States Army Transport *Carroll Victory*. She had the 8,500 horsepower (some Victory ships had 6,000 HP turbines—top speed about 16 knots) geared-turbine power plant.

The 8,500 HP turbines were driven with 675 pounds super-heated steam per square inch, pushing a Victory ship along at 18 knots and better. (There were over 500 Victory ships of the two types built in War II, but some writers fail to make the distinction, and simply state that Victory ships had a speed of 17 knots. This was true for the lesser number of 6,000 HP Victory ships, with a smaller hull. However, the 8,500 HP Victory ships could easily cruise long, loaded, at 18 knots and better.) Anyway, I was happy to be on a ship as fast as the *Carroll*; she was like a speedboat compared to the *Larkspur*, *Bridgeport*, and *Stafford*.

We got underway and dropped down to Philadelphia and took on a load of empty coffins, then headed across.

The confined environment in a ship, day after day, highlights various human traits of the colorful characters one encounters plowing the oceans. First Engineer Bujia in the *Carroll Victory* was such a person. He had been the staff chief engineer in the ill-fated *Morro Castle*, and reports were that he was the only engineering officer who stuck it out aboard the dying ocean liner when a mysterious fire burned her to death within sight of the New Jersey coast, September 8, 1934.

When I first went in the *Carroll*, Mr. Bujia sat at the desk in the chief engineer's office. He wore plain dungarees, a chambray shirt, and an oiler's cap. As was the case with Mr. Voorhees when I first met him in the *Larkspur*, I assumed Mr. Bujia was merely a member of the blackgang, maybe an oiler, waiting to see the chief about something.

I asked to see the chief engineer.

He grunted and told me that the chief was ashore and that he was the First.

With a quick glance at my assignment card on which were the chief's and also the first engineer's name, "Bujia," I offered my hand with the greeting, "Very glad to meet you, Mr. Boojay."

Fire shot out of his Spanish eyes and he burned me at the stake. He jumped up and hopped around on a gimpy leg, ranting and jabbering away. Whether I got good cursing, I don't know, but I did catch something about "another smart-assed punk," mixed in with his Spanish rage. And then he snapped that he was not Boojay, that his name was pronounced Boo-He-Ah.

Mr. Bujia gave me a cold eye and would do little more than grunt when I tried to converse with him, all the way across the Atlantic and into the Mediterranean.

Too late, I learned that many young men in the Army fleet referred to the old salt behind his back as Old BooJay. And Mr. Bujia knew this and apparently thought I was just another smart aleck, brazen enough to call him Boojay to his face. But it was simply a case of ignorance on my part.

We docked in Leghorn, Italy, and the crew was told the ship would be in port there until the next day, and possibly for the next two days. Everyone not on duty went ashore and scattered.

I spent a few hours ashore browsing, and picked up a few nice items for my pretty bride-to-be; a beautiful tapestry and a dazzling handwoven bedspread, complete with cute little golden cupids.

We maintained sea watches in Leghorn, and I returned to the ship to stand my evening 8–to–12 watch. The second engineer beat it ashore as soon as I relieved him.

Shortly I was summoned to the bridge. There, Army Brass strutted impatiently in the skipper's office. Ignoring my commanding officer, a colonel told me that I had to get ready to depart immediately; that the Army wanted the ship in Naples, and he wanted it out of Leghorn within the half hour.

I couldn't believe the colonel was really serious, but he was!

Other than those on my watch, there was only one additional blackgang member back aboard, an oiler, but he was stoned and had already sacked out.

The *Carroll* had been to Leghorn her previous voyage; therefore, many crew members had already holed up with their girlfriends, still others had found taxis to carry them the approximate twenty-five kilometers to Pisa for a look at the Leaning Tower.

It was a twenty-four-hour run down to Naples, and I stammered and offered my objection to leaving crew members who had no reason to know of the sudden change for an immediate departure. Even so, the colonel insisted that I raise steam, on the double.

The skipper, a fine old man from Scandinavia, happy to be master of an American ship, was obviously distressed by the port colonel's demands that we immediately get underway, leaving most of our crew. With a sly wink, he silently appealed to me with a pained expression instead of giving me a direct order, verbally. I sensed he was reluctant as a foreigner to buck the U.S. Army, and wanted me to come up with a valid excuse to delay raising steam in the other boiler, and so, I tried to think fast.

Then with my back to the colonel, I addressed my superior, telling him I would prepare to turn the screw as soon as I could, but that Charlie Noble was, uh, working on the other boiler to, uh, prevent it from filling the engine room with smoke.

The puzzled colonel glared at me. I glimpsed the skipper out of the corner of my eyes. For a moment I thought he would give our unrehearsed ploy away. His throat made little grunting noises like he had just swallowed a bug, and he started scanning navigation charts as though they suddenly needed his attention.

A bird colonel is no dummy, and I was aware of it. But I also knew that some very intelligent landlubbers didn't know who, or what, Charlie Noble was.

I hastened to assure the colonel that my watch would have a full head of steam in both boilers and ready to get underway as soon as possible, though it would take a little longer than half an hour. Actually, the express type boilers in the 8,500 HP Victory ships with heating surfaces of thousands of small water recirculation tubes could raise a full head of steam from a cold boiler in seven minutes in an emergency; not recommended, but it could be done.

Leaving the colonel blowing at the poor skipper, I went below and ordered the fireman/watertender to raise steam on the cold boiler—very slowly. The junior engineer raced ashore to round up all the blackgang and other crew members he could find.

I didn't gloat or think of myself as some hotshot wise guy who pulled the wool over a full colonel's eyes; colonels are trained to fight battles. But suddenly with the war over, a few found themselves messing with ships, which some seemed to know little about. And so, I merely thought it was worth a try to use Charlie Noble to delay our departure. I hoped we *could* get underway before the colonel might learn that Charlie Noble was the smoke stack for the cook stoves in a ship's galley.

The junior found enough crew, including the chief engineer and First Engineer Bujia. Several hours later we did get underway and made it to Naples with little strain.

Word got around about the little incident and there were a few chuckles. The old skipper would greet me in the mess with, "Hey, Third, by golly, how's old Charlie Noble doing?"

A bit amusing and a pleasant surprise, but thereafter I was tops in Mr. Bujia's book. He would greet me with a grin at times, chuckle, and wag his head while grunting with the simple expression, "Charlie Noble. . . ."

We were at Naples for several days, taking aboard 7,600 First-Class Passengers, dead War II soldiers, who were, indeed, listed on the ship's manifest as first-class passengers although they were in boxes, stacked like cordwood in the cargo holds.

When departing Leghorn, several crew members gave their girlfriends train fare to join them in Naples. But when we docked there, each romeo latched on to a Naples girlfriend. Within a day or so, those girls from Leghorn started rolling in, along with those Carroll crew members whom we had left in Leghorn. Some of my shipmates tried to dodge the Leghorn girls, but they searched every waterfront joint in Naples until they found their man. Everywhere I went, I'd see bewildered shipmates with a girl on each arm. And usually the girls would be going at each other like sore-tailed cats, with the seamen trapped in the middle.

Upon such encounters, a weary shipmate would hurry up to me and plead, "Mac, old buddy, good pal, my best shipmate, please take one of these broads off my hands. Won't you? Please!"

I would merely grin and shake my head. Another time in the past, perhaps, because most all were very attractive young women, although cat fighting over a seaman made me believe some were regular little spitfires. But I had found my girl in the moon, and we would be married soon. I was not about to take the slightest chance of getting shanghaied into any unhealthy situations.

After we passed through the Straits of Gibraltar on the way back, the Brooklyn Army Base ordered us to reduce our speed. The Base had adopted a procedure whereby they apparently planned to have ships arrive in New York to suit their whims; that is, not to have arrivals on weekends and holidays or whatever, and they kept daily contact with the *Carroll* by radio to monitor our speed. However, "the best laid plans of mice and men" certainly applies when the elements at sea are involved. Instead of permitting us to plow on across and, at least, anchor out in the safety of the harbor, the POE in Brooklyn kept trying to regulate our speed.

With the engine room telegraph already at "slow ahead," often during each watch the bridge would call down and tell me to reduce the prop's rpm even more! I choked in on the throttle wheel so much on my watches that often the turbines stopped turning. With the high pressure unit of the duplex turbines designed to normally turn at over nine thousand rpm, which are reduced through the huge reduction gear to around eighty-six rpm propeller-shaft speed, that differential is such it is almost impossible to get the throttle set to keep the propeller turning at a constant three or four rpm.

But there we were, plodding along in the North Atlantic, at times barely making headway.

We passed a few hundred miles off the Grand Banks, and deck officers and other crew members rushed down into our machine shop and made large fish hooks! They used up all the quarter-inch and three-eighth-inch steel rods that were in stock for making bolts. When I came off watch at noon one day, they had the cargo booms swung out, fore and aft, port and starboard, using them for fishing poles.

A passing ship sparked us a message, wanting to know if we were a ship or a giant prehistoric sea bug.

The skipper was a prince of a fellow who took his meals in the officers' mess and associated with the rest of us. And once he chortled at noon chow, "By golly, I got the highest priced fishing yatchee in the vorld!"

Perhaps he did; a 15,500-ton United States Army cargo vessel with a fifty-one-man crew, poking along over the North Atlantic with all cargo booms swung outboard, trolling for fish.

Regarding "the best laid plans of mice and men," an economizer tube blew in the port boiler unit and we had to kill the fires and secure the boiler. Later, we hit gale force winds off Cape Hatteras with only one boiler to make headway. Then the Army started sparking orders for us to stop dragging our anchor and make all deliberate speed. We were several hours late arriving in port.

However, when we tied up at the Brooklyn Army Base there was still a large gathering of families and loved ones on hand, solemnly watching as the *Carroll* eased to the dock with their beloved warriors—the *first full* shipload brought home after War II.

There was a big welcoming ceremony for this first shipload, complete with a band, lots of Army Brass, and politicians, including Brooklyn's borough president. (However, there was a great contrast in the atmosphere between this *first* I was a part of and that *first* load of war brides to come to the USA.) I witnessed much grief resurface that day as the coffins were unloaded by the bundles. All the wailing I heard and the pain I saw on those faces really touched me.

Today, a half century later, I still shudder when I recall the wailing cries and the grief-stricken faces of those loved ones of fallen heroes. I could not brush away the deep compassion I felt for those people with the mere thought "war is hell," or with the rationalization "some win and some lose." We had won the war, and the rest of America was light-hearted, happy, and carefree, yet here these people were still paying the supreme price for our victory and hoped-for peace in the world.

It was not an acting scene in some movie. It was real, and there I was, looking on. I realize it is often stated in some form or another that humankind needs heroes. I don't—not live heroes. Because having observed life unfolding these many years and having watched mankind dealing with life to the limits of human endurance, I do not personally believe there is such a person as a live hero. To each his or her own in our way of thinking, but in my heart the term hero is reserved for those who gave their all.

I realize that such conviction is perhaps a paradox, in that a dead hero cannot know any recognition of same, but so be it. Because without grand applause or the roar of the crowd, they performed and did so gallantly with their own self-esteem intact. And when one hauls them back from the battlefields of the world, shipload after shipload, it is a sobering experience. I have stood alone out on deck at night, mindful that there were seven to ten thousand underneath my feet, who, if still living, would have filled the Crump Football Stadium in Memphis. Yet, they lay silent in boxes stacked tightly in the cargo holds. In such moments, the chilling realization about the raw tragedy of war hit me. It was sickening. I was seized to the depths of my guts with the bare truth about a war's supreme cost. With the wind and sea calm, and only the sound of gentle ripples as the ship plowed the ocean heading homeward, the quietness seemed haunting at times. Who they had been, I felt I knew.

Many had been young men like myself, still searching for the girl of their dreams; others had found theirs only to know the joy of their love too briefly.

The voice within still raged: Why! Why! Why! Yet, I knew the reason why. War. But why war? Would mankind ever learn how to avoid war? I could only sigh and gaze out across a moon-splashed ocean and wonder.

I felt a twinge of guilt because I was alive and they were dead. But I salved my feelings with the reminder that the living must go on living. Even so, the thought lingered, a common crutch many use to salve troubled thoughts, "But for the grace of the Big Skipper there go I. . . ."

On watch down in the hole, alone in my room, or strolling out on deck, I would often think about the silent passengers we were hauling home, and it seemed just that I reserve a special place of honor for them in my thoughts. Though only a token, in view of the price they and their loved ones paid, I resolved long ago that they were the heroes, and that never again would I look upon anyone else as a hero who was alive and could love and know the joy of being loved.

We returned to Leghorn and loaded more heroes.

The previous trip a talented artist from Florence came aboard and offered to borrow photographs and paint the likeness in oil or pastel. I had furnished him with a photo of Sylvia in which her long wavy hair framed her pretty face. On this return trip he brought me a beautiful painting of her in colorful pastel—the artist's talent in capturing her likeness from a photo was amazing.

Back out in the Atlantic, we plowed up to and through the English Channel, the North Sea, and made port in Antwerp, Belgium, to pick up War II dead.

With a shipmate, I made the short trip to Brussels and stayed overnight. In Antwerp and Brussels, streets were lit up with dazzling lights. I saw no boarded-up shops anywhere. Neon ESSO petrol signs and hundreds of others glittered everywhere. There were new Chevrolets used as taxis. The drivers drove through the narrow streets like Hitler was still after them; I would see the needle at eighty on a speedometer and I nearly flipped. It didn't matter to me that it showed kilometers per hour, those buildings still flashed by too fast for comfort.

Leaving Antwerp, we stopped at Cherbourg, France. It had been a couple of years, but it still had the same drab forlorn appearance caused by the war. Shops were still boarded up. The streets were still dark and foreboding. I marveled over the contrast between Cherbourg and the Belgian cities.

There were five ships at anchor in the harbor, under the flags of Russia and Poland. Also, there was a new place not there my last visit, called the American Club.

We were at Cherbourg to pick up five hundred American war-dead. It was time enough for a big part of the *Carroll's* crew to get involved in one hell of a free-for-all with the commie sailors at the American Club. It spilled out onto the waterfront street bordering the little canal.

After searching for a bottle of perfume for my future bride, the 8–to–12 third mate and I were returning to the ship and we happened by just as the *gendarmes* rushed to the scene.

The little officer in charge of about a dozen French cops had them lined up at attention, shoulder to shoulder with pistols pointed skyward. He would bark an order, and each time they fired off a round. The gunfire didn't phase the battling seamen. Then the officer barked a different order, and the *gendarmes* waded into the battle, cracking heads with their pistols.

However, every head they pistol whipped was a crew member from the *Carroll Victory*. The deck officer and I bitterly protested to the French sergeant—some of our men were hurt severely.

The cop snarled in distinct English, "Ha. You damned Yanks think you are hot stuff. You need to be taken down a peg or two!" That was a common theme by French people, still vivid in my memory.

We were due to sail the next morning but our skipper "dropped his anchor." He refused to leave the dock until he personally filed a protest with the American Consulate. A representative from Paris came aboard and the skipper had some of the injured, the mate, and me present.

The representative told us that, yes, a protest would be filed with the French government but it would do no good. He added, as an example, that just the week before, an American seaman had been found with his throat slashed, floating not far from where our ship was tied up; and, as far as the U.S. Consulate knew, nothing was being done in the way of an investigation. He ended his visit by telling us that it was a different ball game now that our military had turned the governance back to the French. That although many Americans had given life and limb to hand their country back to them, there were some French people who merely looked upon Americans as rich people whose only sacrifice in the war was to spend a little money. He made the final comment that we should always be alert when ashore in France because we could still get our throats cut over a mere pack of cigarettes.

This incident hung heavy in hearts and minds on our way back home. Needless to say, those who were injured voiced bitter opinions. The mate, also a young man, and I discussed it often. He had the same watch on the bridge as I had in the engine room. We were disillusioned and, off duty, while having coffee in the mess, we wondered aloud to each other if any country gave a damn about America's sacrifice in the war. The old skipper, a master mariner, a learned man of the world, raved about the incident for days during chow and at coffee time in the mess.

He fumed, "By gar, the French, she still be pissy off at America over the Louisiana Purchase. Of all the peoples of the vorld America helped save, by golly, she be the one to thumb her nose at America."

But life aboard the *Carroll* was pleasant. I liked the crew and was reluctant to sign off her. I had suggested that Sylvia could

October 23, 1948. Wedding picture of author and his wonderful seventeen-year-old bride, Sylvia, just before author's twenty-second birthday.

come to New York for us to be married. It was merely a thought, and I didn't really expect it. And her mother, with vociferous support from mine, let me know that if I wanted her only daughter I would have to come home to get her, that she was not about to let her go chasing off to New York to get married.

We were married October 23, 1948, at Walnut Ridge in a simple ceremony by a preacher who was a longtime friend of the family.

To say we lived in a state of bliss would not come close to describing our joy. We floated on a cloud and were totally absorbed with one another. There was no world around us, there was no yesterday or no tomorrow, there was *now* and *us*. We were so in love and enthralled with one another that we were constantly careful not to displease the other.

Time and again I'd gaze at my beautiful bride and wonder in disbelief: how in the world could such a wonderful creature be so in love with a hardtail like me? It was easy to understand why I was so much in love with her—she was my everlovin' girl in the moon. An all-consuming wonderful ache that clutched the inside of my chest and hung on made me know this when I first saw her.

I used all my accumulated leave as time sped by. But the day after New Years, 1949, I boarded the *Tennessean* to head north. When the train pulled out of Union Station in Memphis, leaving Sylvia waving bye at the departure gate, I once again felt like an anchor chain dragged through my heart.

January 5, 1949, I signed aboard the USAT *Lt. James E. Robinson*, another 8,500-horse-power Victory ship.

After I made a couple of voyages that took me to several countries, Sylvia came to New York.

She was fortunate in finding Miss Margaret Rickner, who was originally from Denver, Colorado, and, as a younger woman, had represented a company who catered to movie stars with beauty aids. She was a wonderful woman who kept a few boarders in her big three-story home on Stratford Road in Brooklyn, but she told me that instead of being a boarder, Sylvia was family, because she was like a daughter Margaret never had. They were like two giddy little girls delighted with each other's company.

Margaret still knew some of the older movie queens and other show business people, and the warm-hearted woman showed Sylvia New York and was a great companion to help fill Sylvia's long lonely days while I was at sea.

However, the duration of my voyages kept getting longer; I stayed with cargo ships because we had more porttime when in New York. But we would then be gone a long time, making ports all over Europe and also at places like Turkey and North Africa; everywhere Americans were still stationed, we made ports of call.

An example: The United States had given the Turks two submarines and our Navy personnel were there to train Turkish crews how to operate them. We took them PX supplies and other American goods—we called such voyages "toothbrush runs." It was about an hour's ride by *slow train* to Istanbul. The "slow train through Arkansas" was a cannonball express compared to that train in Turkey. It stopped at every footpath. People boarded the crowded little coaches with goats, chickens, and one grinning local climbed aboard with a sack of manure and took a seat by me. About a dozen of us, strung out like a row of ducks waddling along an extremely narrow sidewalk in "Old Town," (in the old part of Istanbul that is in Asia Minor, across the Bosporus Strait) gained a guide who had overheard us talking. She wore a filthy dress and claimed to have been married to a member of the American Consulate and, for some reason she didn't explain, was stuck in Turkey. She did speak fluent English.

She directed us to the district police station where the chief exchanged Turkey's lira for American dollars at a high rate of exchange, to the advantage of my shipmates and myself.

We were all hungry, and she took us to the "best restaurant in the world"—her words. It was a dingy crowded, long narrow room where skewers of kabob roasted inside the front window. Flies buzzed all about as we were seated. Waiters clearing tables after diners departed merely wiped the silverware with the used napkins, then they placed both items back into a drawer to be used again and again, without being washed.

My watertender and I refused to eat.

Summer of 1949, showing long bridge across Bosporus Strait. Looking from "Old Town" in Asia Minor (Istanbul, also) across Bosporus at modern Istanbul, Turkey, in Europe. Although very hungry, the author declined to dine at what was said to be the "greatest restaurant" in the world, located in dingy Old Town.

Our self-appointed guide sarcastically admonished us, declaring that something must be wrong with us mentally if we were hungry and would not eat.

I told her that if I lived, I would be back aboard ship within hours, then I could eat my fill of food not specked with swarms of flies, and that I could also use eating tools that had been washed in steaming hot water, and, if I didn't live, it would not matter whether or not I was hungry.

We soon crossed back over to Europe on the long bridge spanning the Bosporus and, in modern Istanbul, we came upon a modern hotel. Trans World Airline used the hotel for its flight personnel. The watertender and I dined on juicy, tender steaks; my steak was one of the best I have ever eaten, because I was indeed hungry.

We hauled pack harness and feed for mules sent to Greece, which they used in mountain terrain to fight their civil war. (The United States sent many mules to Greece. Buyers swept across America paying prices for mules higher than many farmers ever dreamed of getting. The old folks back home chortled about that twist of fate greatly accelerating the switch from mules to tractors on the farms in the USA.)

Greek soldiers, put aboard ship as so-called security while we were in port there, stole everything they could get their hands on, literally. A further example of contempt expressed for Americans by the Greeks: It was about a mile to where we could catch a train to nearby Athens. We had to walk. Instead of giving us a lift, Greek soldiers, jeering and thumbing their noses, whizzed passed us in U.S. Army trucks which America had given to them.

Each of my voyages consisted of many miles of ocean and various ports, with stops at the Azores, Tripoli, North Africa, Treiste, and other ports in the Mediterranean area and sometimes way around to the North Sea, all in one trip.

Sylvia never once complained, but I could tell she was miserable with loneliness; a seventeen-year old, who had never been away from family before, thrust into a life of waiting all alone for me in a strange mammoth city.

I did come ashore long enough to pass the examination for my second engineer's license, then within another week or so I was right back out, plowing the sea. We made toothbrush runs going over, then hauled dead soldiers back. Russia and East Germany blinked, and so the Berlin Blockade ended September 30, 1949. But my last voyage ended when I signed off my last ship September 19, 1949—we were still hauling War II dead back.

Although Sylvia never uttered one word of complaint, the distress and anxiety darted about in her sparkling eyes each time I left on another voyage. And when I told her it was time for me to hit the beach so that we could build our home, she gave me one of the most loving hugs ever.

Coming into port from my last voyage, I remember standing at the stern for a long time, looking back over the ocean, thinking: Good-bye, Ole Gal, you've been a mean hellion at times, but, God, you've been one heck of a teacher.

We came home full of blissful happiness. But the world waited with its tail recoiled ready to snap like a steel spring, and it delivered a blow, the likes of which no human ever had survived.

CHAPTER
16

LINER AT LANDING STAGE, LIVERPOOL.   69416

SYLVIA AND I RENTED A COMFORTABLE ONE-BEDROOM
duplex apartment, and we both found pleasing employment in
Memphis. She, in bookkeeping for a large appliance company, and
I took the examination and was issued a first-class Stationary Steam
and Refrigeration Engineer's license, and was a power plant engineer at the Ford Motor assembly plant for two and one-half years.

But I began to feel like I had reached a dead end, a sealed-off
ceiling. The chief engineer was a relatively young man with
several years to go before retirement, and so, there didn't appear
to be any opportunity for me to advance. Thus, feeling that I didn't
have the chance to keep climbing, I became dissatisfied, although
it was an easy job, a very good job, considered one of the top in the
area of its type. Having been bitten by a little knowledge, I wanted
more. Therefore, I took a job with the engineering department of a
national fidelity and casualty insurance company, whose home
office was in New York.

Besides providing insurance coverage against loss, the
company also touted the engineering service it offered to industry,

for any type operation. Their directive to all field engineers, in effect, was: Use what knowledge you have and when you run into a problem you can't handle, we have an inventory of engineering know-how that can handle anything.

Smaller companies, especially, used our services, and it turned out to be interesting and rewarding work, the challenges unlimited with a broad range of opportunities to keep learning.

I was transferred to Little Rock to work the Arkansas territory, and soon got the impression that some of those folks in the home office still looked upon Arkansas as a *territory*.

For example, the director of the company's car fleet wrote sarcastic memos, asking if we had gone into the used-tire business in Arkansas. There were still many unpaved, rocky graveled roads in the Ozark Mountains that were extremely damaging to tires. Mindful of such smart-aleck notes, a few times instead of replacing a punctured tire, I would merely have it vulcanized.

However, I was happy with my job and felt like our home was heaven. Sixty percent of my work was around the Little Rock area, and overnight travel away from home was at a minimum. Other than occasional special assignments to make inspections and surveys of prospective clients, my work was routine. But it covered a wide variety of America's industry and, indeed, it was always interesting. It gave me a general view of America on the move and just what made it tick, in terms of its goods and services—and sometimes its politics, as well.

Sylvia and I found Little Rock to be a friendly city, and we soon had several wonderful young couples for friends. Our lifestyle was modest, we added savings to our nest egg, but easily afforded all our simple desires. We could not have been any happier. The future was in our hands without a cloud in sight.

As memory pegs for recall of a point back in time, *Nautilus*, the first atomic-powered submarine ever built, was launched January 21, in Groton, Connecticut, 1954. March 1, 1954, supporters for the independence of Puerto Rico sprayed gunfire from the spectators' galley in the U.S. House of Representatives, wounding five

Early summer 1950, at sister Lillian's home in Miami, Florida. Sylvia holding two large lobsters she caught on a deep-sea fishing outing in the Atlantic. (Lillian and family moved from Memphis to Miami near war's end, and she became the owner and operator of a successful nursing home. She had in her care once a wealthy man in his nineties who, in his younger days, made a fortune during the Florida land boom. He built an elaborate home on Star Island, connecting Miami Beach, which he owned until the crash in 1929. Later, the gangster Al Capone took up residence in the home when he came to Florida.)

members of Congress. In between these two historical events, around 10 o'clock the night of February 2, 1954, while rounding a hairpin curve on U.S. Highway 70 at the northeastern city limits of Hot Springs, Arkansas, the left front tire on my 1953 Chevrolet company car blew. It pulled me across the center line on the narrow two-lane highway in front of a long limousine, being used as a taxi. The cars hit head-on.

The impact broke the jaw of the driver of the bigger and heavier vehicle. But my head struck the Chevrolet's corner post on the passenger side, bending a head-shaped bow into it, then my face smashed through the windshield before I crumpled to the floorboard.

The steering post was driven into the back of the front seat of my car. I instinctively acted to get out of the way just before impact; I had come upon a terrible accident a few months before in which the driver's head was smashed by the steering column, which was driven back like a projectile when his car crashed into a bridge abutment.

I regained a fuzzy stage of consciousness a few days after my wreck . . . took one look at my face in a mirror and passed out again. My swollen face, I didn't recognize. It was full of ugly stitches and lacerations staring back at me as terrible as any I had ever seen in a horror movie. The next time I looked, after regaining full consciousness nearly two weeks later, it didn't look much better, although the stitches had been removed and much of the swelling was gone, except around my left eye.

In my first conscious in-and-out phase, I felt the cold fear of the unknown with a sense of panic! I had no idea where I was. I only knew that I was flat on my back inside a green tent-like enclosure, with both my ankles strapped snugly to the bed side rails as were both arms, and my head felt like a bulldozer was making a roadbed out of my brain.

I recall my lovely wife's anxious face breaking through the fog from an opening in the oxygen tent, and recall the tears of relief running down her cheeks as she patted my hand and urged me to lie completely still. Also, I recall her saying that I had been severely hurt and that my head was dangerously fractured.

Who knows . . . perhaps a little pain along the way is beneficial to all of us; having felt pain, we then know when we do feel good. But I can't recall the acute sense of that pain. However, I can recall the time and that I had it, and I recall the terrible suffering displayed on the anxious faces of loved ones as they stood by helpless. Also, I recall how frustrated I was, strapped to my bed, flat on my back, night and day, sometimes wanting to urinate so badly I felt I was going to pop.

My devoted wife had a cot in my room and stayed with me almost constantly, and there were also private nurses on duty.

One was a grouchy elderly woman whom I didn't like at all.

One night I kept telling her the darned catheter was not draining.

She kept snapping at me that it was.

Sylvia was beside herself, caught in the middle. She naturally assumed the professional nurse knew her stuff. I had my doubts, because training or no, I didn't think she knew much about drain lines or clapper valves, and told her so.

The nurse would take herself away from her magazine long enough to hiss, "Well, it's still dripping. So, you just shut your mouth, because it's all in your mind."

I hastened to inform her that she didn't know what she was talking about because it was all in my bladder and it was about to pop!

She never bothered to even check the tube or feel my abdomen.

My wrists and ankles were still snugly strapped to the bed, and I couldn't do anything but bitch. I was hurting, flat on my back, unable to get up off the deck; I was miserable. I reasoned that as a nurse, especially at her age, she should not be timid about checking a man's situation.

But she merely kept turning the pages of her love-story magazine, taking an occasional peek to inform me the tube was still dripping and that she knew more about my condition than I.

I finally told her I would bet that I knew more about clogged drains than she did, and asked her if there was a stuck clapper valve in the darned catheter.

She snapped at Sylvia that if I didn't stop "bitching and being so hateful" that Sylvia would have to get another nurse for the late night shift.

Caught in the middle and worried about my critical state, the emotional burden my wife endured was terrible.

The day nurse finally came on. She was a pleasant young registered nurse who had served a hitch in the Navy. Briefly touching my abdomen, she gasped and exclaimed to Sylvia, "My, God, he *is* about to pop. The catheter *is* clogged!"

She removed it but soon had to choke my situation while Sylvia grabbed a bed pan to replace the full urinal.

Still squeezing my situation, the nurse seemed to be in a dither about using the open pan, and I told her to just flop the hose over the side and stand back because I was going to blow the line out. She and Sylvia cackled over that. I was serious!

It was good to hear Sylvia laugh.

I suffered those four weeks at the St. Joseph Hospital in Hot Springs, but I cannot convey enough gratitude for the staff and for Dr. Charles P. Harris, who was called into the emergency room the night of the crash. He told me later that initially he couldn't detect a pulse or other signs of life until I had a convulsion. He had forewarned Sylvia that there was only one chance in fifty that I would ever regain consciousness.

To be told that about someone you dearly love must be one of life's most heart-wrenching ordeals, to wait helplessly and suffer with an anxious heart for days and weeks.

Among several injuries, my head had been fractured all around, and there was a constant noise inside. It sounded like the gushing noise caused when inflating an automobile tire with a hand pump. My left eye was pushed out of its socket, and the lower lid was filled with blood, like a balloon covering the eye. Ice packs were kept on it, but still the protrusion bulged.

Dr. Harris, a young general practitioner at the time, requested a specialist from the Army and Navy Hospital, then in operation at Hot Springs, to examine me.

Dr. Lee, the specialist, put a stethoscope to my eyelid and expressed alarm. He immediately huddled with Dr. Harris. The specialist advised that I suffered an arteria-venus aneurysm. Then, to me in layman terms, he explained that I had a ruptured artery inside a sinuous vein behind my left eye. Within hours, I was rushed to Memphis, Tennessee, and placed under the care of Dr. Francis Murphey, a neuro specialist with international and national recognition for his knowledge and surgical skill.

Dr. Murphey and his colleague, Dr. Semmes, of the Semmes and Murphey Clinic, were waiting when we arrived at the Baptist Memorial Hospital. Despite the best efforts of everyone to display a casual demeanor, I sensed that my condition was very critical and I greatly appreciated Dr. Murphey's candor.

He told me that he had considerable experience with such injuries, which were sometimes suffered by soldiers in the tank corp or by pilots of war planes that crashed; moreover, he said that my ruptured artery happened in the only place in the human body where an artery actually passed through a vein (behind each eye), and that severe skull fractures sometimes caused the artery to rupture inside this particular sinuous vein. He also told Sylvia and me that there was no way to gain access to repair the rupture, and that the only possible solution was to tie off the external carotid artery and pray that it would save me.

He pointed out that due to the overwork caused by blood escaping out the rupture, my heart was dangerously enlarged, twice its normal size, racing like a motor spinning a car's wheels, going nowhere. He expressed amazement that my heart had endured such stress for so long, but advised that something had to be done immediately before it stopped. He warned that at worst a tie-off could be fatal or that it could affect me mentally.

Early the next morning Dr. Murphey opened my neck under local anesthesia. My most vivid memory of the operation is that the novocaine really made my nose itch! A lot more than the little dab any dentist ever injected when working on my teeth.

The surgeon cautioned me not to talk while he made the incision; after which, he applied a clamp to the external carotid artery and at time intervals made little tests by sticking the bottoms of my feet with a pin. Then I would give him a thumbs-up to let him know that I could feel it. He then placed a hand at the incision and asked me several foolish questions, I thought; but, he was testing my mental reaction.

I kept wiggling my nose, and he finally asked what was wrong. I told him that the stuff they shot me with was itching the heck out of my nose and I wanted it scratched. A very somber man, he nonetheless grinned and instructed the nurse to give my nose a good rub, and said the clamped artery surely was not hindering my ability to gripe.

He then permanently tied off my external carotid.

The bulge receded somewhat, but my eye was still pushed out and the loud bruit, or gushing noise, inside my head continued. The poor man was obviously at wit's end.

He informed me that tying off the external carotid was usually decisive one way or the other, that it either killed or cured. Also he mused aloud that due to the length of time since the rupture occurred, calcium had apparently formed and was possibly complicating matters. Again explaining the grave situation, he advised Sylvia and me that it was perhaps possible the danger could be lessened by tying off a crossover artery inside my forehead to prevent blood flow from the right side crossing over and pumping back through the rupture.

Within a few days, we gave it a go.

Wow. It is claimed that one cannot feel anything when his skull is cut on or sawed. Ha. The vibration makes you feel like you are crawling out of your skin. It is a weird sensation.

The crossover tie-off did little to relieve the condition. The gushing noise continued.

The doctor became increasingly concerned about my heart holding out and he called in other specialists for consultation. I didn't understand much of their medical lingo, but I understood their puzzled frowns; the complications of my injury had them stumped also.

Sylvia had a small bed in the room and, all through those long days and nights, she stayed with me constantly, even though I was tended by private nurses around the clock.

This experience causes me to believe that it's much harder in many aspects on a devoted loved one who can only stand by helpless and look on, hoping and praying, and by his/her presence giving comfort, than it is on the afflicted. Because, after all, when a trauma hits you and you are down, you accept it for what it is; there is not a thing to do but pray and think about getting well.

But I had many visitors. Actually too many at times. Thus I have a definite opinion about visitors running to hospitals; if one is very sick, he does not need visitors, except a companion like my Sylvia. A get-well card will do just fine; and, if one is not very sick, he does not need visitors, anyway. . . .

And everyone should be required to remove high-heeled shoes and clack-clack-clacking cowboy boots before stomping through the halls and corridors of any hospital. I'll guaran-dang-tee, if you are not very sick while confined to a hospital bed, you will get sicker than a horse after a couple of days listening to clacking heels stomping up and down uncarpeted halls.

Also, patients who are already prepped with joy-juice at night for early morning surgery should have a muzzle put on them.

When I was at my worst, feeling miserable, hurting, having trouble sleeping, such a lady was placed in the room directly across the hall from mine. She was having abdominal surgery early the next morning and, the night before, her room was flooded with visitors stomping in and out with those high heels and cowboy boots.

The nurses kept urging them to hold it down, but the patient and her friends kept up their loud cackling and howling. She had either already received her prep for the surgery and was high on that or, as I suspected, her friends were juicing her with slugs of sko-cat, because she was having a ball!

Sylvia asked them in her polite, pleasant way to please not make so much noise, and they were very rude to her.

Of course, one is pretty darn sore the next day after surgery, and I told Sylvia that the merrymaker was in for a shock the next night. Sure enough, she then lay over there moaning and groaning, calling out for the nurses.

The new Baptist Memorial Hospital was not yet complete, and the old building didn't have modern voice communication connecting rooms to the nurses' station. Patients had to flip a switch at their bed for a light outside the room then wait until a busy nurse looked down the hall to see it. And this could seem to take a long time, depending on a patient's distress.

The lady across the hall started groaning, "I gotta pee." She kept it up, "Oh Lord, I gotta peeeeeEEEE!"

I knew the feeling, and I yelled as loud as I could to tell her that she could borrow my urinal. There was a brief silence, then she shouted, "What . . . !"

I answered, "Yes, Ma'am, I'll be glad to loan you my urinal. You want to give it a try? You might even have fun with it."

"Hush your damned mouth, you son of a bitch," she squalled, "or I'll come over there and ram that thing up your ass."

Of course family, friends, and loved ones mean well. Bless them, they are concerned about you and they want you to know they are. They all want to cheer you up, but I suspect darn few of us know the correct way—if there is one. Surely, it is because we feel such anxiety about a critical situation and the pain suffered by loved ones that we are at loss to know what to say when we visit.

As an example, my dear old dad would irritate the heck out of me. Bless his heart . . . it was his way that he thought might reassure me. He meant well, and I was aware of it; however, he would visit often and sit on the foot of my bed and (everytime!) tell me about someone who was worse off, and how much worse off I could be, and to be thankful that I was not worse off.

After Dr. Murphey laid back my scalp, then cut into my cranium and made the tie-off of the crossover artery, acute infection developed in my scalp. He expressed great alarm and ordered large jolts of penicillin pumped into me every four hours around the clock. I was little more than skin and bones with barely any flesh left in which to pump that *clabbered milk*.

Some weeks later when I was strong enough with the support of two nurses to walk down the hall to the scales, I weighed eighty-nine pounds, so God only knows how much less I weighed when I was being slugged with that thick antibiotic.

Even when gentle nurses were as careful as possible, the injections hurt. But a few of those ladies really rammed that darned plunger home, and I howled and squeezed my buttocks so tight, I fear my voiding equipment completely sucked plumb back into my belly. I told a nurse that if the coward kept hiding I might have to start using a lady's urinal.

One compassionate little student nurse in her senior year always came in with the longest face, as though it was about time to pull the curtains on me. She always tried to appear casual; however, her long face depressed me.

I told Sylvia that I would sure like to see the nurse smile for a change.

One night when the nurse came in to clabberize my rump with that long needle on the jug of buttermilk, she asked, as if she didn't know, "By the way, Mr. McEwen, just how did you lose the sight of your eye?"

I suddenly remembered an old joke I had heard Dad tell. I feigned a serious expression, and said, "Well, little lady, it was like this: Awhile back, a group of us was riding horseback to church and we came to a washout in the trail. The ladies were all riding sidesaddle, and when our horses jumped the ditch, one of the women fell off. Her skirt ruffled up, exposing her foundation. The preacher was along and he bellered to all us men not to look, or we would go blind. But, you know, I just had to risk one eye."

The little nurse from Ohio did not think it was a corny joke. She broke down and cackled. And from then on, she would breeze into my room and each time she always wore a smile and often had an amusing tidbit to tell Sylvia and me. A simple little episode, but one that was rewarding to someone who had nothing to do but lie on a hospital bed, waiting to get popped in the rear every four hours with a jack hammer.

But, through it all, I marveled at Sylvia's endurance.

A few days after we got to Memphis, it was confirmed that she was pregnant. At times I would be vomiting in one side of the pan and she would be vomiting in the other side of the same pan.

Now two love birds can suck the same soda through straws all they wish, and moo and coo over one another all they please, and that, indeed, is a great experience. However, when the two can share the same pan in which to vomit, and wink at one another while doing so without holding their noses, and hold hands at the same time, then they know that they are in love.

The infection was killed.

A few days later, Dr. Murphey came rushing into my room after 10 P.M. He informed me that he had come straight from the airport after returning from a medical convention in Denver, Colorado. There he said my case was on the agenda and was discussed by medical experts from all over the world. (Medical profession reader, if you would like to research this, it was written up in medical journals. The meeting in Denver occurred somewhere around the last of March 1954.) Then the doctor jarred me by saying that in all the annals of medicine there could be found only one other case that ever existed with such complications as mine.

Of course I was eager to hear about it.

Dr. Murphey explained that as a last resort, in addition to the patient's external carotid artery having been permanently tied off, his internal carotid was also tied off but that it was fatal.

I thought, it was just my rotten luck, that I was right back in a probable damned if you do and certain damned-if-you-don't situation. Strangely, I thought about keeping steam up and the old *Larkspur* being battered by the storm-tossed sea.

I thought Dr. Murphey, although highly skilled in his profession, was a down-to-earth person. He would often explain the human anatomy relating to my condition in simple terms, easy to understand. In a sense it was like Mr. Voorhees explaining a ship's power plant, with its miles of piping, electrical circuits, and hundreds of various controls, to a novice seaman. Actually, there is indeed a good analogy between a steamship's power plant and the human body.

Dr. Murphey appeared to be physically exhausted at that late hour as he sat studying my demeanor. I had discovered that he put in many long-hour days caring for critically injured and ill patients and he genuinely cared about them, just as he was there in my room after a long day, deeply concerned about me. A sense of compassion for him flashed through my thoughts.

He suggested that he could remove a bit of muscle tissue from elsewhere in my body and insert it into my external carotid with hope that the tissue would plug the rupture. He further advised that, as far as he knew, such an experiment had never been tried, but that my heart could not hold out much longer unless a way was found to relieve the extreme burden it endured.

I asked what would happen if the tissue failed to plug the rupture and passed on to lodge inside my head.

He grimaced with a shake of his head, which told me all, as he patiently waited in silence.

I swallowed hard and thought about it. There was no cause for much hope, yet, I still had hope.

He broke the silence and advised that the only other option was also a long shot; that he could apply a clamp to my internal carotid and test the results and pray for a miracle.

Again I thought with a bit of bitterness, what the heck, storm raging, hull cracked, and no water in the boilers . . . it's go-for-broke time again—but this situation was far different!

I had found my dream girl and we were tremendously happy. I had managed to get a firm grip on the world's tail, but only for too short a time. It wasn't fair to have to let go so soon, but I was so weary that my thoughts rebounded from a blank wall, and my mind was very tired.

I sighed and tried to hide my bitterness, to say, "What the hell, Doctor. Let 'er rip. Give it your best shot."

The next day he was very careful, going back inside my neck by cutting along the scar left by the incision he had made to tie off the external carotid.

With a clamp on my internal carotid artery, he stuck my feet with the pin from time to time and asked me those *silly* questions, but I didn't mind. I knew he was testing to determine what affect clamping the artery had on my mind. He frequently released the clamp, then he would leave it clamped for progressively longer periods. At times he placed a hand at the incision, then we talked; we talked about anything that popped into our thoughts. He grinned about my itching nose and chuckled, instructing the nurse that she make sure to keep me content by rubbing it often. He became more jovial, and I saw him smile more than I had ever seen him do.

I began to think: O boy, we're going to make it!

I felt good!

Maybe too good. I don't know why . . . sometimes a young'n' just can't control a situation, but I felt good all over.

The nurse and anesthetist wha-whawed, they laughed so hard.

Dr. Murphey looked down at me with a big grin like a mule eating briars.

I cut my good eye down past my belly and saw a neat little tent poked up in the sheet over my lower body. I grunted. Dr. Murphey again put his hand to my neck and asked if I wanted to say something.

I told him no except that I felt like an idiot.

Shaking his head, he grinned, and said, "Oh, no. You are far from being a idiot, young man. That's one of the best signs you could give me. I believe you're going to make it just fine."

Indeed, with the clamp in place I could not hear the gushing sound any longer. He then tied off the internal carotid artery permanently.

I now had a tied-off crossover artery, and the left internal and external carotid arteries permanently tied off for life, but my engine was still hitting on one cylinder.

A miracle? I didn't know or worry about it, I was too consumed with relief and joy, knowing that I was still alive!

However, that night in the wee hours I woke up and realized that I was not breathing. But I felt fine. Everything was very quiet in the hospital. Bright moonlight poured through a west window. The private nurse was apparently taking a break; she was not in the room. I turned my head on the pillow and saw Sylvia's pretty face. She was awake, eyes wide open, just looking at me. I was amazed, because I didn't feel any discomfort, any urgency or panic. Rather, I felt a peaceful calm, as though I floated like a feather on my bed. For a mere instant, long enough for the foolish thought to pass through my mind, I marveled that I was omnipotent, that I actually had the power over myself not to breathe! Then just as quickly I was hit with chilling fear. I knew I was in danger. I had to think consciously to mentally start my breathing process again. I would think "breathe" and then I would breathe.

I had no distress and had not made a sound that I was aware of. But Sylvia lay on her bunk, facing me, eyeing me intently. Finally she raised up and said, "Honey, are you alright?"

I told her I was just fine. And I was, considering my condition at the time. I blew her a kiss and closed my eyes, pretending to go back to sleep. I lay still and thought about what had just happened.

That experience was only for a matter of seconds, perhaps two or three minutes, but I kept thinking "breathe" for some time. When daylight seeped through the window, I felt normal and breathed easy.

I never mentioned it to Dr. Murphey. But I cannot recall why I didn't tell him; it was an incident that was unpleasant to think about, and perhaps I just simply procrastinated, not in any hurry to bring it up. In fact, it was some years later before I ever mentioned it to Sylvia. It was a phenomenal experience, a bit scary.

Not that I ever wished to on a permanent basis, but there have been times when I have tried to see how long I could will myself not to breathe. Not very long. Doubtless can anyone hold his breath, except perhaps a hysterical person.

I concluded that perhaps there had been a bit of circuit breaker adjustments going on in my brain and a few essential breakers momentarily kicked out and were a bit tardy kicking back in, causing my breathing impulse to temporarily lose its automatic function.

I never had the experience again, but I refrained thereafter from taking the little sleeping pill each night.

Over the next three and one-half years there was considerable patching done on me. Needless to say, if a head-on doesn't put a person's light out, it delivers a devastating blow that shatters the body somewhat.

The ulna nerve in each of my arms had been damaged, making the ring and little fingers of each hand useless, until Dr. Murphey transplanted the nerves to the inside bend of my elbows, so that the ulna nerves are not stretched, and are thus relieved from stress. It worked fine, except two fingers on each hand are still sort of numb and floppy.

I taught myself to type about forty words per minute using all fingers, years ago. It was very effective therapy. But I learned on a manual typewriter, and, because of my lazy fingers, now these new fangled electric typewriter and computer keyboards sometimes flitttttttt all over the page or screen on me.

I had a ruptured ear drum, optic nerves for both eyes were damaged, and my line of vision was pulled in towards my nose in a fixed position. I had to turn my head to see across the bridge of my nose with my good right eye for more than a year, until muscle tissue was transplanted to straighten the eyeball.

Nearly all my teeth were cracked, chipped, and sliced, which the doctor said was caused in large part from sheer grinding pressure with my jaws clamped shut while I was unconscious. I had a mouth full of gold when the dentist got through fitting me with permanent bridges, caps, and inlays, etc. Each time I drank something hot or cold it was like spikes shooting into my forehead. And the list goes on and on. . . .

The last surgery as a result of the accident was in September 1957, over three and one-half years after the wreck, which was to transplant muscle tissue to also straighten my sightless left eye, for cosmetic effect.

I suffered terrible headaches, and Dr. Murphey put my head and neck in traction to see if that would help. It did not. He sighed, looked me in the eye, and advised, "Lee, you may have to learn to live with those headaches. We don't know all the answers, but we do know that it's not uncommon after a serve head injury for a person to suffer headaches the rest of his or her life."

He had been prescribing big bottles of codeine, but when I learned that the steel ball was going to keep on bouncing in my head, I accepted it and switched to aspirin. Since 1954 I have taken from four to six aspirins everyday. Sometimes they seem to help and sometimes they don't. But, nonetheless, I did, indeed, learn to tolerate the headaches and get on with my life.

But taking aspirin all these years has possibly been a blessing in disguise in another way: Knowing that only partially blocked carotid arteries often cause fatal or damaging strokes, taking aspirin for my headaches may have also kept my blood flowing. I have read various articles that claim medical experts now believe that simple aspirin is very effective medication to keep the blood thin and the heart ticking.

But whatever, rest assured that I am truly thankful to my Maker. And to quote ole Satchel Page, the late great black baseball pitcher who pitched after he was gray-haired, I, too, don't look back, "because something might be gaining on me. . . ."

Hopefully, learning of my good fortune will strengthen the hope of others who are concerned about clogged or blocked arteries.

The sense of pain and discomfort of those traumatic years have long been encased in a tranquil cradle of my mind. But, in no way can I stir my senses to recall the torture I once felt, to sense once more the intensity of the pain. However, I can, of course, recall with a shiver that it did indeed happen, and I can vividly recall the worry, fatigue, and anxiety on my darling wife's lovely face. She suffered right along with me those long days and nights.

But two precious lights of joy came into our lives during that time. We became proud parents of Lee Junior, our fine handsome son, and two years later, Gale, our beautiful daughter—there was a powerful wind storm in Memphis the day she was born, and we just had to name her Gale. Also, she was born the same day in September 1956 that the first transAtlantic telephone cable went into operation, and when she was at home as a teenager, I often wondered if the telephone-cable event and also the windy weather that day had been some strange omen of things to come, because our beautiful daughter sure was windy, especially on the telephone talking to other teenagers.

Aside from me being in and out of hospitals for corrective surgery and recuperating to undergo additional surgery, we had happy lives. Not only did Sylvia, a wonderful mother, pamper and care for our active children, she continued to shower me with attention.

We purchased a modest home in a new subdivision in Memphis, and I geared my thoughts to preparing myself for the

November 18, 1954, in Memphis, Tennessee. Proud mother, Sylvia, holding Lee Junior, who was one month old.

day I could get back into harness again. My company offered several various correspondence courses to keep engineers up-to-date about industry and company procedure, and I continued to study them. And I constantly nudged my district supervising engineer and also the home office in New York about any clue regarding my job-future. I was always given assurance and told to relax, take it easy, and get well.

My face rapidly improved, but was still visibly scarred, and my eye was still inflamed somewhat and I was still skin and bones. My appearance looked ghastly to me, and I wondered if I would ever again have the courage to stand before a group of people and address them.

While still in and out of the hospital for corrective surgery, but after gaining more strength, I enrolled in a public speaking course, seeking to regain self-confidence—Ha. I won the prize for the best minute-and-a-half impromptu speech one night. During the session, the director instructed the men, with permission from the women, to blindly stick a hand into a woman's purse, as it came our turn to speak. Then we showed whatever we withdrew to the class. We were instructed to then instantly start a minute-and-a-half impromptu talk on a subject pertaining to the article.

When it came my turn, I felt around inside a purse and found what I thought might be a book of matches. I held the little package before the class, and the matches turned out to be a package of condoms.

The class roared with laughter, including the dear woman's husband. She snatched the package from my hand and fled the room.

The director instructed me to proceed with the talk.

The Lord only knows why it did, but the image of a fish bladder suddenly came to mind; as children we used to play with the inflated bladder of a drum fish, and this I told the audience. Then I started a spiel about man's ability to invent from ideas formed because of things seen in nature.

This theme was greeted with snickers, and instantly I switched to the ingenuity of mankind to improve inventions; from fish bladders to children's toy balloons and from toy balloons to, uh. . . .

Memphis Christmas, 1954. Author on leave from hospital to gain strength for additional surgery and to be home for the holidays. Holding son, Lee Jr., who was three months old.

The class continued to laugh without letting up.

That was one very long minute and thirty seconds!

But the class voted me the prize, the popular book by the late Dale Carnegie, *How to Win Friends and Influence People.* Anyway, since that incident, I will not stick my hand into a lady's purse, not even my wife's, unless I can look to see what I am grabbing.

My company had been very considerate and humane to my family and me, but, then I was declared totally disabled, and I was told that I had to look elsewhere for gainful employment.

Often, before my mishap, other companies had made me job offers. I had serviced large and small companies: oil refineries, natural gas pipe lines, chicken plucking plants, and various types of manufacturing and construction. Also, I was a commissioned boiler and pressure vessel inspector, I inspected steam power plants, and I could certify welders and boiler makers to make repairs in accordance with the ASME boiler and pressure vessel construction codes, etc. And it was reassuring to be told on occasion by management of various other firms that I always had a position with them if I ever wanted to change jobs.

However, when I started making the rounds, attitudes had changed; not from indifference, but because of fear of the unknown, I believe. Everyone expressed great alarm about my arteries being permanently tied off. They all seemed to react in common, such as: "My God, Mac, we would like to have you with us, but you are subject to a stroke at any moment . . . you know our operation, and there is just no place we can fit you. . . ."

I did a lot of praying and fought off depression and would not allow myself to dwell on bitterness about such reactions. But I could never get beyond the medical; the major concern was always the same, that I was subject to a stroke.

Call it fear of the unknown or whatever, prospective employers simply had never been faced with such a creature who was still walking around even though he had two carotid arteries and a crossover artery permanently tied off. Many didn't even wait for a medical report, because of the common knowledge, even by laymen, that people have strokes everyday when carotid arteries are only partially blocked.

Frustration in my search for gainful employment sometimes caused me to feel that I was a freak! I had to suppress and defeat extreme thoughts that suggested I would be better off finding gainful employment if I was without both arms and legs instead of my tied-off arteries.

I was still some thirty pounds underweight, weak and frail, and Dr. Murphey cautioned me to let up, to take it easy. He would wag his head at me, seeming to be perplexed. Finally one day he lectured that I had to make myself understand that my whole body had suffered a tremendous impact, and that I had to stop trying to rush things; that the medical profession could do all possible, but that it would take years for my body to fully overcome the trauma it had suffered. He summed it up by telling me that I was not as I once was, that I never would be, that I would always be without what once was a part of my being.

He sighed, then said, "It's a matter of time. Your body has to have time to compensate. Any human body does, and yours is no exception. Just relax and be thankful to your Maker."

Even so, I was convinced that I would somehow still grab the world. Perhaps it appears foolish, but I had a mental block; my mind simply wouldn't think of myself as a cripple, and the urge to get back out and take on the world gnawed at me.

Of course, I only had to flex my weak hands, dwell on my headaches, or close my good eye and know blindness, to be reminded that some important bodily functions were amiss, but, nonetheless, I would think: What the heck, I'm still me, the same being as always. It was not that I harbored thoughts about showing the world what I could do—instead I was anxious to get back out and take on the world for my own personal satisfaction—knowing for myself what I could do.

But it would be awhile, yet, before I would get a good grip on that tail. Although I kept trying to grab it, it continued to switch and it decked me again and again and again, hard each time, even slinging two different cancers at me a couple of times on down the trail, which I successfully tussled.

LINER AT LANDING STAGE, LIVERPOOL.   69418

CHAPTER 17

THE REST OF THE FAMILY WERE QUITE NATURALLY concerned about my little family's future. I sought to relieve Dad's concern and let him know that Sylvia and I had saved a substantial nest egg and, if nothing else, we would go into some type of little business.

My younger brother had been farming Dad's land, but ventured into the grain buying business. Dad then sold his farm in Arkansas and bought a farm in the boothill of southeast Missouri, in an area where he was pastor of a rural church.

Within forty-eight hours after I had sought to put my parents' minds at ease about my welfare, I got a long distance telephone call from Dad. His first words were, "L. R., your brother is in a jam and you've got to help him out." (I go into this for only one reason, and that is to honor the fantastic goodness and charity in a wonderful human's heart, that of Sylvia's.)

Dad told me that the grain market had dropped and that farmers were bringing in their receipts to be paid for grain previously delivered to my brother and his father-in-law, with whom he was in business. Dad said that there was not enough money to pay off the farmers, or to cover some checks already issued.

Once again, the feeling gnawed at me, that "uh-oh, here I go again. . . ."

Dad stressed that the bank would only hold off two days before bouncing checks, and therefore there was little time before a scandal got out.

I still balked—there were persistent rumors that my brother gambled heavily in dice games, and I wanted a little time to, at least, check on his operation—the future and interests of my own immediate family had to be considered.

But family pressure persisted.

I asked for Sylvia's opinion. She did not hesitate in making the simple statement, "Honey, right or wrong, you have no choice. He's your brother; we've got to help him all we can."

Sylvia's innate goodness has amazed me through the years, but never have I been more in awe of her as I was then. There we were with two small children, living on a mere $244 monthly disability insurance payment that would end in a little over a year; a future uncertain, yet she didn't blink an eye or equivocate. She simply felt we had to help my brother. He was family, and that was it. Thus we agreed to give J. authority to draw drafts on our bank account. Dad and others in our family had far more net worth than we, but it was known we had the cash.

Sylvia, through education and experience, had become a proficient full charge bookkeeper, and we rushed over to find out all we could about the shortage in the business's cash flow.

J. assured me that a mere fifteen thousand dollars—chicken feed as he called it—would cover everything until he could get enough grain delivered to the big grain processing companies in Memphis; after which he said he could draw drafts on them for more than enough to repay me and continue to operate without word ever getting out to the farmers that they had been in danger of not getting paid.

In a way, J. B. also gambled on the grain market. At harvest time he committed grain to be sold on the May Futures Market in the coming spring, but he could draw cash advances only on grain delivered, limited to a percentage of lower market prices around harvest time. (Thus, as I was soon to discover, he didn't have enough grain to deliver to the big elevators to cover his cash-flow shortfall.)

Over the weekend, we took our children to Sylvia's folks who lived near mine in southeast Missouri, where her father was also the pastor of a church in a little community. When we returned to Harrisburg the following Monday afternoon, to our horror, we found that drafts for over $27,000 had been drawn on our account in Memphis. Except for about $2,000, our nest egg had been sucked empty. Consider this: In 1958, a new Chevrolet or Ford car could be purchased for around $2,000; a three-bedroom brick veneer house, constructed with lumber of far better quality than that used in building many homes today, could be purchased for around $8,888 to $9,999. In short, the purchasing power of $27,000 in 1958 was about that of $200,000 in 1998.

We were shocked because our account had been wiped out, but Sylvia took a deep breath, smiled, and urged me not to fret about it. She commented that it was a family matter, pure and simple, and that we had been tossed the ball. There was nothing left for us to do but make the best of it.

Again, I wish to stress, that this little phase of our lives is mentioned *only* to highlight the natural goodness and tenacity of an exceptionally wonderful human. Being away from our children—Gale was then just past her first birthday and Lee barely past his third—a week and sometimes two weeks at a time, was an awful emotional drain on a young mother who loved her babies very much. But she endured with a smile. Always, she wore her warm wonderful smile.

The nation was all in awe about the first artificial satellite to orbit the earth—the USSR's sputnik that was launched in October 1957. But Sylvia and I hardly noticed, as we hustled daily to get soybeans to Memphis so that we could draw on them from the big grain companies in order to keep operating the business. But my condition was still weak. I could do little more than make sure that soybeans we purchased were graded properly for moisture and foreign matter, and keep the flow going to Memphis.

Sylvia and I labored to recover as much of our money as possible, then we wanted to return all of the business to my brother.

February 11, 1958, Sylvia drove about eighty-five miles up to southeast Missouri to see our children, whom she had not seen for nearly two weeks. J. B. was home with his family watching television. I stayed late that evening at the grain elevator in Harrisburg, Arkansas, making sure two of our trucks were loaded in time to travel the sixty miles to Memphis before midnight. After the first of the year, trucks were not unloaded until the next day if they arrived at the big elevators in Memphis after midnight.

We were loading out of a tall pile of soybeans that had been bought that day, which had been stored by the farmers in driers. The beans were firm, like little marbles. But the big eighteen-inch auger-conveyor in the center of the concrete floor had reduced the elevator-pit side of the huge pile, leaving a deep trough; beans had stopped feeding into the open auger.

I crawled on top and gave the pile a kick. I slipped, and an avalanche of beans poured down and carried me with them and pitched me out across the naked auger on my back.

At the end of the big building, where the auger passed underneath the base of the wall to empty into the elevator pit on the other side, there was an opening on each side of the big screw-type auger. As luck would have it, my left foot jammed through one of the semitriangular holes to wedge between the auger and the base of the wall. My left foot was twisted off.

I saw it tumble on and drop out of sight into the elevator pit. The twirling auger snatched at the seat of my pants as I lay across it.

Frantically, I sought to keep my palms from slipping on the little soybeans scattered about on the concrete floor, to keep my hands from getting caught in the relentless steel spiral. And, finally, I managed to plant my palms on each side of it.

I don't remember feeling any pain. It happened in a matter of seconds. My mind was too busy, concerned with first things first. The hungry auger had me by the seat of my britches. Chewing away, grabbing for my rear, the twisting iron monster was snapping ever closer to my hanging testicles.

Although chilling horror had me in its grip, apparently a man's subconscious mind is geared to react fast to such a threat . . . reason somehow squeezed through and zapped my sense of panic. With the auger chewing away at the flesh of my left leg, I was careful not to let my hands slip and get caught, and I flipped my body off, then jerked my leg out of its twisting, merciless jaws.

A local doctor quickly cauterized my mangled leg and hustled me by ambulance to Memphis.

Dr. Murphey had cautioned me to be careful and not get a lick on the head or anywhere that might cause a blood clot; that my brain primarily depended on my right-side arteries; and that a clot would be fatal. I didn't know whether my mangled left leg presented such a danger, but I asked that Dr. Murphey be notified. However, he happened to be bedfast with a brief illness and he asked Dr. Milford, an orthopedic surgeon, to attend me.

They had me stretched out on a table flat on my back in the emergency room of the Baptist Memorial Hospital in Memphis, and two young interns were discussing my condition while waiting the arrival of Dr. Milford. The interns agreed in their discussion that my leg would have to be amputated above the knee.

My attention sharpened to a razor's edge, and I protested, "Oh, no, I'll be damned if that's so!"

Dr. Milford loomed big over me when he arrived and he too informed me that my leg would have to be removed above the knee.

I again protested.

I'm always amazed how quickly one gets feedback from the subconscious in such situations. Images of wounded soldiers we brought home in those hospital ships flashed through my mind. I instantly recalled that those who still had their knee joint were more mobile than those without their knee. It wasn't that I was being a smart-ass or being disrespectful of Dr. Milford's medical expertise; it was simply a matter of nut-cutting time, with little time left. Already, the anesthetist was standing by with a big hypo, ready to put me to sleep for the surgery.

Expressing bewilderment at my stubborn attitude, Dr. Milford hastened to explain that not enough suitable flesh was left below my knee with which to make a stump to support a prosthesis.

I argued that I knew there was plenty of bone left and that I didn't want the knee joint cut off.

Beside himself, he insisted that the flesh had been chewed and mangled and that so much scar tissue would be left, even if the stump healed, it was highly unlikely that I would be able to withstand the pressure of a prosthesis.

I suggested he take part of my rump and graft a stump. He deeply frowned, shook his head, sighed in exasperation, and crisply stated that it was impossible to provide a functional stump by means of grafting.

Already they were marking my thigh for surgery, and I snapped, "Dammit, I'm telling you, don't cut my knee off!"

The poor doctor put himself squarely before me by leaning down close to my face. "Look, Mr. McEwen," he stressed, "even if there was enough suitable flesh, there is so much dirt and other contamination ground into it, your stump will never heal. I don't believe we could inject you with enough antibiotic to prevent dangerous infection. I'm forced to amputate above the knee. If I don't, you will certainly have to endure another operation when infection does set in."

My subconscious was keyed up and whirling, flashing feedback. I insisted, "Dammit, Doc, I heal good. Cut a toe with an ax in the log woods, just pour some kerosene on it and go ahead. You just soak my stump with kerosene and don't worry about infection."

Panic had me in its grip, and I was desperate. I knew I was going to be put to sleep within seconds and, then, I could not fight for what I was convinced to be best for my well-being—it's a terrible, helpless feeling, this flat-on-your-back tussling!.

I believed the surgeon was doing what he thought was best to prevent me from suffering another operation later, but I was more than willing to endure it if there was any chance at all to save my knee joint.

"Kerosene . . . " snorted Dr. Milford. Turning to the others, he added, "Did you ever hear of such a ridiculous. . . ." He cut himself short, and firmly stated, "Look, fellow, I understand your concern but you must also understand that I have no choice. I'm very sorry, but I have to amputate above your knee."

No, indeed, I didn't feel too significant, flat on my back with little to fight with. I did the only thing which I felt was left for me to do. Raising to prop myself with elbows, I snapped, "Doctor, if you cut my knee off, I'm going to sue the hell out of you."

He fell out of his saddle.

The look on the good man's face would have scared a ghost. My brother was standing back, leaning on a wall with his head tucked, and Dr. Milford turned to him and wailed, "Is he serious? Does he really mean that?!"

Poor ole J., what a spot to be in. Worry and anxiety fixed in his face, he looked at the doctor, and replied, "Yes sir, I'd bet on it."

I woke the next morning to find myself stretched flat on my back in a hospital bed, with my left leg hoisted in traction. I still had my left knee but barely two inches of bone below it. A heavy iron weight hung from the end of my stump.

Dr. Milford visited me early and was very cool, but I was not surprised. He explained that the flesh and skin fitted over the end of the bone to make a stump could not be disturbed, and that my leg had to remain in constant traction. Therefore, since the bandaging could not be opened to allow examination, my temperature would be taken every hour, night and day, to detect any increase that would indicate fever from infection.

I had experienced many things back along life's trail that tugged at my heartstrings, but nothing more touching than my own little son, who was a few months past his third birthday. Trying to keep back her own tears, Sylvia put the little fellow astraddle my chest at my request. My child sat there choked up. Tears streamed down his cheeks. His lip quivered as he looked down at his father.

Those were really tough moments. I wanted to cry but could not. I cried inside.

I mustered a smile and pulled my precious little boy to me in a big hug. I assured him that everything was going to be okay, that soon I would have an artificial leg, and we could still go fishing and hunting together just like nothing ever happened. And I made him a solemn promise that he would never have to think that his daddy was a cripple.

He was concerned about me hurting a lot. I assured him that I didn't hurt one little bit, that they gave me medicine that made me feel fine. With a sigh of great relief, his face brightened and he hugged his daddy's neck a long time.

And darling Sylvia, bless her heart . . . God, I thought, how can she withstand any more strain like this? But, with her head high and always with her wonderful smile, withstand it she did.

Dr. Milford kept a close check on me, visiting me often, still somewhat cool and aloof.

Sylvia's mother stayed at our home in Memphis and cared for our children, and Sylvia stayed with me almost constantly.

After a couple of days, Dr. Murphey was up and about and he along with Dr. Milford visited me. Dr. Murphey just sat looking at me, silently wagging his head. He was visibly shaken.

"Lee, what in the world is going to happen to you next?" he wailed.

I felt a sense of guilt and also compassion for him. He had worked so long getting me rebuilt. I pictured an automobile which someone had labored for days and years to rebuild, only to find it wrecked again. But lying there on my back, being disturbed every hour from fitful sleep at night to find a thermometer stuck in my mouth, and attended by a physician who didn't smile, I also felt somewhat perturbed.

I growled, "Heck, I don't know, Doctor Murphey, but I'll tell you one darned thing for sure, when I leave the hospital this time, I'm finding a water hole somewhere way out in a desert and there I'm going to squat, away from everything that moves."

He wagged his head with a wry grin, and chuckled, "Yes, but, son, with your luck, it won't do any good, a rattlesnake will probably bite you."

He and Dr. Milford conversed, Dr. Murphey asking how I was doing. Dr. Milford informed him that so far so good under the circumstances. Then told him, right smack dab in front of me lying there, that I was the stubbornest patient he had ever tended. He told Dr. Murphey about our confrontation in the emergency room and stated that I would just have to suffer the ordeal of surgery again to remove my knee. He told him about my kerosene recommendation, and declared that there was little chance my stump would heal.

Dr. Murphey took my temperature. He seemed pleased. He asked what exactly the chances were of saving my knee.

Dr. Milford, sighed, and replied, "Very slim, maybe one in a thousand."

Again, a slight grin played at the corners of Dr. Murphey's mouth, and after winking at me, he said, "Well, from my experience with this man, barring any complications, he heals well; it's worth it if there's any chance to save his knee."

The stump did heal without any sign of infection. There was considerable scar tissue to contend with, but Dr. Milford had expertly folded the flesh back in such a way that the scars were at the back of my stump, subject to minimum pressure.

Dr. Milford was a very good physician and surgeon, a fine human being, and he displayed joy and relief because the stump did heal and because I had the great advantage of my knee joint. He told me he was compelled to say that it was one time he was very glad a patient had argued with him.

Such behavior has always greatly impressed me—such an expert in his field—and convinces me that it takes a big man to do that. I wondered how many times in life do any of us ever admit we are glad someone argued with us. . . .

However, even though my stump healed fine, the trauma of my foot having been torn off caused nerve damage that influenced the knee joint to draw my stump back in a fixed position. Thus I could not be fitted with a prosthesis. I would somehow have to get my knee to straighten and flex.

Dr. Murphey was asked to lend his neurological expertise. He tried a variety of tests: Novocaine was injected into my spine and the knee would then relax, and I could freely flex the joint. But as soon as the sedation wore off, the stump drew back to its fixed, bent position. Dr. Murphey wagged his head in frustration, commenting that I was becoming a very interesting specimen, from a medical viewpoint. He advised that he believed the problem stemmed from a somewhat mysterious phenomenon; that damaged nerves had a way of remembering severe trauma and doing their own thing, regarding not functioning properly.

I spent days and weeks at home, with Dr. Murphey's hope that the nerves would relax.

With fitful sleep, even after sedation, my amputated leg would thrash about involuntarily, rudely disturbing Sylvia's sleep and making it impossible for her to get the rest she needed to care for two small active children. And even when awake, while watching television or sitting at the dining table, my leg would suddenly go into a jerking frenzy.

How Sylvia stood up under such tremendous stress as mother and wife is mind boggling. Often I marveled aloud about it, and she sweetly smiled, giving my cheek a little pat, softly cooing, "It's love, honey, the sweet nectar of pure love. It supplies one with boundless energy."

But I knew that she suffered in her endurance. She had lost much weight, and her beautiful young face, strained with extreme fatigue, had aged her looks well beyond her years. And, yet, as wife and mother, always she showered us with her warmth and good cheer. I would gaze long at her brave smile with my heart overflowing with love and admiration, and she never looked more beautiful.

While waiting to see if time would cause my stump to relax, we went through several frustrating weeks of trial and error.

The doctor discussed this condition with me in simple terms, again, as though we were in the engine room figuring out a solution to a mechanical problem. Although he had doubts it would correct my problem, Dr. Murphey thought it might be worth a try to sever the sympathetic nerve on my left side. He patiently explained that it would require cutting me open on that side to get to the nerve, underneath my stomach along my spinal column. He left the decision up to me.

I didn't feel any sense of bravado or feel that I was some type of a real tough hombre. On the contrary, I felt just as amazed as anyone else might in such a circumstance; that the human body, any human body, is so complex, often delicate in many ways, yet within itself is indeed a mysterious organ with much stamina. A person who has had his or her body jarred a couple of times, soon adapts, I believe, a pragmatic attitude about getting the body-engine functioning again.

Just as Dr. Murphey feared, the clipping of the sympathetic nerve didn't help. My stump remained in a ridged fixed position.

With my approval, the good doctor finally did what he said he would never usually do, except to relieve severe pain in cases of terminal illness. He kept me awake on my stomach and meticulously performed a selectotomy—cutting the nerves along my spinal column between my shoulder blades. That deadened the left side of my body.

Immediately I could then flex the left knee about in its normal function.

I lost the feeling along my left side for awhile. But, gradually through the years, I experienced partial return of a weird type of feeling. For example, normal feeling is as we all know it to be; when stuck with a pin, a person feels like he has been stuck with a pin. But when my left side is merely pricked with a pin, it causes a feeling as though a dull pin has been pushed all the way into my body. A little strange, but no problem . . . I don't go around sticking myself with a pin anyway.

I was soon fitted with an artificial leg, and I attended therapy sessions offered by Campbell's Clinic, a popular orthopedic clinic in Memphis where Dr. Milford was also a part of the medical staff. Such famous people as major league baseball catchers came to Campbell's Clinic in Memphis to keep battered knuckles in their fingers repaired.

The clinic had a therapy specialist who had been a sergeant in the Army. She was as tough as nails, but she taught how to achieve the best use of a prosthesis. I was cautioned by her at the outset that the way I learned to walk—how well I learned to walk, or how sloppy I learned to walk—would stick with me the rest of my life, because once implanted it was almost impossible to un-learn bad habits later.

At the outset, I used a training path with rails on each side for support.

The rather stout therapist was very patient, telling me what I did wrong. I was not kicking the prosthesis on out like a normal stride, or I hesitated before trying to take a step, etc. She closely watched every step. And she didn't raise her voice or rant and rave if I kept making the same mistake over and over. She merely kicked me in the rump and told me to do it right. Really, she was a very kind woman, but some of her kicks were well placed and firm.

I fussed that she was getting lower and lower at times, and that if she ever missed and her foot went through the fork, she was coming dangerously close to parts not suited for the toe of her shoe!

She would fake an innocent little smile and coo, "Oh, now, you don't say. But, honey, it's your artificial leg we are really concerned about, isn't it? Now, shape up and do it right, and you will have nothing to worry about!"

The lady was good; she knew how to get attention.

Often down through the years I have been told by people that they didn't know I wore a prosthesis. And so, it's very important for an amputee to learn to walk the best one can at the very beginning.

There have been times, and still are, when a relative or close friend of someone who has just lost a leg has come to me and requested that I talk with the person. I do, because I know the terrible, even hopeless, feeling one has the first time he or she tries to walk with a slug of wood or fiberglass for a leg. You think, my God, I will never be able to walk with a log hanging from my stump.

I strongly believe that such is a matter of individual adjustment in each case. Furthermore, I also believe the worst thing a family member or friend can do, is to say to a loved one who has lost a leg and is perhaps having difficulty getting adjusted, "Just look at so-and-so, he has a peg leg and can do anything anyone else can do."

This is wrong, I believe, on two counts: First, all the false claims and pretenses aside, a person with only one natural leg will never be able to do everything as good as a person with two healthy legs. However, since God has given us a planet upon which there is so much to do in life, none of us, healthy or otherwise, can ever possibly get around to doing it all. And, therefore, a person with a prosthesis will find more than enough activity for joy and recreation, and life can be just as interesting, wholesome, and fulfilling as it ever was.

Second, I believe it is a hindrance to a person who is struggling to come to terms with his self and his situation after having just lost a part of his body, to be told over and over by well-meaning friends and family members how well someone else is doing with an artificial leg.

I state without equivocation that such a person does not give a fiddler's damn about how well someone else is doing. At such a time, and rightly so, a victim's thought process is busy adjusting to his or her own particular circumstance.

But successfully adjust we do. Pure and simple, it's a matter of the uncanny ability God gave us with which we adapt.

After I was able to get about again, the joy shown by Sylvia and our children was a pure delight. Each day started with the family so exuberant it was like the gift fairy had paid us a visit.

For example, at night while gathered around each other in the living room, my little daughter and son would often rush to sit in their dad's lap. Sometimes both would sit on the floor and pet my stump, always inquiring if it still "hurted."

Assured by me that it felt just fine, even so, little Gale would caress the scars. Each time she would kiss my stump then look up at me with sparkling, loving eyes, to say, "There, Daddy, I make you feel more better."

Gale was then about two years old and Lee about four, and the unabashed love that their tender faces warmly glowed at their father as they petted his mangled leg really tugged at my heart-strings. And a glance at Sylvia warmly smiling with moist eyes as she looked upon such scenes, made me know that, in spite of all we had suffered, I was truly one of the most blessed people who ever lived.

Through their Memphis operation, after weeks of working through channels, a national grain company made a mutual agreement with my brother. They furnished him operating capitol and he agreed to give them first option to buy the large volume of soybeans his little operation bought from farmers.

He delivered a check to me for $27,200, and insisted over and over that I need not get out of the business. He extended sincere thanks to Sylvia and me for helping him protect his family from scandal and nearly broke down in his effort to apologize for my loss.

He has been dead for over thirty years, and to the best of my knowledge, no one else but the family and the local banker ever knew that J. had been in a jam. And, as far as I know, not a single farmer had cause to know that they would have lost if the bank had bounced checks which they had received as payment for their soybeans and grain, had Sylvia not said: "J. B. is your brother, we have no choice, we've got to help him."

After forty years of silence about this, she should be given tremendous credit for her unselfish role and her innate goodness. She richly deserves it. Dad had lived and associated in the area for many years and in his later years he preached at several churches in little communities all around the area, and he was very concerned about the integrity of the McEwen name.

We did our best to preserve it. Then we got on with our lives, focusing on our little children's future.

But finding a nook in the mainstream of life was often frustrating and difficult for my family. I discovered that, even with the Vietnam War, there was no demand for banged-up marine engineers. Indeed, I would soon learn, from firsthand knowledge, that one-eyed, peg-legged seamen were an invention of Hollywood and the movies.

CHAPTER 18

LINER AT LANDING STAGE, LIVERPOOL.   69418

WE SPENT MONTHS, BEWILDERED, TRYING TO CHOOSE from a variety of business opportunities. Bewildered, we soon learned that franchisers, so-called franchisers, and con men have ways of finding out if a prospect really has a few dollars in the bank or has other net worth; thus, when word got around that we were looking, they hounded us relentlessly.

We finally bought an associate home and auto retail store in Texarkana, Arkansas. It was supposed to be a franchise with a national retailer, but it was actually no more than a buy-and-sell agreement (as most so-called franchises are, in my opinion).

The parent company owned and operated retail stores in the largest cities, nationally. In addition, they wholesaled their private labeled merchandise to associated dealers. These dealers owned and operated their retail stores as associated stores in the smaller towns and trade areas. In short, the parent company was the wholesale-middleman who contracted with manufacturers to make private labeled merchandise, and we retailed the items under the parent company's name. But they reserved the right to withdraw the use of their name whenever they desired, after a sixty-day notice. Thus, in reality, our so-called franchise protection was a thin shell.

The first day, October 6, 1958, our associate store had $11.90 total sales for the day, and we had been assured that the store was located in a 90 percent foot-traffic location. . . !

It was on Broad Street, then the main street in downtown Texarkana, next door to Dillard's, one of the town's four largest department stores, and there were no big shopping malls back then. Indeed, it was the original Dillard's, the first of the many other Dillard stores now scattered in big shopping malls across America, and now listed on the New York Stock Exchange.

While the U.S. Marines dug their heels in to protect the elected government from being overthrown in Lebanon, we dug our heels in at Texarkana, determined to make the best out of our business. We rented an old house on the Texas side for $75 per month. We scrimped and did without, and literally lived on $244 per month disability insurance—which would stop after another twelve months.

In short, we plowed everything into building up our store's inventory. But after five years of struggle and sacrifice, the handwriting was on the wall. An old, old story known to many down through time: bad credit customers killed our business.

Also, in this area and all over, it was the beginning of the enormous growth of discount chain store expansion. As they did in other small and large towns all across the South, the chains moved in seemingly overnight. And many popular items were retailed by the discount stores for prices lower than it cost us to buy them from our middleman-wholesaler.

We never cut and ran, but we worked hard for those five years to achieve success. But then control of the parent company was bought by a major finance company that specialized in making loans to consumers for household furnishing and the like. Over the five years, we had obtained the goodwill of some very reliable customers who established credit accounts, which were a tremendous asset because most of our business was credit sales. However, it had cost Sylvia and me dearly to build up a significant number of accounts, consisting of honest customers who paid what they owed, while we learned something about selling on credit. Consequently, most of our net worth became tied up in bad credit paper which we had to pay off because of those customers who did not pay. We then owned the past-due credit accounts to collect if we could. And out of over thirty-five thousand dollars past due and owed to us, we recovered less than one thousand dollars! (Thirty-five thousand dollars was a lot of money in 1963. As a comparison to today's dollar-value, just imagine that all of your financial wealth today totaled around three hundred thousand dollars and that it was invested in your private business, and most all of it loaned out to people who will not pay you back; and that, indeed, all you eventually recover is a mere ten thousand dollars. Anyway, one thousand dollars did not supply a family's needs for very long.) In short, our store became a company-owned store.

But not to fret, that we were alone with such problems. I have since traveled across a big part of America and looked on with a bit of sadness as little "mom-and-pop" businesses in small to medium-sized towns folded everywhere.

A sign of the times, of centralization, which some experts claim is a sign of progress. But, for the long haul, I don't believe that the rush to centralize every aspect of our society is a sign of progress for the individual. . . .

Despite our ups and downs, we found that the love and joy of each other and our children far surpassed everything. Sylvia found permanent employment in the office of a small manufacturer of hospital equipment and health devices.

Searching for a way to be useful, I blended certain chemicals to make an effective no-frills, with no fancy bottle, shampoo for cleaning carpet and furniture upholstery. A friend who was a chemist advised me, and also, I had a general knack for making cleaner; I had helped Dad and Mom make lye soap on the farm and, aboard ship, I had learned to mix alkali boiler feedwater treatment

Gale and Lee Jr., Easter Sunday 1959. Gale not yet three was unhappy about being so dressed up—she liked to rough it as a child. Lee not yet four years of age. Living on 15th Street in Texarkana, Texas, at the time.

with acid until I got a neutral pH glob that was very good to wash bunker-C fuel oil out of dungarees. (After I got it right. But such chemical mixing can be extremely dangerous . . . don't try it without expert advice and guidance.)

Anyway, I traveled the South and parts of the Midwest, wholesaling my shampoo to carpet and furniture retailers.

I ate lots of bologna and, now and then, slept in my car. At such times, kindhearted service station managers granted me the privilege of shaving and taking an FCB bath—that's face, crotch, and butt—in their rest room lavatories. Also, not often, there were occasions when I ate nothing but a loaf of bread for a day or two at a time, conserving my limited funds for gas to make sure I could get back home.

The Big Skipper surely must have been looking out for me because during all this time of traveling with meager funds—over twenty years—never once did I have costly mechanical problems while on the road, often traveling over one thousand miles away from home. And my vehicles were usually pretty well worn.

Our existence was often a little skimpy, but we had food and shelter, and our children were getting an education. However, it was frustrating that I could not do more. Our children both wished to go to college when they finished school, and Sylvia and I were determined that they would, but we didn't yet know how we could pay for it.

Along about that time, I stopped to buy gasoline just east of New Orleans. I was on my way home after two weeks of sleeping in my car, shaving, and washcloth-bathing in service station rest rooms, and had little in the way of profit to show for my two-week effort. I met a Merchant Marine at the service station, and we had coffee and scuttlebutted at a nearby cafe. The mariner was a family man about my age and had been going to sea since War II. He had a master's license, but had been sailing as second mate for some years and was happy to have had the job.

I was appalled when he told me that the United States' Merchant Marine fleet had dropped to eleventh place among the nations of the world, and that finding a berth aboard a ship had for some years been difficult. However, with the United States deeply involved in Vietnam, he was getting a ship as captain. On the one hand he was happy to have a ship again as skipper but not happy that it had been made possible because young Americans were fighting and dying in another war.

Our country was pulling War II cargo ships out of *mothballs* and hurriedly sending them to sea with supplies. The news media reported that the Merchant Marine Academy at Kings Point graduated engineer and deck cadets six months early to provide help to man the reactivated ships. Also, America asked other nations to help carry badly needed supplies to our men and women in Vietnam.

The mariner told me that, then, at the very moment we were talking, there were American-made ships flying French Colors tied up at docks in New Orleans, and the government of France refused to permit them to haul supplies to Americans in Vietnam.

Damn . . . ! Hearing that made my blood boil!

Peeling off the four hundred miles to Texarkana that day, I fumed and time passed quickly. I thought about mothers and fathers who had paid untold millions in taxes to build those ships that were later traded to France for the salvage of the *Normandie,* a floating pile of scrap. They rebuilt a nation's merchant fleet in

Daughter Gale, from article from Texarkana Gazette newspaper. Senior Band Queen Razorback Band, Texarkana High School.

exchange for a mere three million dollars' worth of scrap iron. The USA, with its great influence, was very charitable in making sure France was *given* the German passenger liner *Europa* and given other generous war reparations; and now that nation, a nation that folded at the outset of War II like lettuce in hot oil, refused to haul supplies to America's sons and daughters who were in a life and death struggle.

A large number of those reactivated vessels were Victory ships; I knew their power plants. But the Coast Guard refused to renew my second engineer's license.

Then I wired President Lyndon Johnson and simply told him I could operate the power plant in a Victory ship without any problems. Why, not! The president put his pants on just like I did (I think), and if one can't get results any other way, then go to the top, I always say. I asked for a waiver of my blind eye and peg leg. I got a reply from the Adjutant General of these United States who, in effect, told me that the situation was not serious enough to use one-eyed, peg-legged marine engineers.

Of course, I then learned for certain that peg-legged seamen and those with a black patch over an eye was stuff that Hollywood invented to dramatize movies.

I was not at all pleased with our involvement in the civil affair of Vietnam but I sure supported those American men and women over there who were putting their lives on the line. I could have stood an engineer's watch in a Victory ship's, or any other merchant ship's, power plant, and could have been useful. I don't wear a black patch over my blind eye but I would have put one on if that would have helped.

Regardless, Sylvia and I continued to be happy watching our children grow and develop, and by taking part in their interests at school and other activities.

Gale became a First-Class Girl Scout and Lee became an Eagle Boy Scout. They were both in the school's bands from beginners on through high school.

Sylvia and I served as copresidents of the Band Boosters' Club for a couple of years, and Sylvia served another year as secretary. We wanted to help but, most of all, we wanted to show our kids that we dearly loved them and wanted to be a part of their interests. They were active in church, and we encouraged them to engage in other wholesome activities. And we knew where they were at night.

Parents of school children and others urged me to run for state representative one year. I had to borrow the three-hundred-dollar filing fee. Lee was my campaign manager and he made signs by hand and ran all over town, putting them in people's yards.

Lee Jr. standing on the right. He and Gale attended Texarkana College one year before finishing at University of Arkansas.

Texarkana, 1975. Son, Lee Jr.,
twenty years old, and daughter,
Gale, eighteen years old. Sitting,
the author and Sylvia.

My opponent was the local Chevrolet/Cadillac dealer.

We lost by 995 votes.

Lee would frequently lament, "Daddy, if we could have just split those votes, just got 448 of them . . . !"

I was disappointed when we lost. When the St. Louis Cardinals lose a baseball game I am disappointed, for about a minute. My biggest disappointment was for Lee. He had worked tirelessly making signs to help his daddy win.

Four hundred seventy-five thousand U.S. troops were in Vietnam, and President Johnson also had another war going on at home; his war on poverty. Taxes were also sucked out of working folks' pockets to pay for his Model Cities Program, Office of Economic Opportunity, and other federally funded social engineering programs.

Well-meaning friends, some with posts in government, told me I was foolish for being stubborn, that I should get *mine* while the getting was good. Those well-meaning friends and relatives kept raving at me, asking what was I trying to prove.

They kept urging, "The giveaway programs are shoveling out money by the scoopfuls, you ought to go ahead and get 'yours,' everyone else is getting 'theirs'!"

Sylvia would tell them to leave us alone, that we were doing just fine. Actually, the bottom line is, I already had *mine*; the most precious, loving wife any man could have and two wonderful children.

February 21, 1972, President Nixon was in China on an eight-day "journey for peace" visit; Alabama Governor George Wallace was seriously wounded May 15 by a gunman while campaigning for the presidency; the Watergate break-in of the Democratic National Committee happened June 17; and our son graduated from high school that year, and our daughter would follow in two years. Both earnestly wanted to continue on through college.

I dressed in my best J. C. Penney suit, shined my shoes, and visited the local Social Security office. I told the interviewer that I didn't want disability sustenance payments, but that I merely wished to check into the possibility of only getting assistance to make sure my children could attend college. The woman looked at my newly cleaned and pressed suit, giving me a good inspection with a frown slowly forming, and with unfriendly eyes, she grunted, "Humph, what's wrong wid chu?"

I saw red . . . The safety valve popped on my boiler.

I glared back at the Affirmative Action Make-fit, and said, "There's not a darn thing wrong with me, young lady. I just have a peg leg, one eye, one brain, two floppy hands, I'm hitting on one cylinder, I have headaches, especially at times like this, but I'm just fine."

"Well," she retorted, "we gotta have a doctor's repoat to certify you got somethin' wrong wid chu befoe we can even listen 'bout no claim. Unnastand what I'm saying?"

"Certify . . . ? First off," I exclaimed, "I don't have the money to waste for a doctor to tell me something I already know!" Pulling up my pants leg, I howled, "Here, dad-gum-it, you want it certified, I'll certify it for you. I'll even take the danged leg off and prove it's. . . ."

She squealed and cut me off as I started to remove my pros-thesis. I should have been more tactful, used more decorum and all, but an expression of contempt begets contempt. I stomped my peg leg out of the Social Security Office.

Anyway, our children went to the University of Arkansas, the original university in Arkansas with the highest prestige.

Something that should be brought to the forefront: Many would-be eggheads and legislators in Arkansas had, and have, such an inferiority complex, in my opinion, that several years ago they rushed to attach the "University" handle onto many little colleges at little crossroad communities all over the state. A few additional colleges in Arkansas had the plant to offer universal studies; however, in my opinion, several others did not and do not. Such glut of universities—so-called—in the state has diluted the image of the original University at Fayetteville, which is most deserving of being called the University of Arkansas. Indeed, in traveling over much of our great country and meeting and talking to people of all walks of life, I'm always dismayed to find that folks see through the pretense of calling nearly every college in Arkansas a university. For that reason, in my opinion, we, again, are the "laughing stock"—God! We have had some pretentious dummies running things in this wonderful state . . . one, a professional con artist in my opinion, is now president of the United States!

Anyway, it didn't burden taxpayers of this great nation for our son and daughter to complete college at Fayetteville. Also, our children did not select easy courses just to ease their way through the university in order to show off a college degree. Lee got a degree in electrical engineering. Today he also has a master's degree from the University of Evansville, Indiana, and he is a senior engineer with an energy company. Gale has her master's in business administration and accounting; she also has a teacher's certification, for which she had to go back to college to earn.

While attending the University of Arkansas, Lee worked as custodian at the Baptist Student Union Building, where he got room and board. But he sometimes had to work until midnight, then find time to study his engineering courses. However, he made above average grades.

Gale worked in the office at the college and also made above average grades. She went back to college to get a teacher's certification after her son and daughter were born, and drove a two-hundred-mile round trip each day for well over a year to get it and to also be home at night with her husband and children.

Hindsight reveals my efforts to help carry the financial load and feel useful did little more at times than give me hope.

And underlining it all, I was ingrained with fear that if I broke and "played the part" of being a cripple, I would become the "part" inside. And I cringed at the thought that my children might be caused to look upon their father as a cripple. I do not mean because of my obvious physical loss, which didn't bother them. Rather, had I "played the part" and accepted within myself the image of a useless cripple, then surely this would have been sensed by the developing minds of my growing children, and they could have grown up with an image which might have caused them to pity their father.

A late relative, who was an attorney, often advised, "There are enough government benefits available, which I can get for you, that will assure you of not having to work the rest of your life. But you will have to 'play the part.'"

Ha! Sylvia and I played the part of self-supporting parents, instilling pride in children we brought into this world, so that now they too stand proudly on their own two feet. Nothing heroic about it, just plain facts of responsibility, pure and simple.

However, if indeed there is such a person as a live hero, that dear woman is at the top of the list, because Sylvia carried the brunt of the load, by far, every step of the way and kept her wonderful smile and loving disposition while doing so. God, she is truly a courageous and great woman!

For years, a limited number of carpet and furniture dealers, widely scattered across the South and Midwest, would tell me from time to time that customers raved about my rug and upholstery shampoo being good stuff; that it was also effective to clean urine stains caused by household pets. These dealers kept urging us to create a label to identify a product specifically as a pet stain cleaner. Thus, after several years, we developed an effective pet-urine odor killer. By blending it with the stain cleaner, we created a good stain and odor remover.

With a bit of luck, as a small family vendor, I had the product in a major supermarket chain for seventeen years, and things were brighter for us, financially (until pressure and influence of a big name-brand company took my shelf space in the supermarkets).

However, at no time did we roll in money, although we did pay off our modest home, and my pavement pounding during those years was greatly reduced. And we were happy; Sylvia and I found lots of joyous time together and time to visit our children and grandchildren.

In the summer of 1986 we finally got to take our dream vacation. We had often talked about visiting the tall redwoods of California and had planned to do so when summer arrived in 1954, the year I got jarred that February night so long ago near Hot Springs.

I caught a cold from one of the grandchildren and had been fighting it for over a week. However, except for a lingering hoarse voice, it seemed better. And so, after having waited some thirty years, we hurried on across country familiar to us, making Kingman, Arizona, our third night's stop. Early the next morning we beat it on up and marveled at Hoover Dam. Then, without even stopping, we highballed it through daytime Las Vegas like she was a drunk sleeping it off in the hot summer's sun.

We hummed on up through Nevada until we could cross over into California at the northern end of Death Valley.

Both Sylvia and I are natural scenery lovers, thus we leisurely stopped and started all the way down through Death Valley to the little salty ponds—with little fish in them—at North America's lowest spot below sea level, 280 feet below. We stopped and read probably every historical marker along the way.

An old steam engineer should have known not to leave the car's engine running with the air conditioner on but, because the humidity was very low, it didn't seem all that hot. We later learned that it was the hottest day of the year in Death Valley, 121 degrees!

It grew dark as we waited for the engine to cool.

We strolled about, looking at the stars and listening to the night sounds; still a lot of life in Death Valley. I showed Sylvia her lovely face in a big bright rising moon. She gave me a little hug and assured me that I was moonstruck. But I think she was pleased because after the car cooled, while adding water to the radiator, I stopped and watched as she stood motionless, her stunning silhouette painted in the soft glow, as she gazed up at the moon.

We made it into Lone Pine about 11:30 that night. The owner of the nice little motel chuckled at our adventure. He was a retired California State policeman, and told us that he had made many trips down in the valley over the years to rescue folks who were stranded with frozen overheated car engines, which they had left running with air conditioners on while stopping to browse around.

We traveled on up through pretty Owen's Valley and entered Yosemite Park from the east. Beautiful and interesting, but over-flowing with people; bikers, campers, and the like. Much too crowded for us, and after traveling along the rushing Merced River, then taking a look at famous Yosemite Falls, we hurried on our way to places less crowded.

After rubbernecking along, through downtown San Francisco, we headed for the Golden Gate Bridge in late afternoon when folks were rushing home from work. Dudes passed me on both sides, honking, revving their car's engine, and yelling, "Hey, hick, drive it or park it!"

San Francisco looked unlike the drab image pictured in my mind. A very colorful and beautiful city, Sylvia and I thought.

We shut down for the night at Petaluma and got an early start next morning, heading north along the coastal highway for the tall redwood trees.

Awesome.

Standing under those tall giants, awesome!

I asked a park ranger if I could take one of the big trees back to Arkansas and start a toothpick factory. She smiled and winked at Sylvia then told me, yes, that I could have one if I could get it into the trunk of my car but that she was not going to help me load it. Anyway, she was a very nice person.

After an overnight stay near Crescent City and another in Portland, Oregon, we found our way to nearby Mt. St. Helens.

We were the only people way up there at the lookout point and we stood a long time, gazing in wonder at the blown-out north side at the top of the famous mountain, now, said to be two thousand feet shorter.

As I eased our car around sharp bends, up and down a narrow roadway which had been cleared with bulldozers through the flattened trees, Sylvia and I were gripped in awed silence as we gazed over hundreds of square miles of total destruction on the north side of the volcano. Up steep mountains and broad slopes, through valleys, fanned out for a radius of over twenty miles, everywhere we looked, there was nothing left standing; a stark landscape covered with ashes and hundreds of years of life gone dead in a matter of minutes.

We, like most, had seen on television the flattened timber that was slapped down when the mountain blew its top, but we were not prepared for the naked view close up. The scenes we had viewed on television were like comparing flattened fence posts to the enormity of what we looked upon. The broken huge Douglas firs were just that; a carpet of big trees all flattened in one big sweep like they were mere stalks of grain laying in a wheat field. Also, from the volcano in an arc that fanned out twenty miles or more along the crest of mountain ridges, the trunks of big trees on the lee side had been spared, and were still standing, but their exposed tops had been sheared off. It appeared as though some giant saw had run along the ridges, clipping the tree tops even with the mountain crests. Awesome!

Awesome, always one of my favorite words to describe the spectacular, yet it seemed so pitifully inadequate to describe the feeling I experienced while Sylvia and I lived those brief moments among the evidence of such incredible force only nature can deliver.

Overwhelmed with the vast destruction, I thought of the old combat soldier standing on the fantail of the *Larkspur* after our two days fighting the hurricane so many years past. I hoped he was somehow still alive and kicking, and I wondered what the old topkick would have to say about St. Helens, were he there to witness what Mother Nature had caused in just a few moments of her fury.

As we left the area and continued on, I mused to Sylvia, "You know, honey, a person's journey on earth is really little more than a whisper, isn't it. . . ."

She looked at me, squeezed my arm, and leaned to touch my scarred cheek with her soft lips, then she murmured in my ear, "Yes, darling, but it's such a lovely journey."

After Moses Lake and Spokane, Washington, Sand Point, Idaho, and Libby, Montana, we reached Glacier National Park. Again, awesome was the breathtaking beauty as we drove through the park, stopping along the way, from the west to the east.

The soreness in my throat was gone, but my voice had grown hoarser. I attributed it to the thinner air of the high mountain altitude.

In the high mountain thin air, I was quickly reminded of my tied-off carotid arteries and the short oxygen supply to my brain. Up on high mountains, I feel fine inside a car with its air conditioner stirring the thin air, but after a few minutes outside a car on a tall mountaintop my legs start sagging like they are feathers.

Anyway, after we came out of the park's east side, we decided to take a short drive into Canada. A young guard at the border apparently had difficulty understanding me. She asked nonchalantly where we were from, and I just as casually replied, "Arkansas."

She asked what country.

"What do you mean, what country!" I fretted. "Dang, young woman, the good ole US of A, where'd you think!"

She bent to drop her face to the open car window, exclaiming, "Oh, Arkansas . . . yessss, hmmmm, Arkansas. How many guns do you have with you?"

"Guns? Ma'am, we don't have any guns. We're just up here roaming around, looking at the pretty country. We're not hunting."

I fell back as she thrust her face through the window and stuck it before mine to gasp, "Yes, but from Arkansas, and you don't have at least one gun with you . . . ?"

I looked at Sylvia, shook my head, and wearily sighed in disbelief. I again turned to the, now, alert border guard, and stressed, "Look, Ma'am, I've told you, we don't have any guns on us, in, on, or under the car. We—Don't—Have—Any—Guns, period."

She studied my face while warning me about Canada's strict gun laws. I assured her that I knew all about them and, again, that we did not have any guns. She stood back toying with her chin as she kept appraising me, but she waved us on.

We drove the twenty miles or so up to the pretty little town of Cardston then we dropped back to the USA.

Drinking in the splendor of the big sky country, we drifted along in awe, across Montana and Wyoming. In Montana, we stood where Custer made his last stand. Stopping overnight in Sheridan, Wyoming, then, after a gander at Mount Rushmore, we cruised out of South Dakota. Leaving Nebraska, we quickened our pace when hitting the familiar country of Kansas and Oklahoma.

There we were, with only a couple of years until our fortieth wedding anniversary, grey peppering our hair, yet I believe we would not have been any happier had we made the trip long ago, when we dreamed about it as young lovebirds.

At times on the 7,500-mile sojourn we would drive long stretches in silence consumed with the joy of each other's presence and the love that flowed between us. As we absorbed God's beauty unfolding over each mountaintop, around each curve, and out across the wide plains, often Sylvia would slip a dainty little hand to pat me and softly murmur, "Honey, it's really wonderful."

While getting back into our daily routine at home, Sylvia kept insisting that I see a doctor about my hoarse voice. But I felt good, was somewhat busy, and prone to feel if something ain't broke don't fix it.

But she has sticka u-nus, lots of it. After a couple of weeks she made an appointment for me.

The doctor looked down my throat and frowned, informing me that he saw a small polyp on my right vocal cord. He prescribed antibiotics. After I took them, I saw him again within a few days. The pills hadn't worked, so he put me into a local hospital, with a tube in my arm, dripping antibiotics into a vein. The outlaw on my vocal cord stayed put.

At that time, Gale, our daughter, worked for the hospital administrator; therefore, she knew many of our local doctors, and she suggested a specialist.

He was a young man, Dr. David Whitt, and I liked him right off, because he didn't dish out a lot of BS. He put me to sleep and plucked a bit of tissue from the polyp for a biopsy . . . told me he had hopes, because it didn't cut like it was malignant.

But within a few days, after he received the pathologist's report, we went to his office and learned the dreaded news. It jarred the devil out of me, but there was nothing left for me to think but that I had been decked before and that I would have to dig in one more time.

But I would have rather ridden out another hurricane with the ship's hull cracked on both sides than see the anguish in Sylvia's lovely face. How much more can that dear woman endure, I thought.

For most of our lives together she had been bent back and forth with bad news, like a strip of metal. For example, when I was traveling a lot, she often told me that her greatest fear while I was on the road was that she might get another one of those late-night phone calls telling her that something else had happened to me.

And once again, the instant shock and anguish was there in her eyes when we learned the terrible news.

One can be told that having cancer is possible, but still there is hope it will not be so, and when finding their worst fear has become a fact, it jars, it's real. No more hope that it might not be.

She stood blinking in silence for a moment, her face drained of color. Then swallowing hard, instantly she forced a smile and swept the alarm from her face. She dabbed at her moist eyes, then looked long at me, showering me with her warm smile. Then she moved to me with that wonderful hug of assurance.

Such feelings are too great for simple words to describe, yet known by untold millions who have experienced the power of love in such moments.

Of course one had rather be thinking about going fishing or anything other than think about what the next few weeks, months, or whatever might be like, but somehow you feel inside that everything will be all right, regardless. Hope . . . one prays and clings to hope, and it helps immensely to have a doctor in whom you have great confidence.

After the surgery, I am convinced that I nearly died in the recovery room within a matter of seconds.

Then shortly thereafter, after I had been moved to intensive care, my heart started doing a jitterbug. To add to our strain, as had once happened in the past, I had another grouchy nurse, and she tried to prevent Sylvia from being in the room with me even for a few minutes. This distressed me, but because of such delicate surgery and because of a hollow tube stuck in my guzzle, I was warned not to try to talk. But you can bet I did some explicit writing on my pad for the doctor. I was a real tattletale!

However, the relief nurse was a nice person and allowed Sylvia to remain with me for brief periods, after which she would assure me that Sylvia was present just outside the door.

The stamina of a loving woman is awesome. But, like the many months of our other life-and-death visitations in the years gone by, I worried that she would wear herself down.

As for myself, I don't believe I was a contrary patient in the recovery room. I really don't. I sensed that I was on the edge of death and I was just a human who struggled to stay alive. This, when four well-meaning, but unwary, strong nurses had darned near drowned me when I woke up in the recovery room.

Also adding to my stress was the grouchy nurse's antics with Sylvia. That, I believe, caused my heart to do the hop, skip, and jump. In short, I merely fought with all I had available: that instinct of self-survival.

I suppose my last visitation was the kind of stuff that can be embellished with exaggerated BS. But I feel that simple facts are revealing enough without someone attempting to enlarge the scope of such experiences, deluding themselves to feel they are superhuman and believing others will think so, too.

I have no desire to offend anyone who may wish to think they are a special superhuman after they have perhaps survived some terrible, dangerous ordeal. However, such is not for me because the many times I reflect back along life's trail, I think of my feelings as a young man; when we hauled so many other young Americans home from the battlefields of the world, who lay dead, stacked in the cargo holds. Always, at such times, the thought comes to me that it is somewhat vain for anyone who is still alive to pretend that they can express the feeling experienced when a human has endured all the pain and suffering possible for a human to endure. When one reaches the limits of endurance they die. Thus it is impossible for anyone alive to know how much trauma one can endure.

While there's no way that people alive can say how much we can take, those young Americans stacked in my ships' cargo holds surely knew, for a mere instant, anyway. Because, when they reached that point when they endured all humanly possible, they then passed beyond. Forever on earth, they would be unable to express just how it felt to have reached the point of enduring all a human can stand.

Heroes? Yes indeed, I like to think *they* were. However, I know for certain that there is no such person as a *live* hero or super-human. But, mind and body, any body, is tremendously resilient with the capacity to heal itself and survive. Thus, I believe it is that simple without trying to embellish a trauma or visitation.

With surgery, Dr. Whitt had cut the outlaw out of my right vocal cord, then he skillfully designed a make-do vocal cord with the remaining muscle tissue so that I could eventually talk without having to use a mechanical device. He then left orders for me to be kept under a mixture of oxygen with added moisture. This, I am told, is common procedure after such surgery, to keep the throat moist, thus not hindering the healing process.

Even though I had told Dr. Whitt all I remembered about my medical history, there are things one tends to forget. Indeed, as Dr. Murphey had long ago cautioned, due to the shattering damage a body suffers in such accidents as a car head-on, little side effects are likely to pop up from time to time, which time will usually heal, and some which it may not.

Such has been the case of a condition that has infrequently disturbed me in the past. A few times, perhaps a dozen or so, over the past forty years, I have been jarred awake at night suffocating; choking, windpipe cut off, unable to breath even the stir of a gnat's wing.

Each time my mind screamed: "This may be it. You'd better get on your horse and do something quick or your light's going out!"

Indeed, I soon learned to flop my head down over the side of the bed, squeeze back panic, and shortly, after straining every muscle in my chest, I would start breathing normally again. I also learned how to prevent those wake-up calls. Such incidents usually occurred after a big late-night dinner, perhaps with too much greasy food. Then after going to sleep, oily liquid regurgitated and sucked into my windpipe. Eventually, I learned to stop stuffing myself with food late at night.

I didn't remember to mention the condition to Dr. Whitt. And he, of course, had no way of knowing added moisture to the oxygen would trigger a spasm.

I was jarred back into the world in the recovery room, once again realizing I was choking—drowning.

I snatched the oxygen mask off and gave my chest muscles a hard workout, trying to suck air through my blocked windpipe to feed my starved lungs. At such times without a tube stuck in my throat, it sounds to me like the lingering bawl of a 'coon dog resounding through the woods after it has treed its quarry.

First, one nurse hurried to my side and slapped the oxygen mask back over my face. I snatched it off and tried to howl in protest but had no breath; I was hindered by the hollow tube stuck through my neck into my trachea. The nurse sternly warned me not to talk.

I wanted to scream at her but couldn't; I was drowning, but was unable to even force a little squeak to let her know it (boy, that's a horrible, helpless feeling!). Flat on my back, I fought with her, trying to flip over and get my head over the side of the bed.

In a flash, four nurses, two on each side, were holding me down and plopping the dadgummed oxygen mask back over my face.

I snatched it off!

They kept slapping it back on!

This all happened in a very short period of time, but my lights were dimming fast, the nurses becoming mere blobs.

Luck, coincidence, or whatever, I personally thank the Big Skipper for the doctor who happened to rush into the recovery room, and I thank the doctor. I believe he saved my life. Whatever his mission at that moment, he dropped it and rushed over to check on the commotion at my bed.

Whether it was my strained face as I desperately tried to suck air, the alarm I displayed, or both, he quickly waved the nurses aside and allowed me to move my head off the side of the bed, giving me support as the liquid drained out.

Heave by heave I began to get my breath.

He waited until I breathed deeply.

Recovered, I then scribbled on my pad that the oxygen was drowning me and that, years past, I had been in a head-on car wreck, and my windpipe seemed to be screwed up at times.

He read my note, took a look at my chart attached to the bed, then spoke to the nurses.

No other attempt was made to slap that death mask on my face.

Dr. Whitt had given me a thorough examination with one of those see-more scopes that is inserted down a person's throat for a look-see, and he said that no abnormality was detected in my lungs or in any bronchial tubes. Informed about the trauma I experienced in the recovery room, he said he believed that nerve damage I suffered long ago perhaps caused my windpipes' shut-off valves—my terminology—from properly closing at times.

At this writing, twelve years have passed since that particular experience in a hospital. Monitoring my progress closely, some seven years ago, and again about three years past, Dr. Whitt gave my throat a clean bill of health.

Of course I breathed a sigh of relief each time, and I would muse to myself, "Stay dead, the outlaw, and long live Dr. Whitt. May he forever have the Big Skipper's blessing."

As it was with my other mishaps, now it all seems like a long dream, regarding any pain and discomfort. As already mentioned, the pain one can never recall, nor do I wish to, of course; I can only recall that I had some pain on back down the line, but no sense of recall to once again vividly feel the acute pain itself. However, the light moments and the little incidents that were amusing are still vivid memories, giving me a few chuckles. And above all, the tremendous relief, comfort, and joy in knowing that Sylvia was always near, watching over me and showering me with love, are more than vivid memories.

But fate was not done with me, yet. Once again the tail would thrash; out of the *hole* the unexpected would jump up and deck me.

Picture of Donegon bottle.

After a bout with pneumonia during the 1996–1997 holiday season, at the end of January a cough persisted. My doctor had a CAT scan run on me. A small spot in my right lung showed in three of the frames.

Rather than bother with getting a hole poked in me to pluck tissue for a biopsy, which I was told would be almost as major as surgery to remove the spot, I chose to go ahead and let the surgeon remove the outlaw. (I consulted other doctors, including Dr. Whitt, and all doctors recommended that I get the spot removed, regardless of whether it was or was not malignant.)

January 28, 1997, Dr. A.D. Smith, a pulmonary specialist and lung surgeon, removed about 10 percent of my right lung and got rid of the spot. It was malignant.

I can't tell that I'm missing that small part of my lung. I feel great. Check-ups and X-rays confirm that the surgery did indeed get all of the cancer.

I believe the last visitation was a bad-news-good-news situation; of course, the lung cancer was bad news, but the good news was it was detected early and, therefore, the surgeon was able to get it all without any complications and without hindering my ability to breathe. Further good news was, I didn't have to endure chemotherapy or follow-up radiation treatments.

By pointing out the "good news," I hope it will help support the truth about how tremendously important early detection is in order to have a fighting chance to cure cancer. My doctor told me that had it not been for the CAT scan—early detection—the cancer could have spread from my lung to my heart and other parts of my body before it was known. In short, but for the early detection *later* could have been too late.

This last tussle and all the others back along the way now seem like a dream. No indeed, the terrible sensation of pain one can never recall.

But it is easy to recall the delightful, warm moments Sylvia and I have had together through the years. And we still share them. For example, each time I pause to fume at the flitting keyboard for this newfangled computer contraption, I glance over to see a smile creep into Sylvia's beautiful face as she sits listening to me fuss while she sews on another dress for our granddaughter, or writes letters to our three grandsons in Kentucky.

I prop my chin in hand with an elbow on the desk and sit gazing in wonder at her while she still gently wags her head in amused fashion.

Each time, I feel compelled, and I say something like, "Honey, we're really in love, ain't we?"

She'll lift her pretty face to glow at me with her sparkling eyes and warm smile, then sweetly she will murmur, "Yes, darling, we really are." Touching fingers to her lips, she'll blow me a kiss and then go back to her delight in doing little things for our grand-children. A similar scene that is often repeated but it never seems redundant. Always, each time, such warm moments send a fresh thrill though our hearts.

I turn back to tussle with this blamed keyboard, and sit here frowning at the F1, 2, 3, 4, and all the other F-eees.

Oh well. . . .

I'm happy to be *able* to say that Sylvia and I are still going strong, loving every minute of life that God gives us with each other. We have just returned from another 7,586-mile sojourn out through the mountains and plains of the northwestern and western states—God . . . folks, we have a beautiful country in America, both Canada and the USA. . . . There are many parts of the world that I have not seen, but there are many parts that I have been to, and nowhere have I seen any place with all the awesome natural beauty that we have in our own great country. . . . God sure blessed America!

Anyway, on the trip through eighteen states, we celebrated our 17,910th through our 17,932th wedding dayversary . . . when our 18,262th wedding dayversary arrives this year, I'll submit a notice to the local newspaper—why, not . . . ! As we all know, in every Sunday newspaper, there are notices about fiftieth wedding anniversaries, but I have never seen a single one about a 18,262th wedding dayversary.

I'll never completely retire as long as I can keep mojoing. I'm not trying to prove anything. I simply get a kick out of what I am doing. I am still flabbergasted and pleased that letters and occasional phone calls keep coming from pet lovers all over America who want to thank me for my stuff.

Some are from those who have used my household-pet cleaner stuff for over twenty years; many are from those whose life companion has gone on to rewards hereafter, leaving a loved one behind all alone with loving memories and a devoted pet for joy and comfort.

'Tis a simple thing, I do. Even so, I will keep piddling with my cat and puppy pee stain and odor cleaner, because it makes me feel a little useful, still.

I never got to build my fair lady that castle young men dream they will build; I know I did. But I did capture the golden crown

Son and his family visiting Mom and Dad Christmas 1997, Texarkana. From left: grandsons, Michael James McEwen, age fourteen; Matthew Lee, age sixteen, John Thomas, age nine. Daughter-in-law Loretta standing with Lee McEwen Jr.

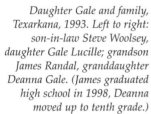

Daughter Gale and family, Texarkana, 1993. Left to right: son-in-law Steve Woolsey, daughter Gale Lucille; grandson James Randal, granddaughter Deanna Gale. (James graduated high school in 1998, Deanna moved up to tenth grade.)

in having Sylvia to cherish and the joy of her love all these years. And because of our enduring love for each other, we feel that together we have been a success.

Even though our lives only represent a mere whisper that brushed this earth, surely, our having passed this way will be listed in the Big Skipper's record of mankind's progress on this planet. The type of progress consisting of family responsibility for their own and to society, which we believe is necessary to preserve order with peace and goodwill for all.

Therefore, we are humbled, yet proud, that we were able to instill in our son and daughter these virtues.

Also, we are blessed because our offspring are devout and God-fearing children, who are also much better educated than we were and therefore better equipped to be more protective of our great planet and to pass these qualities on to our grandchildren, and they to theirs, into infinity.

For Sylvia and me, the journey has been, and is, a great joy. It is so because there is no greater terrestrial love than the love one woman has for one man and that he has for her.

Indeed, true love is such a wonderful, mysterious force that it has defied all human efforts to clearly define it despite the many great love stories told and written down through the ages of civilization. Even so, God saw fit for the devoted love of a woman to give me the will to live. Thus, I have wondered many times if perhaps love exists

for its own sake and merely chose humankind for its abode and source for sustenance.

Regardless, it surely must be an omnipotent force of God's with the awesome mystical power to heal when all else is futile.

And now as the night slips down in my twilight years, I believe I really did get to be somebody, because my girl in the moon made it so.

Texarkana 1993. Forty-fifth wedding anniversary of Sylvia.

The author and his wife, Sylvia, on their 18,262nd wedding dayversary (50th wedding anniversary), October 23, 1998.